English-French Translation

English-French Translation: A Practical Manual allows advanced learners of French to develop their translation and writing skills. This book provides a deeper understanding of French grammatical structures, the nuances of different styles and registers and helps increase knowledge of vocabulary and idiomatic language.

The manual provides a wealth of practical tasks based around carefully selected extracts from the diverse text types students are likely to encounter, from literary and expository, to persuasive and journalistic. A mix of shorter targeted activities and lengthier translation pieces guides learners through the complexities and challenges of translation from English into French.

This comprehensive manual is ideal for advanced undergraduate and postgraduate students in French language and translation.

Christophe Gagne is Senior Language Teaching Officer in French at the University of Cambridge and a Fellow of Churchill College, Cambridge, UK.

Emilia Wilton-Godberfforde is Lecturer in French at the Open University and a life member of Clare Hall College, Cambridge, UK.

D1571782

English-French Translation

A Practical Manual

Christophe Gagne and Emilia Wilton-Godberfforde

 Routledge
Taylor & Francis Group

LONDON AND NEW YORK

First published 2021
by Routledge
2 Park Square, Milton Park, Abingdon, Oxon OX14 4RN

and by Routledge
52 Vanderbilt Avenue, New York, NY 10017

Routledge is an imprint of the Taylor & Francis Group, an informa business

British Library Cataloguing-in-Publication Data
A catalogue record for this book is available from the British Library

Library of Congress Cataloging-in-Publication Data
A catalog record for this book has been requested

ISBN: 978-1-138-83880-2 (hbk)
ISBN: 978-1-138-84195-6 (pbk)
ISBN: 978-1-315-73193-3 (ebk)

Typeset in Times New Roman
by Apex CoVantage, LLC

Contents

Acknowledgements

For some time we talked about wanting to put this book together, and the framework for this was forged long ago. We carved out the time to write this while working in our respective posts and are thankful to our departments and colleagues for their support (both in the Faculty of Medieval and Modern Languages, University of Cambridge and The Open University). We would, above all, like to thank our students with whom we have had the pleasure to work. Their enthusiasm and commitment has been inspiring, and they have helped us in testing out ideas and exploring different ways of working with a variety of texts. We would also like to thank Ángeles Carreres, María Noriega-Sánchez, Carme Calduch and Tita Beaven for their encouragement and guidance. The "Conversations in Translation" series at CRASSH, University of Cambridge, convened by Ángeles and Maria but also Monica Boria and Marcus Tomalin, has further contributed to our work, and we are grateful for the opportunity to have shared our ideas in this innovative research group. We would also like to thank Sandra Smith for all her help.

We also wish to acknowledge the help of Sam Vale, Rosie McEwan, Autumn Spalding and all the team at Routledge who have worked with us from the start. Particular thanks also go to Katie Meade at the OU for her advice regarding copyright and contracts.

We are grateful to all who have helped us secure the permissions for material that we have included in our book (especially Sebastian Kamps for the epigraph; The Fitwilliam Museum for "The Man with Flowing Hair"; QED Publishing for "Give Us a Smile Cinderella" and les Editions Scholastic for the French version; Sandra Smith and Clairborne Hancock at Pegasus Books for reproduction of "L'Etranger" graphic-novel; Gallimard for the Raymond Queneau poem, "Pour un art poétique"; the Kinsley Amis estate for "The Helbatrawss"; Oxford University Press for James McGowan's translation "The Albatross" and Coach House Books (Christian Bök) for the five translated poems of Rimbaud's "Voyelles").

Finally, we wish to thank our loved ones, near and far, in France, the UK and much further afield. We celebrate that this book, initially mapped out in the buttery of the MML, will now be in the departmental library and hopefully on many other bookshelves!

Introduction

If you are reading this, there is a good chance that you have a strong curiosity about translation or about the French language (or indeed both). The principle underpinning this book is, precisely, to combine an exploration of translation with an investigation into the French language. More specifically, we want to use translation as a way of examining the relationship between English and French, and this first entails examining the languages at a grammatical and sentence level. There is rarely an absolute one-to-one fit between French and English forms and, at a textual level, there are also different conventions that apply when writing in English and French. Translation also provides the opportunity to explore linguistic variation and, looking at texts from this perspective, can allow for a fascinating exploration of how language works in different forms, in different contexts and for different purposes. We encourage a bilingual perspective and underscore the major issues to which we must attend when attempting to produce a "translation". In this way, we explore translation as an activity in itself. We touch on key theoretical considerations in this regard, but our answer to what constitutes translation emerges through the processes of practically working with the language, unpacking how it is put together and how we might make sense of it, and then attempting to rework it into another language.

When working on translation, cultural differences also become salient. Crucially, it is not just how we talk about things that differs, it is also what we talk about. Reference points are different. There are differences in relation to common everyday knowledge; for example, an everyday notion might exist in one language but not in the other, or a word that denotes the same object in the real world might have different connotations. Throughout this book, we alert our readers to such issues and aim to provide systematic steps and techniques to handle the range of difficulties translation can pose.

However, we firmly believe that approaching such rich and complex issues need not be a dry and laborious task. Therefore, while aiming to provide a structured methodical approach to translation that will help learners improve a wide range of skills, we have, above all, endeavoured to elicit the reader's excitement and showcase the creative flair translation so often requires. This playful dimension is important and needs to be appreciated so that learners can develop as continually motivated problem-solvers.

How, more precisely, do we envisage learners developing their skills? Our book is designed to enhance:

- an understanding of translation as a complex communicative activity
- a contrastive awareness of English and French
- the ability to translate from English and to French (and also French to English)
- language skills in French with particular emphasis on advanced features of grammar, register and style (but also in terms of lexical range)
- pragmatic and intercultural competence
- familiarity with a number of key notions and debates within the discipline of translation studies and knowledge regarding the practical task of the translator.

In this way, it is ideal for use in the teaching of advanced French at university. Suitable for specialist linguists, it is nonetheless a helpful resource for students of other subjects who want to flex their translating muscles and are interested in intercultural competence and creative writing. We uncover how the task of translation raises so many different issues, all of which are crucial to any university degree in language, literature and culture. We do, of course, envisage this course being a useful tool for students in translation modules/courses, and since it covers the basics of translation theory, it can be used as introductory reading for first-year translation students. Teachers can select material that aligns with the aims of their course and adapt and extend the proposed activities as they see fit. It is intended for use in the language classroom, and the activities lend themselves to collaborative work, however, equally these can be used in the context of independent study. It is assumed that the student will already be familiar with using reference materials, including dictionaries and databases. We do not discuss machine translation or how to use translation software since this is not a manual for translators in the workplace but rather a textbook guiding the reader to find strategies for specific linguistic and stylistic issues.

The trajectory of our study is one that starts at the micro-level (or word-level) and moves outwards, to look at language at the sentence-level and within syntactical arrangements in the two languages, and then at a more macro-level, within a larger textual/genre-based context. Chapters 1 through 4 adopt a more linguistically-led investigation and draw attention to recurring structural patterns in both languages as well as proposing the most common linguistic procedures translators adopt (such as modulation and transposition). Chapters 5 through 7 extend the discussion by examining broader questions of translatability, translation loss (or "betrayal"), the challenges of translating poetic language, and working with speech in audiovisual material. Our study by no means claims to provide an exhaustive account of translation (whether in terms of language, genre, text-types or theory) but rather, seeks to alert the reader to a variety of recurring difficulties that are linguistic, stylistic and ideological. These are showcased with a range of examples (children's literature, adverts, signs, aphorisms and idioms, extracts from newspapers and magazines with music reviews, interviews, sports coverage and current affairs, book titles, political speeches and slogans, legal texts, extracts from novels, poetry, song lyrics and filmic dialogue). These serve as a reminder that all sorts of texts can contain features that are worthy of analysis (be they from the sublime realms of poetry or from the ridiculous and seemingly mundane language of signposts).

We have attempted to provide an ambitious range of material and have found Eurostar's bilingual *Metropolitan Magazine* a pertinent source of examples which also give the reader a taste of the kind of language and commercial material they might well have to deal with as professional translators. We have included eye-catching images (photographs, slogans and signposts) where linguistic issues are incorporated into the visual and graphic format. Furthermore, we encourage the reader to seek out similar examples in the everyday world around them and think through possible translations when, for example, they come across graffiti, slogans or slick advertising messages in the different languages. However, we also underline the usefulness of attempting translations of literary texts, not simply as a way of becoming familiar with a range of Francophone texts and authors, but because identifying the authors' conscious manipulation of language and rhetorical strategies can alert us to features which can then be better pinpointed and appreciated in any kind of text. They can then subsequently be rendered into the target language (TL) more carefully.

Each chapter presents a detailed discussion, followed by practical activities. These activities replicate the very issues we have highlighted and help provide a step-by-step way of thinking through different problems. Targeted activities are provided along with lengthier translation tasks. They provide the learner with the space to test their understanding and adopt the proposed techniques. The guidelines for the tasks have been written in French since we believe this will enhance the students' ability to think in the TL and creates the appropriate mindset. The activities are designed to be both instructive and ludic explorations. Most of these activities are supported with a "key". This is more the case for activities where a suggested answer is a way of testing understanding (with lexical, grammatical items, for instance, or of specific translation techniques). The more open-ended creative explorations clearly have no single right/wrong answer and we have thus not always provided a "version". Learners can, of course, compare and contrast their renderings with classmates and defend and reshape their versions accordingly, and independent learners will not feel constrained by any template we might have been provided or risk viewing their own rendering within the shadow of an "authoritative" version.

Our work is situated within a multilingual paradigm and embraces the benefits of translation pedagogy in additional language learning. As Maria González-Davies underlines, "translation is certainly making a comeback that is far from Grammar-Translation practices. Its role as a natural learning strategy is now embedded within established approaches related to student-centred (language) learning" (Carreres et al., 2018, xiii). Our volume aims to make a contribution in this light and engages with the "plurilingual turn", or the "translation turn" as authors of *Mundos en palabras* (2018)[1] describe it. In such a way, we embrace the role translation can play for enhancing multilingual and intercultural skills. Although we unashamedly grapple with grammar, our approach is a far cry from the dry method of testing grammatical knowledge through prose translation exercises. Rather, we embrace the communicative approach. In so doing, we present translation as a fundamental communication and mediation skill.

We are, of course, indebted to a range of scholars whose work has energised and inspired our own. This includes, but is not limited to, Vinay and Darbelnet's seminal book (1958) and reflexion on translation techniques and the work it has fuelled, Chuquet and Paillard's excellent book (1987), and Claude Demanuelli and Jean Demanuelli's interesting work on literary texts (1990). More contemporary influences include Lawrence Venuti's highly impactful work on the translator's visibility (1995); Guy Cook's focus on pedagogic translation (2010); Mona Baker's excellent coursebook which uses modern linguistic theory, now into its third edition (1992–2020); and David Bellos' engaging and accessible writing on the subject of translation (2012). Additionally, fascinating exchanges with literary translators, colleague and friend Sandra Smith in particular, and other fellow teachers have nourished our work. Another excellent stimulus has been provided by the *Cambridge Conversations in Translation* seminars organised by Ángeles Carreres, Monica Boria, María Noriega-Sánchez and Marcus Tomalin at Cambridge University between 2015 and 2019.

Our book does share many of the theoretical and educational principles that underpin the Routledge *Thinking Translation* series. However, we consider this book to be unique in the way that it places particular emphasis on translating into French. It also integrates issues and materials that have appeared more recently. We were further motivated to produce such a handbook since our students repeatedly lamented the lack of English textbooks that provide clear conceptual and pedagogical frameworks on translating from English into French. They also expressed their frustration at being unable to find material which provides different kinds of texts, registers and genres to translate from English to French. We noticed that there was certainly a need for a textbook that is designed with the undergraduate and non-native speaker of French in mind. This book therefore aims to provide such a resource and help students develop a methodical and critical approach when analysing material.

On a final note, we believe our linguistic and professional backgrounds enhance the bilingual and pedagogical approach of the book. Since one of us is a native speaker of French and the other a native speaker of English, we provide different perspectives which have made our collaboration particularly fruitful. Furthermore, we bring with us over 20 years of experience of working as language teachers at university (with a range of students in the UK and also in France). We have piloted many of the exercises during our classes and can confirm that students have found them useful and also enjoyable. We are well aware of the specific perspective needed when teaching inverse as opposed to direct translation.

We bring our knowledge of how students deal with texts in the classroom, and this provides us with a distinct ability to present our information in a way that is conscious of the obstacles an English speaker might stumble over when having to transform the material into French. Additionally, having both worked as professional translators, we felt well positioned to design a book that encourages students to work on a variety of texts and to do so in a practical and methodical fashion that sharpens their skills. Our aim, however, as we have already shown in this introduction, is not to provide a professional handbook, but rather to awaken the readers to the pleasures and perils of translating and thinking across languages and cultures.

Note

1 Carreres, A., Noriega-Sánchez, M. and Calduch, C. 2018. *Mundos en palabras: Learning Advanced Spanish through Translation*. Abingdon and New York: Routledge.

References

Bellos, D. (2012). *Is That a Fish in your Ear?: The Amazing Adventure of Translation*. London: Penguin Books.

Carreres, A., Noriega-Sánchez, M. and Calduch, C. (2018). *Mundos en palabras: Learning Advanced Spanish through Translation*. Abingdon and New York: Routledge.

Chuquet, H. and Paillard, M. (1987). *Approche linguistique des problèmes de traduction anglais – français*. Paris: Editions Ophrys.

Cook, G. (2010). *Translation in Language Teaching*. Oxford: OUP.

Demanuelli, C. and Demanuelli, J. (1990). *Lire et traduire: Anglais-français*. Paris: Masson.

Venuti, L. (1995). *The Translator's Invisibility: A History of Translation*. London: Routledge.

Vinay, J.-P. and Darbelnet, J. (1958). *Stylistique comparée du francais et de l'anglais*. Paris: Didier.

Chapter 1

Le Mot juste

> *To be comfortable in another language you need roughly half of the words you possess in your native language – 25,000. As about 40 percent are variants of other words and can be easily inferred, a good estimate of truly unique words you need to start with is 15,000 words.*
>
> *This is a huge number and double what you are expected to learn in 8 years at school. Fortunately, you do not always have to learn them all.*
>
> *Take the word evolution. In Spanish, Italian, and French, the word translates into evolución, evoluzione and évolution. As you can see, many words are almost identical between some languages and come with just slight differences in packaging. Once you understand the rules that govern these differences, you have immediate access to thousands of words.*
>
> *(Bernd Sebastian Kamps, 2010: 13)*

Summary

One of the main objectives of this chapter is to draw attention to the fact that there is rarely a one-to-one relationship between the signifiers encountered in French and in English. The "signifiers" we shall examine here will be words, or lexical items. In focusing on word meaning, or lexical semantics, we will look at ways in which French and English make different choices when it comes to categorising experience. Firstly, we acknowledge how there are many similarities and borrowings within the two languages, owing to the communal ancestry of the two languages. We also attend to significant lexical differences between French and English and the ways in which we must be mindful of the fact that full equivalence between lexical items is rare. Throughout our examples, we have recourse to lexicological notions to identify the complex way words are patterned, linked together, fossilised and made new. Crucially, we show how a familiarity with these specific features can be useful for navigating between the two languages when translating.

Introduction

It is easy to assume that translation is easy, especially when it comes to vocabulary. All you need is a good dictionary, and off you go. Imagine that you are at

Figure 1.1

a museum and you see a 17th-century portrait of a man with the following caption: *man in armour with yellow flowing hair*. A simple sentence to translate. You remember studying colours in the first few weeks of your French course – yellow is *jaune* and has always been *jaune*, just like brown is *marron*, and what about ginger, is it red, or is it something else? Anyway, you came up with *Homme en armure aux cheveux jaunes et ondulés*. You have nailed it (well done for suggesting *ondulé* and for making *cheveux* plural), except that unless you are describing a *Playmobil* figurine, using the adjective *jaune* to describe the colour of a person's hair is bound to get a few sneers from your Francophone friends. Similarly, using the word *femelle* when trying to explain to your feminist friends that feminism is not solely a female issue, *le féminisme ça n'est pas que pour les femelles* (said in an attempt to express the idea that *feminism is not just a female issue*) might incur the ire of your feminist interlocutors, and for very good reasons. Regardless of their actual take on the issue, such a statement is likely to be interpreted as an insult. *Et pourtant*, I hear you say, *c'était dans le dictionnaire*. Of course it is in the dictionary, and you certainly did not mean to insult anyone, and using *femelle* to translate *female* works in a large number of contexts. It is just that certain forms that share formal properties in both languages are not semantically equivalent, or not in every context. An "equivalent" term might be restricted to certain usages and carry different connotations and associations (in French, *femelle* is restricted to animals and using it to refer to women is thus highly offensive).

1 Linguistic systems and conceptual categories

The fact that linguistic systems organise the world into different conceptual categories obviously makes the task of translating difficult. What does it mean when we suggest a word or concept is "untranslatable"? As Emily Apter underlines (Cassin, 2017: xiv), one of the risks "of the casual use of 'untranslatable' is the suggestion of an always absent perfect equivalence. Nothing is exactly the same in one language as in another, so the failure of translation is always necessary and absolute". That said, this rather neglects the fact that "some pretty good equivalences are available" and that such a proposition rests on "a dream of perfection we cannot even want, let alone have". As Apter underlines, this longing for perfection is unwanted, since, if there were a perfect equivalence from language to language, "the result would not be translation; it would be a replica".

As Jonathan Culler pointed out in his introduction to the work of the linguist Ferdinand de Saussure:

> If languages were simply a nomenclature for a set of universal concepts, it would be easy to translate from one language to another. One would simply replace the French name for a concept with the English name. If language were like this the task of learning a new language would also be much easier than it is. But anyone who has attempted either of these tasks has acquired, alas, a vast amount of direct proof that languages are not nomenclatures, that the concepts [. . .] of one language may differ radically from those of another. [. . .] Each language articulates or organizes the world differently. Languages do not simply name existing categories, they articulate their own.
>
> (J. Culler, 1976: 21–22)

Saussure himself famously pointed out that *sheep* and *mouton* might have the same meaning (as both terms can be used to refer to the same animal), but do not have the exact same value within their respective linguistic systems (i.e. *sheep* does not have the exact same value in English as *mouton* does in the French lexicon because of the presence of the term *mutton* in the English lexicon). Additionally, *to know* is not the equivalent of *connaître*, as in some cases it can also be translated by *savoir* (Vinay and Darbelnet, 1958).

Observations of this kind are not simply anecdotal. The interdependency of linguistic items within a system is a crucial notion in linguistic theory, as is the notion labelled by Saussure as the "arbitrariness of the sign" (i.e. *there is nothing in the actual form of the word that has any direct connection with the object it refers to in the real world*). The arbitrariness of the sign means that the way the world is conceptualised in the different languages of the world is never identical between two languages.

However, the fact that language B does not have a lexical item that perfectly matches a lexical item in language A does not mean that the concept in question cannot be communicated in language B. If, as conceptual systems, languages tend to show a lot of differences, they also do have a lot in common. From a cognitive point of view, natural languages are, after all, the product of the human brain, and, from an anthropological point of view, they are used the globe over in similar ways. As Lakoff and Johnson (1980) have rightly shown, the metaphors that appear in idioms in different languages often operate on the same principles – language A and language B might not have exactly the same idiom (i.e. idiom A might not be translatable word for word in language B), but the principles at play are identical. Whether you have a *frog* or a *cat* in your throat is significantly different and yet conceptually very similar from the point of view of the processes involved in creating an idiom of this kind. A spade might not be called a spade in French, and surveying garden tools and implements, or any kind of inanimate object, will not help find the right French term to stand in for a spade. In fact, it is an animal that is required: *appeler un chat un chat*. That said, both *to call a spade a spade* and *appeler un chat un chat* operate on the principle of *calling a something a something*. We are therefore dealing with a structure that is productive in both languages and can easily lend itself to a range of adaptations, depending on context.

2 An Historical overview of the two languages

In addition to sharing properties because of the very nature of language, French and English are also closely related historically and culturally. The Old French motto *Honi soit qui mal y pense*, originally used as the motto of the British chivalric Order of the Garter in the 14th century, can be found on every British passport. Similarly, the motto *Dieu et mon droit* can be found on many official buildings in the United Kingdom and as far afield as New Zealand and Australia. However tempting it might be to see the presence of these French mottos in the English-speaking world as purely anecdotal (or as a manifestation of a British eccentricity, a remnant of a long-gone form of Francophilia), they are in fact a reminder that following the Norman Conquest of 1066, Norman French was the primary language of the English Royal Court and ruling elite. And it continued to be for well over three centuries.

This situation had a profound effect on the English lexicon. According to eminent experts, such as David Crystal (Crystal, 2003), after the Norman Conquest, the influx of words from the continent doubled the size of the lexicon to over 100,000 items, and many French terms were borrowed and integrated into Middle English (*authority, accuse, abbey, art, action, advise*, the list is considerable). Besides, it was not solely words that were borrowed from the French language but also affixes and their derivational patterns (*con-, trans-, pre-, -ance, -tion, -ment*). This created many commonalities between the two languages, which gives English language learners of French a great advantage, since for an English speaker a large section of the French lexicon is already familiar, as are some of the processes by which new words are created. If we add to this the fact that English also borrowed several thousand words from Latin in the 14th and 15th century, via Spanish and Italian, we can rightly expect the similarities between the French and English lexicons to be even more significant. According to Crystal, "by the end of the Renaissance, the growth in classically-derived vocabulary, especially from Latin had doubled the size of the lexicon again" (2003). Some of the Latin-derived words found in the English lexicon might not be identical to those encountered in the French language, but most will show a definite *air de famille*. Consider, for instance, the adjective *kingly* and its synonyms *royal* and *regal* in English – *kingly*, which has a Germanic origin, has no counterpart in French, while *royal*, which comes from the French, does: *royal* (same spelling). So too does *regal* which comes from Latin and corresponds to the adjective *régalien* in French.

Owing to the essentially dual origin of the English lexicon (Germanic on the one hand and Latin and French on the other), there are many *doublets* (pairs of words) in English (note, in passing, that the term *doublet* itself comes from Old French). One of the most noticeable manifestations of this phenomenon is the presence of a term to designate an animal (ox, calf, sheep) and of another one for the meat (beef, veal, mutton). This is a distinction which probably originates in the fact that while the peasantry who looked after cattle in the Middle English period (1100–1400) spoke English, the aristocracy and ruling elite who consumed the meat spoke French (Paillard, 2000). This also explains the presence of synonyms such as *bring up* and *educate, wound* and *injure, looking-glass* and *mirror, might* and *power, folk* and *people, clever* and *intelligent* and so on – and of terms based on a figure of speech called *hendiadys* (literally two for one), which is used for emphasis and in most cases consists in two words linked by the conjunction "and" *(e.g. nice and clean)* where one term has a Germanic origin the other one a Latin one: *I pray and beseech you, my last will and testament, by leaps and bounds* (Paillard, 2000).

Taking note of the communal ancestry French and English share can, from the point of view of translation, provide ways of overcoming translation difficulties at a lexical level. When faced with a particularly difficult word to translate from English into French, it is always a good strategy to try and see, for instance, whether there might be a synonym in English which might correspond to a cognate word in French.

If, for instance, you have to translate the following sentence:

She was given a reward

but cannot think of a word in French to translate *reward*, try to think of a synonym in English for *reward* – *recompense* or *prize*, for instance (for which there are terms in French which are almost morphologically identical):[1]

On lui a remis une récompense.
On lui a remis un prix.

3 The Trouble with polysemy

Overall, however, it is important to keep in mind, as indeed others have pointed out, that in spite of the numerous clues sharing a common ancestry provides, "full cross-linguistic synonymy is the exception not the rule" (Hervey and Higgins, 1992: 90). If we look at the following,

Figure 1.2

leaving aside the issue of the tastelessness of the pun, it is clear that the intended humour of the message is based on the polysemy (i.e. multiple meanings) of the term *erection* (e.g. *penile erection, erection of a building*). If the pun can easily be understood by a native speaker of French – the French term *érection* shares the same Latin source (the noun *erectio* and the verb *erigere*) and can be used in French with both meanings as in English – it would be unthinkable for a French scaffolding company to have a slogan such as *Spécialistes de l'érection*. This is because the second meaning (*penile erection*) is in contemporary French much more salient than the first one (*erection of a building*); contrary to the verb *ériger*, which can be used to refer to the erection of a building but not, in contemporary French, for *penile erection*. The fact that two terms are formally identical and etymologically related does not guarantee that they can be used interchangeably. Polysemy occurs and will occur whether the words in question are formally related or not. Let us take the example of bathroom and *salle de bain*, which seemingly refer to the same part of a house. If you wanted to go to the toilet and requested the bathroom in English, your host would understand exactly what your request was. However, if you asked a French speaker "Où est la salle de bain?" they would assume you wanted to have a wash and would direct you to the *salle de bain*, not to the toilet.

4 Friend or foe?

The French and English lexicons show a lot of similarities, and translation difficulties can often be overcome (or even *surmounted*!) by going back to their communal root. Awareness of etymological connections greatly helps develop one's translation and vocabulary learning strategies since there are many lexical items that show kinship across the French and English lexicons, what we could call *bons amis*. However, we also need to be mindful of the fact that full equivalence between lexical items is rare. There are indeed numerous *bons amis*, as English-speaking learners of French will know, but there is also a considerable amount of *faux amis*, alas, a much more commonly known category, no doubt due to their vast number. Because *faux amis* (i.e. deceptive cognates) are so numerous, we will only outline briefly what the different categories are since several studies have dealt with this issue quite comprehensively: dictionaries such as Koessler and Derocquiny (1928), Kirk-Greene (1981), Thody, Evans and Rees (1985), Van Roey et al. (1998), for instance, but also English-French translation handbooks (Vinay Darbelnet, 1958; Chuquet and Paillard, 1987; Armstrong, 2005). First of all, following Chuquet and Paillard's 1987 typology, it is useful to distinguish *faux amis complets* from *faux amis partiels* – the first category involves words which show a strong formal resemblance but have nothing in common semantically (*axe, coin, hate, supply*, etc.) and constitute the category which is the least troublesome since the risk of confusion is low. However, the risk is greater for items that show a strong resemblance in form as well as kinship in meaning. This is the case for terms such as *agenda, attend, lecture, location, surname, trespass, mundane* and so on, which can never be translated by the formally equivalent French term (*agenda, attendre, lecture, location,* etc.). In this sense, they are *faux amis complets* and are, to an extent, easier to handle than *faux amis partiels,* which also show formal and semantic similarities but can sometimes (however, not always) be translated by the term that is formally equivalent in French (*actual, education, formal, book, chair, cake, oil, order, response, sympathy, charity, surgery, golf,* etc.).

Some cognate lexical items might also be used to denote the same reality but have different connotations – that is the case for items such as *routine, juvenile* and *politician. En français: il faut casser la routine* – in English, *routine must be preserved*! In French, *la routine* refers to the tedium and monotony of everyday life rather than a regular pattern of events. Similarly, if *juvenile* can be used in French (as in English) to denote bad behaviour: *la délinquance juvénile,* it can also be used to denote something positive: *un sourire juvénile.* It is interesting to note that this term does exist in English but is used by dentists to refer to teeth that are abnormally short from birth and not a youthful facial expression. Similarly, *politician,* which is neutral in English, tends to be the equivalent of *femme/homme/figure politique* rather than *politicien-ne*; the latter can be used in French too (and perhaps more so in Canadian French than in European French) but often appears in a context where politics and the actions of politicians are decried. It is used with pejorative adjectives such as *verreux, lamentable* and *corrompu* or, if used as an adjective, with nouns such as *manipulation, manoeuvre* and *querelle.*

The lack of one-to-one correspondence (or *anisomorphism*) between English and French terms that share a communal ancestry is not confined to items that English has borrowed from Latin or Old French. If we look at English words that French has recently borrowed, it is clear that alongside *straight borrowings* (i.e. where both meaning and form are borrowed), there are a number of *adapted borrowings* (i.e. where the English form is gallicised, e.g. *conteneur* rather than *container*) and *semantic calques* (which occurs when, in the case of an already existing lexical item, a new meaning is borrowed: *développer, réaliser, supporter*).

The English suffix *-ing* has become highly productive in contemporary French. However, it is often added to an English verb base to form nouns that do not correspond to English usage. A lot of *-ing* words such as *camping* and *parking* are in fact *faux ami partiels*: as in English, *le camping* can denote the activity of camping, but in French it can also denote the place where one camps (i.e. a *camp site*). *Un parking* also denotes the place where one parks (*car park, parking lot*) – there is therefore a metonymic shift (from action to place), hence lexical items such as footing (*faire du footing,* meaning *to jog*). These might, understandably, surprise English speakers. Consider also the following: *un lifting* (*a face lift*), *un pressing* (*a dry cleaning business*), or where the suffix *-ing* is added to a French verb base: *le bronzing* (*sun bathing*). There are also cases where only the English root is borrowed, in the case of *speakerine* (a female radio or TV presenter, a term slightly quaint these days) or *un catcheur* (*a wrestler*). *Ball* *trap* is another *faux anglicisme* that English speakers might find puzzling; it means *clay pigeon shooting* or *trap-shooting*, as might *pipi room* (an informal word for *the toilet*, incidentally also used in Italian).

A lot of contemporary verbs are also created by adding the French suffix *-er* to an English root (*flipper, zapper, speeder*) and usually have a meaning quite distinct from their meaning in English (*flipper* means *freak out*, *zapper* can only be used in relation to TV channels, *speeder* means to rush or to feel nervous).

There are, of course, a lot of false Gallicisms in English too (items that do not correspond morphologically and/or semantically to the original French etymon): *bon viveur* (rather than *bon vivant*), *folie de grandeur* for *folie des grandeurs*, *deluxe* for *de luxe* or *haut de gamme, ensuite* (*bathroom*) for (*salle de bain*) *privée* ou *attenante*, a *chandelier* for *un lustre*, *a foyer* for *un hall* or *un vestibule*, a *double entendre* (*un sous-entendu* or *une allusion*) – although *double entendre* comes from the French, it is obsolete in contemporary French (see Solano, 2015 for an in-depth overview of Gallicisms).

These items illustrate the fact that once borrowed forms enter a linguistic system, they always undergo a process of assimilation into the TL system. This assimilation is not always straightforward and borrowings raise morphological questions. Both in French and English, speakers are often unsure of what the plural form of nouns borrowed from Latin might be – what is the plural of *corpus*: is it *corpuses* or *corpora*? *Referendums* or *referenda*? This also happens with English nouns that are used in French. Let's consider the case of the English suffix *-man*, which has become quite productive in French; should French or English morphology prevail when used in the plural? Should the plural of *tennisman* (i.e. *tennis player*) or *rugbyman* (i.e. *rugby player*) be *tennismen/rugbymen*, or should it be *tennismans/rugbymans*? Note that both *rugbyman* and *tennisman* are cases of the pseudo-anglicisms *rugbyman*, since they are lexical items that do not correspond to English usage.

5 Morpho-semantic categories (polysemy, synonymy, hyponymy, etc.)

Having a clear idea of the semantic relationship between lexical items in the lexicon is a useful skill for the translator. In what follows, we will be looking at different kinds of lexical relationships. *Polysemy*, when lexical items can have different acceptions (i.e. meanings) has been mentioned, as has *synonymy* (lexical items which are formally distinct but have the same meaning). It is worth stressing that pure synonymy, inter and intra-lingually, is rare. For example, *father* and *daddy* correspond to the same person in the real world; however, these lexical items cannot be used interchangeably in every context, as Umberto Eco points out (Eco, 2008), with the example of the Balzac novel title *Le Père Goriot*. *Le Père* cannot be translated as *daddy* here because you would only use the latter to address your own father in an affectionate manner. Interestingly, *Father* cannot be used either because in English it is only used to refer to one's own father or to a *man of the cloth*.

Antonyms are also essential items in the translator's toolbox. Where a synonym will not work, if dealing with an affirmative sentence, an *antonym* (i.e. a word opposite in meaning to another) combined with a negation might well do the trick. If, for instance, you want to rewrite the following sentence and avoid using the adjective *cold*:

The water is too cold.

One obvious solution is to propose:

The water is not hot enough.

When translating, this might be a useful strategy if you have to translate a term that you cannot immediately find a synonym for, or if there is simply no equivalent in the TL. There are three different types of antonyms: (1) binary opposites where the two meanings do not lie on a continuous spectrum: dead/alive, off/on, day/night, identical/different; (2) gradable antonyms: hot/cold, warm/cool, heavy/light, old/young, early/late; the two meanings lie on a continuous spectrum; and (3) relational antonyms: teacher/pupil, husband/wife, doctor/patient, and so on.

Let us now consider *homonyms*. Homonyms are lexical items which have the same form but a different meaning. They can be either (1) homophones (words that sound the same) or/and (2) homographs (words that are spelled in the same way).

Let us look at the translation of the following picture book for children, *Give Us a Smile, Cinderella*. The king who wants his son to get married suggests organising a ball – *We'll hold a ball* – to which his son responds: *What, a football?*

"We'll hold a ball!"
he cried excitedly.

"What, a football?"
asked Rupert.

Figure 1.3

"No! Not a *football*," said the king.
"A *ball* ball! A big posh party.

Figure 1.4

The humour stems from the ambiguity of the term *ball* which can be used to refer to (1) a formal occasion where people dance or (2) a spherical object used in a game, hence the misunderstanding. We are dealing with two distinct words (homonymy) rather than with one word with two different acceptions (polysemy), as these terms have a different etymology; 1 and 2 come from two different etymons: the Proto-Germanic *ballu-z*, and the Italian noun *ballo* from the verb *ballare* (to dance), respectively. It goes without saying that translating a pun based on homophony always poses a challenge, as two words that mean different things but sound the same in the source language (SL) are unlikely to correspond to two words that share those same characteristics in the TL.

The English term *ball* corresponds to two distinct French words which are also homophones, *une balle* for (1), *un bal* for (2) – note that *un ballon* is however more common when referring specifically to the spherical object people use when they play football. While *balle* and *bal* are homophones, and could therefore trigger a misunderstanding, which is what we are looking for here, one noun is masculine and the other is feminine, and the risk of confusing one for the other is therefore less likely to occur (*il faut une balle* cannot be confused for *il faut un bal*). Besides that, the misunderstanding is reinforced in the source sentence by the use of the verb *hold* in the sentence, "we'll hold a ball". So, the translator might be able to use *bal(le)*, but will have to be quite creative to provide something that will work. Alternatively, the translator could opt for a different strategy and create an ambiguous utterance that does not necessarily rely on the use of a homophone; what matters is that the whole utterance lends itself to two distinct interpretations.

In the French edition of the book, the French translator uses *un bal* in the French translation, trying to create an ambiguity based on the partial homophony of *bal* and *ballon*, as phonetically the first syllable of *ballon* is identical to *bal*.

Il se trouve qu'un prince charmant nommé Rodolphe habite vraiment dans un château tout proche. Son père, le roi, voudrait qu'il se marie et il lui vient une excellente idée! Il s'écrie avec enthousiasme :

— Nous allons donner un bal!

— Un bal... lon? demande Rodolphe.

Figure 1.5

Although a misunderstanding is created, the French utterance does not quite have the immediacy and transparency of the English original, and it is hard to imagine that it will have the same effect on the French reader. The reader will clearly realise that there has been a misunderstanding but will probably not perceive it as particularly humorous.

— Mais non! Un *bal*, pas un *ballon*, répond le roi. Une grande soirée dansante très chic!

Figure 1.6

Another very useful notion when analysing the semantic relations between lexical items that belong to the same linguistic system is the notion of *hypernymy* and its structural counterpart: *hyponymy*. A *hypernym* is a word with a generic meaning constituting a category into which words with more specific meanings are included. For example, *dog* is a hypernym of *animal*; *collier* is a hypernym of *dog*. The generic term is called a hypernym, the specific one a hyponym (e.g. hypernym: *dog*; related hyponyms: *poodle*, *bulldog*, *labarador*, *German shepherd*, etc.). Why is this useful to a translator, you may be wondering? Firstly, if the translator cannot find a word specific enough in language B to translate a specific term in language A, s/he might opt for a generic term. Secondly, it is important to note that there are cases where language A uses a hypernym and language B a hyponym (and vice versa).

The English lexical item *room* can for instance be translated into French by *pièce* if referring to the number of rooms in a house, *chambre* for the place where one sleeps, or *bureau* for the place where one works (Chuquet and Paillard, 1987).

Other examples from English into French where English uses a generic term and French a more specific one:

> *River*: fleuve, rivière
> *Driver*: conducteur, chauffeur, automobiliste
> *Brown*: roux (sugar), brun/châtain (hair), marron (objects)
> *Bell*: cloche (church), clochette, sonnette, sonnerie, timbre, grelot
> *Boot*: botte, bottine, brodequin, grosse chaussure

The same phenomenon can be observed in the opposite direction (French hyperym → English hyponym):

> *Bord*: edge, border, rim/brim, side, hem, brink, verge, shore/strand
> *Esprit*: mind, spirit, wit
> *Education*: education, upbringing, learning
> *Souvenirs*: memories, souvenirs, memoirs
> *Grincement*: grating, squeaking, scratching, creaking, scraping, screeching, gnashing

The above examples are taken from Chuquet and Paillard (1987) and Demanuelli and Demanuelli (1990). Paillard (2000) provides the following:

> *A clatter of dishes*: un bruit de vaisselle
> *A scraping of chairs*: un bruit de chaises
> *Sabre rattling*: des bruits de bottes

Conclusion

In this overview, we have sought to give the reader a sense of some of the different issues involved when focusing on lexis. Our main objective has been to show that there is rarely a one-to-one relationship between French and English lexical items, in spite of what could be anticipated between two languages that share a common ancestry. Both languages partly developed from Latin, which largely accounts for the morphological commonalities between the two languages – a vast number of affixes can be transposed from one language to the other (*con-, trans-, pre-, -ance, -tion, -men*t) and means that there is great transparency. However, these similarities are deceptive; they often are the *arbre qui cache la forêt*. As we have seen, false friends are numerous and (pseudo-)Anglicisms and Gallicisms are far from being transparent. The same is true for connotations, which can vary greatly even when two words are equivalent from the point of view of their connotative meaning.

The objective of this chapter has been to try to develop a better understanding of how lexis is organised in each language (internally and in relation to one another). The exercises in the next section are designed to further explore the challenges encountered thus far.

6 Activités de mise en pratique

I Etymologie comparée

Compléter les séries bilingues ci-dessous sur le modèle proposé. Noter les cas pour lesquels le mot anglais d'origine française ou latine n'a pas exactement le même sens ou les mêmes connotations que le mot anglais d'origine germanique.

Mot français	Mot anglais (origine française ou latine)	Mot anglais (origine germanique)
abandoner	to abandon	to relinquish
commencer	to commence	to begin
adolescence		
anniversaire		
breuvage		
chef		
copieux		
détester		
enfant		

Mot français	Mot anglais (origine française ou latine)	Mot anglais (origine germanique)
exécuter		
fraternel		
maternel		
paternel		
pensif,-ive		
sentiment		
vendre		
voyage		

II Noms composés: concret vs. abstrait; composition et dérivation

Comme le signalent Vinay and Darbelnet (1958), le français utilise souvent des termes abstraits là où l'anglais utilise des termes concrets facilement reconnaissables. On a très souvent affaire en anglais à un nom composé (deux noms autonomes sont combinés: a horse show) là où en français on rencontre un nom suivi d'un adjectif relevant d'un processus de dérivation (pour former l'adjectif, on combine une base et un affixe: hippique). On obtient alors pour "a horse show" (nom + nom) "un concours hippique" (nom + adjectif formé à partir d'une base savante: "hippo" plutôt que "cheval").

Compléter sur cette base les séries ci-dessous.

Terme abstrait en français	Terme concret en anglais
Un concours <u>hippique</u>	A <u>horse</u> show
Un arbre <u>généalogique</u>	A <u>family</u> tree
Un témoin <u>oculaire</u>	
Un globe <u>oculaire</u>	
Les papilles <u>gustatives</u>	
Les empreintes <u>digitales</u>	
La fréquence <u>cardiaque</u>	

Terme abstrait en français	Terme concret en anglais
Les dommages <u>cérébraux</u>	
Une lotion <u>capillaire</u>	
Une odeur <u>corporelle</u>	
Un implant <u>mammaire</u>	

On observe ce même phénomène pour certains noms français constitués à partir d'une base savante (grecque ou latine):

Une otite	An ear infection
Un orthophoniste	
Un oto-rhino-laryngologiste	
Un pédiluve	
Un ophtalmologiste	
Un antalgique	

On retrouve également ce phénomène (nom ou adjectif abstrait en français, nom ou adjectif concret en anglais) pour des syntagmes ne comportant pas une base savante en français:

Les tâches ménagères	housework
La table d'honneur	
Le bureau central (d'une entreprise)	
L'embouchure d'un fleuve	
	a time zone
La sécurité alimentaire	

III Hyperonymes et hyponymes

Traduire les phrases suivantes en faisant attention aux mots soulignés:

1 Prince Charming had a privileged <u>upbringing</u>.

Aladdin only received a very basic <u>education</u>.

2 Grandmother's cottage in the wood has two <u>rooms</u> upstairs and two downstairs.

Although the princess didn't want to sleep, she had to stay in her <u>room</u> and rest.

3 Hansel has <u>brown</u> hair and wears <u>brown</u> shoes.

Gretel likes eating <u>brown</u> sugar and has <u>ginger</u> hair.

They live in a house made of <u>ginger</u>bread.

4 Cinderella hurt her <u>leg</u> when running from the palace at midnight.

Do you know how many <u>legs</u> unicorns have?

5 Sleeping Beauty did not hear the church <u>bell</u> this morning.

The Cheshire Cat did not have a <u>bell</u> around his neck.

6 Poor Little <u>Red</u> Hen; whenever she asks the other animals for help, she gets no assistance!

The Big Bad Wolf approached Little <u>Red</u> Riding Hood and asked her where she was going.

7 Do you know what shoe <u>size</u> the giant is?

The dragon lives in a house the <u>size</u> of a mountain.

8 A girl <u>stitching</u> or doing domestic chores waiting for Prince Charming is sexist!

The Beast had a nasty wound that required <u>stitches</u>.

9 *Puss in <u>Boots</u>* is about a cat who uses trickery and deceit to gain power.

"Forget about Seven-league <u>boots</u>; we don't live in a fairy tale. I will put my climbing <u>boots</u> on and climb up the tower", said the prince to Rapunzel.

10 The National Dog <u>Show</u> had just started when the 101 Dalmatians arrived.

Jack went to buy some beans at the agricultural <u>show</u> in Paris.

IV Emprunts anglais utilisés en français

On rencontre en français beaucoup de termes empruntés à l'anglais. Ces emprunts confèrent très souvent aux énoncés un aspect "cool", une connotation de (pseudo-)modernité qui explique en grande partie qu'on les retrouve fréquemment dans le parler des jeunes (ou des "djeuns" pour reprendre un terme de plus en plus usité). Dans le texte ci-dessous, une adolescente parle de Kevin, un garçon qu'elle a connu au lycée. Réécrivez ce texte en remplaçant les termes en italique par des termes relevant du français standard.

Kevin était vraiment un mec trop *cool*. Avec lui, on savait toujours à quoi s'en tenir. Un mec vraiment *au top* qui *speedait* jamais, ne *partait jamais en live*, toujours super *relax*. Je savais que je pouvais vraiment compter sur lui. J'aimais bien son côté *clean*: toujours bien coiffé, bien habillé, et jamais d'embrouilles. En plus, il était super *fun* et avait *un look* un peu bcbg que j'aimais bien. J'adorais quand il mettait son *blazer* ou parfois son *duffel coat* . . . il était à l'opposé des *bad boys* qu'il y a partout. Malheureusement, il a déménagé et on s'est perdu de vue . . .

L'autre jour je faisais du *shopping* quand j'ai eu *un flashback*, je me suis revue marcher avec lui dans les couloirs du centre commercial, je sentais sa présence, c'était *trippant*. Et puis j'ai vu un type qui de loin lui ressemblait: j'ai vraiment cru que c'était lui, j'ai failli tomber *KO*. Mais en fait c'était un type que j'avais croisé au lycée, un *has been* de première, un type complètement *space* qui se prend pour une *rock star* mais qui, en fait, est *un loser* complet. Ça m'a vraiment fait *flipper* de me tromper à ce point.

Chaque fois que j'ai un coup *de blues*, c'est à Kevin que je pense. Ça me donne un petit coup de *boost* de penser à lui. Je me dis que *la life* vaut d'être vécue, qu'un jour on va se retrouver, et que ce sera le *big love*. On s'aimera comme des fous et ce sera le plus parfait des *happy end*. En attendant, il faut que je fasse attention au *burn-out* parce que ça c'est pas *cool*.

V Traduction d'un conte pour enfant

Traduire ce texte extrait de l'ouvrage "Give us a Smile, Cinderella", qui est une adaptation du conte pour enfants Cendrillon:

Once upon a time there was a young girl called Cinderella. She lived in a big house with her mean old stepmother and two horrible stepsisters, Griselda and Prunella.

They made poor Cinderella do all of the housework while they lazed about eating cakes and sweets.

Griselda and Prunella were so lazy that they couldn't even be bothered to brush their teeth!

Their teeth went yellow, then green, then brown, and some of them even fell out.

The stepsisters often had toothache too, which made them even meaner. Poor Cinderella worked hard all day. But no matter how tired she was, she always brushed her teeth twice a day – once in the morning and again just before bedtime.

When she went to sleep, Cinderella dreamed that she was married to a handsome prince, lived in a beautiful castle and never had to do any housework ever.

As it happened, there was a handsome prince called Rupert in a castle not very far away. His dad (the King) wanted Rupert to get married and he had a brilliant idea!

"We'll hold a ball!" he cried excitedly.

"What, a football?" asked Rupert.

"No! Not a football," said the king. "A *ball* ball! A big posh party. You're bound to find the girl of your dreams and we'll have the wedding the week after!"

So that was settled.

A few days later the invitations to the royal ball were sent out.

"Look! There's one for me!" gasped Cinderella.

"Yes, but you can't go!" sneered Griselda.

"That's right," said Prunella, "you've got nothing to wear".

COMMENTAIRES SUR LE TEXTE

Le texte appartient au genre particulier que constitue le conte pour enfants. Il s'agit d'une réécriture d'un conte traditionnel (Cendrillon) qui fait appel à un certain nombre de savoirs préalables liés au genre que constitue le conte (types de personnages: prince/princesse, situations, formulations qui sont typiques de ce genre de textes). On s'attend en outre à ce que le lecteur connaisse le conte originel et possède une familiarité avec les personnages principaux, les situations rencontrées et la trame du récit, connaissances qui conditionnent évidemment les attentes du lecteur. Le texte est constitué d'une narration (première partie du texte) suivie d'un dialogue (deuxième partie du texte). Le narrateur est dans le texte source un narrateur de type troisième personne (narrateur omniscient, omniprésent).

Signalons les différences typographiques que l'on observe entre les dialogues anglais et français. En anglais, les guillemets doubles encadrent les interventions des personnages tandis qu'en français il n'y a pas de guillemets, c'est un tiret long (tiret cadratin) qui signale la prise de parole:

As it happened, there was a handsome prince called Rupert in a castle not very far away. His dad (the King) wanted Rupert to get married and he had a brilliant idea!

"We'll hold a ball!" he cried excitedly.

"What, a football?" asked Rupert.

"No! Not a football," said the king. "A *ball* ball! A big posh party. You're bound to find the girl of your dreams and we'll have the wedding the week after!"

Il se trouve qu'un prince charmant nommé Rodolphe habite vraiment dans un château tout proche. Son père, le roi, voudrait qu'il se marie et il lui vient une excellente idée! Il s'écrie avec enthousiasme:

– Nous allons donner un bal!
– Un bal . . . lon? demande Rodolphe.
– Mais non! Un bal, pas un ballon, répond le roi. Une grande soirée dansante très chic! Tu y rencontreras sûrement la fille de tes rêves et vous vous marierez la semaine d'après.

TRADUCTION PROPOSÉE

La traduction proposée, réalisée par Isabelle Montagnier, est tirée de l'ouvrage *Souris, Cendrillon!* qui a été publié au Canada (Toronto) par les Editions Scholastic.

Je vais vous raconter l'histoire d'une jeune fille nommée Cendrillon. Elle habite dans une grande maison, en compagnie de sa méchante belle-mère et de ses deux horribles demi-sœurs, Gisèle et Prunelle.

Elles obligent la pauvre Cendrillon à faire tout le ménage tandis qu'elles paressent et se gavent de gâteaux et de sucreries.

Gisèle et Prunelle sont si paresseuses qu'elles ne prennent même pas la peine de se brosser les dents!

Leurs dents jaunissent, puis verdissent, brunissent, et certaines tombent.

Les deux sœurs ont souvent mal aux dents, ce qui les rend encore plus désagréables.

La pauvre Cendrillon travaille jour et nuit. Mais même si elle est très fatiguée, elle se brosse toujours les dents deux fois par jour: une fois le matin et une fois juste avant d'aller se coucher.

La nuit, elle rêve qu'elle se marie avec un prince charmant, qu'elle habite dans un magnifique château et qu'elle n'a plus à faire le ménage de toute sa vie.

Il se trouve qu'un prince charmant nommé Rodolphe habite vraiment dans un château tout proche. Son père, le roi, voudrait qu'il se marie et il lui vient une excellente idée! Il s'écrie avec enthousiasme:

– Nous allons donner un bal!
– Un bal . . . lon? demande Rodolphe.
– Mais non! Un bal, pas un ballon, répond le roi. Une grande soirée dansante très chic! Tu y rencontreras sûrement la fille de tes rêves et vous vous marierez la semaine d'après.

Tout est donc réglé.
Quelques jours plus tard, les invitations au gand bal royal arrivent.

– Regardez! Il y a une invitation pour moi s'exclame Cendrillon.
– Oui, mais tu ne peux pas y aller, se moque Gisèle.
– C'est vrai, renchérit Prunelle. Tu n'as rien à porter.

COMMENTAIRE DE LA TRADUCTION PROPOSÉE

Temps verbaux   On notera que contrairement à ce que l'on observe dans le texte source où le prétérit constitue le temps verbal le plus majoritairement utilisé dans la narration, c'est pour le présent de narration que le traducteur a opté dans le texte français. Le fait de ne pas utiliser les temps du passé dans la narration française va de pair avec un certain *nivellement* en ce qui concerne l'aspect verbal. En effet, si le passé simple ou le passé composé avaient été utilisés comme temps de la narration, il aurait alors fallu alterner entre l'un de ces temps et l'imparfait pour distinguer entre les différences aspectuelles qui apparaissent dans le texte source (passé simple ou passé composé pour les action ponctuelles, imparfait pour les actions en train de se produire et pour celles qui sont habituelles: aspects duratif et fréquentatif).

Lexique   Le texte comprend un certain de *noms propres* qui correspondent aux noms des personnages, contrairement à l'idée très répandue selon laquelle les noms propres ne se traduisent pas. Il va ici de soi que le nom du personnage "Cinderella" ne saurait être conservé tel quel en français: Cendrillon s'impose ici comme la seule solution possible. Pour ce qui est des noms des deux horribles demi-sœurs: "Griselda" et "Prunella", on notera qu'ils ont été modifiés en Gisèle et Prunelle, noms qui correspondent à des formes francisées (la terminaison en -*e* pour les prénoms féminins français étant plus fréquente que la terminaison en -*a*). On notera également que le prénom du prince "Rupert" a été modifié en Rodolphe (du point de la fréquence, le prénom anglais "Rupert" est très peu usité en français). En proposant Rodolphe, le traducteur fait donc le choix de proposer à ses jeunes lecteurs un prénom plus facilement reconnaissable.

Notons que la francisation des noms propres est courante en ce qui concerne *les noms de personnages historiques* (Christophe Colomb, Léonard de Vinci, Galilée), *les noms de lieux* (Londres, Edimbourg, Pékin, Le Caire), *les noms d'auteurs ou de personnages de l'antiquité* (Platon, Socrate, Euripide, Alceste, etc) pour lesquels seules les formes établies vont pouvoir être utilisées.

Signalons que le très hyperonymique verbe "say" qui apparaît dans la dernière phrase du dialogue ("That's right," said Prunella, "you've got nothing to wear.") correspond à un terme hyponymique ("renchérir") dans la traduction française. On observe ce phénomène ("say" en anglais →terme plus spécifique que le verbe "dire" en français) dans de nombreuses traductions, particulièrement lorsque le verbe "say" est répété.

Il est intéressant de noter que la structure "to go + adjectif de couleur" qui apparaît dans la phrase suivante:

> *Their teeth <u>went yellow, then green, then brown,</u> and some of them even fell out.*

. . . correspond en français à un verbe spécifique (jaunir, verdir, brunir):

> *Leurs dents <u>jaunissent, puis verdissent, brunissent,</u> et certaines tombent.*

Procédés de traduction   Du point de vue des procédés de traduction, on notera *la modulation* (cf. Chapitre 2 sur les procédés de traduction) utilisée pour traduire la formula "once upon a time" attendue en ouverture de conte. Plutôt que de proposer la formule stéréotypée "il était une fois un/une + nom" que l'on rencontre habituellement, le traducteur opte pour "je vais vous raconter l'histoire d'une jeune fille" qui modifie en outre la relation texte-narrateur, puisque la narration est prise en charge par un narrateur première personne, contrairement à ce que l'on observait dans le texte source.

VI Traduction d'un extrait de roman, Deaf Sentence, *David Lodge*

David Lodge – Deaf Sentence

When they were back in the privacy of their bedroom, and while they were restoring it to some kind of order, he apologised for the debacle of the night.

"You drink too much, Desmond", she said. The "Desmond" was an index of her displeasure. Even an acidly ironic "darling" was better than "Desmond".

"It was Lionel's fault, producing that bottle of malt".

"You didn't have to drink it. Anyway, it's not just last night, it's most nights. You're getting addicted".

"Nonsense".

"It's not nonsense".

"All right, I'll prove it", he said. "I won't have a drop to drink today".

She looked at him appraisingly. "You know we're eating out tonight – at the *soi-disant* French restaurant?"

"Yes".

"And you won't have any wine?"

"No".

"Even if the food is not up to much?"

"Even if it's horrible. As I confidently expect".

She laughed. "Well, if you keep to your resolution, darling, I'll be amazed – but delighted."

Analyse du texte

Identifier dans un premier temps la situation décrite dans cette scène: qui sont les personnages, quelle relation les unit, à quels événements récents font-ils référence? Identifier ensuite les difficultés linguistiques que pose le texte (difficultés lexicales, constructions susceptibles d'appeler une transposition ou une modulation (cf. Chapitre 2), modifications grammaticales inévitables). Traduire dans un deuxième temps le texte puis lire attentivement la traduction proposée ci-dessous. Comment les difficultés identifiées ont-elles été abordées? Le texte comporte-t-il des changements qui n'avaient pas été anticipés? Ces changements sont-ils justifiés ou superflus?.

Lorsqu'ils eurent tous les deux retrouvés l'intimité de leur chambre, et tandis qu'ils remettaient un peu d'ordre à la pièce, il s'excusa pour la débâcle de la nuit.

"Tu bois trop, Desmond", dit-elle. Ce "Desmond" était révélateur de son
5   mécontentement. Même un "chéri" prononcé avec une ironie mordante
était préférable à "Desmond".

C'est la faute de Lionel, c'est lui qui a sorti cette bouteille de malt.

– Tu n'étais pas obligé d'en prendre. Et d'ailleurs, ce n'est pas
seulement hier soir, c'est presque tous les soirs. Ça devient une
10   habitude chez toi.

– Ridicule.

– Ce n'est pas ridicule.

– D'accord, je vais te le prouver, dit-il. Je ne boirai pas une seule goutte
d'alcool aujourd'hui.

15 Elle le dévisagea comme si elle cherchait à le tester. "Tu sais que nous
dînons dehors ce soir – à ce *soi-disant* restaurant français?"

– Oui.

– Et tu ne boiras pas de vin?

– Non.

20 – Même si la nourriture n'est pas à la hauteur?

– Même si elle est affreuse. Et je parie qu'elle le sera.

Elle éclata de rire. "Eh bien chéri, si tu tiens tes résolutions, je serai
surprise – mais ravie".

La Vie en sourdine, traduction de Maurice et Yvonne Couturier

Commentaire linéaire de la traduction proposée

- *Lorsqu'ils eurent tous les deux retrouvés* (1): noter l'utilisation du passé antérieur dans cette subordonnée, que la présence de la conjonction de temps
  lorsque justifie (noter également que le passé simple est utilisé dans la proposition principale: *il s'excusa*).
- *intimité* (1) correspond ici à *privacy* dans le TS, terme difficile à traduire en
  français puisqu'il peut aussi correspondre à *vie privée* (*right of privacy* →
  respect de la vie privée, *invasion of privacy* → *atteinte à la vie privée*), *confidentialité* (*privacy statement* → *déclaration de confidentialité*). De la même
  façon, *private* peut être traduit de diverses manières: *a private detective* →
  un détective privé; *a private message* → *un message personnel*; *I hate talking about private matters* → *je déteste parler des affaires intimes*; *a private
  consultant* → *un consultant indépendant*.
- *chambre* (2), *pièce* (3): noter que ces deux termes sont utilisés pour traduire
  le terme *bedroom* – le premier met en avant le caractère spécifique de cet
  espace, le second a une valeur plus générique.

Débâcle (3): *debacle* dans le TS, terme d'origine française dont le sens correspond au sens figuré du terme français (en français, le sens propre est celui de la rupture des glaces d'un cours d'eau). Le terme *fiasco* fonctionnerait également bien dans ce contexte.

Ce "Desmond" (4): noter que l'article défini du TS est traduit par un démonstratif.

Noter la collocation *ironie mordante* (5) qui est très idiomatique.

C'est lui qui . . . (7): noter la structure syntaxique (clivée).

soir (9): correspond à *night* dans le TS (cf. *Saturday Night Fever, La Fièvre du samedi soir*).

Ça devient une habitude chez toi (9–10): modulation de *You're getting addicted*.

Elle le dévisagea (15) – noter l'utilisation de ce verbe qui a le sens très spécifique de regarder quelqu'un avec insistance et qui n'a pas d'équivalent en anglais.

Comme si elle cherchait à le tester correspond à un seul terme dans le TS: *appraisingly*.

Soi-disant is translated here by *soi-disant*!

Elle éclata de rire (22) pour *she laughed*, *éclater de rire* rend l'aspect inchoatif du processus explicite (en anglais *laugh* peut-être inchoatif ou statif).

Note

1   Although reward comes from the Old French word *regarder*, there is not a noun based on that etymological root that means anything close to reward in French; with *recompense* and *prize* there is an obvious equivalent term, the almost morphologically identical French nouns *récompense* and *prix*.

References

Armstrong, N. (2005). *Translation, Linguistics, Culture: A French-English Handbook*. Bristol: Multilingual Matters.

Cassin, B. (2017). *Dictionary of Untranslatables: A Philosophical Lexicon*. Princeton: Princeton University Press.

Chuquet, H. and Paillard, M. (1987). *Approche linguistique des problèmes de traduction anglais – français*. Paris: Editions Ophrys.

Crystal, D. (2003). *The Cambridge Encyclopedia of the English Language*. 2nd ed. Cambridge, UK and New York: Cambridge University Press.

Culler, J.D. (1976). *Saussure*. Hassocks: Harvester Press.

Demanuelli, C. and Demanuelli, J. (1990). *Lire et traduire: anglais-français*. Paris: Masson.

Eco, U. (2008). *Experiences in Translation*, trans. A. McEwen. Toronto and London: University of Toronto Press.

Hervey, S.G.J. and Higgins, I. (1992). *Thinking French Translation: A Course in Translation method: French to English*. London and New York: Routledge.

Kamps, B.S. (2010). *The Word Brain: A Short Guide to Fast Language Learning*. Beyenburg, Cagliari, Paris: Flying Publisher & Kamps.

Kirk-Greene, C.W.E. (1981). *French False Friends*. London: Routledge & K. Paul.

Koessler, M. and Derocquigny, J. (1928). *Les Faux amis: ou, les pièges du vocabulaire anglais (conseils aux traducteurs)*. Paris: Vuibert.

Lakoff, G. and Johnson, M. (1980). *Metaphors We Live By*. Chicago: University of Chicago Press.

Paillard, M. (2000). *Lexicologie contrastive anglais-français: Formation des mots et construction du sens*. Paris and Gap: Ophrys.

Solano, R.M. (2015). Drawing a distinction between false Gallicisms and adapted French borrowings in English. In: C. Furiassi and H. Gottlieb, eds., *Pseudo-English: Studies on False Anglicisms in Europe*. Berlin and Boston: De Gruyter Mouton.

Thody, P., Evans, H. and Rees, G. (1985). *Faux Amis and Key words: A Dictionary-guide to French life and Language through Lookalikes and Confusables*. London: Athlone Press.

Van Roey, J., Granger, S., Swallow, H. (1988). *Dictionnaire des faux amis français-anglais*. Paris and Gembloux: Duculot.

Vinay, J.-P. and Darbelnet, J. (1958). *Stylistique comparée du francais et de l'anglais*. Paris: Didier.

Chapter 2

Transposition and modulation

Summary

In the previous chapter, we discussed the fact that a one-to-one relationship between the lexical items encountered in French and English should not be posited as a given. We saw that because linguistic systems organise the world along different conceptual lines, equivalent terms are usually restricted to certain contexts and are the exception, not the rule. This chapter will further explore the issue of transferability of meaning. Owing to the fact that there is not a one-to-one correspondence of linguistic forms between the SL and the TL, the translator is obliged to reformulate or "transpose the message" (to use Vinay and Darbelnet's terminology).

Introduction

The Canadian translation scholars Vinay and Darbelnet (1958) demonstrated, in their seminal *Stylistique comparée du français et de l'anglais*, that although literal translation (i.e. word-for-word) is in some cases possible, in most cases, utterances have to be reformulated in order to produce something that is not grammatically or stylistically flawed in the TL. They argued that translators need to develop *strategies* to compensate for the lack of equivalence between the SL and the TL. Although their contrastive analysis is based solely on English and French, their study, which considers how meaning is distributed differently in both languages, is commonly held as one of the first systematic attempts at analysing and classifying the procedures used when translating.

The stimulus for their work on translation strategies (between the English and French language pair) arose from an epiphanous journey they made from Montreal to New York. Their interest was aroused by the difference in tone of the road-signs they came across during their trip. They saw a systematic difference between the formulation of the messages that appeared in the English road-signs and the French ones. Although the utterances they encountered were the same from a functional point of view, something differed in their nature. For instance, warning motorists against speeding, for instance, was communicated via the use of "slow" in English (an adjective with implied imperative meaning). However, this instruction was rendered through the form of an infinitive *ralentir* in French. They also discuss the case of "slippery when wet" (two adjectives linked in causal relationship by the adverb of time *when*) which becomes "glissant si humide" (where one adjective is conditional upon the other).

Observations of this kind led Vinay and Darbelnet to define the notion of "démarche de langue" as "préférence que marque une langue entre des structures également possibles" (Vinay and Darbelnet, 1958: 7).[1] For instance, the fact that, in English, passive forms show a higher degree of frequency than they do in French is indicative of the English preference for the passive voice, and the translator should take this into account. However, there are many instances where it is grammatically and structurally possible in French to have a passive where English uses such a form, and yet a different form is used in the French. Vinay and Darbelnet also point out the preference for noun forms in French, for instance, where English has a verbal form: *before she left*, French will tend to use a nominal form: *avant son départ*. It is, however, not impossible to have a verbal form in French either: *avant qu'elle parte* or a nominal one in English: *before her departure*. Nominalisation (i.e. a noun phrase (NP) generated from another word class) is therefore a stylistic, not a grammatical, phenomenon (a preference which is dictated by the French *démarche de langue*), hence the title of Vinay and Darbelnet's book which describes their approach as a "*stylistique comparée*". Vinay and Darbelnet's objective is to get a better understanding of the arbitrary choices English and French writers make when they write in their respective languages. Their aim is to develop a "méthode de traduction". They stress that the method can only generate observations of comparability of use in context for a given period of time since use will vary over time. Thus, instances of correspondence of function of given forms between source text (ST) and target text (TT) will only hold true for synchronic instances of use. Although identifying recurring patterns is crucial, it is just as essential not to lose sensitivity to context and not view the regularities identified by Vinay and Darbelnet as rules that govern how meaning is transferred in any context and believe them to be entirely predictable at any given time. As others have pointed out, it is important, for instance, to note when discussing *nominalisation* that although the "the translator is statistically more likely to transpose *from* a noun when translating into English, and *to* a noun when translating into French" there are "plenty of exceptions to the statistical norm" (Hervey and Higgins, 1992: 234).

Vinay and Darbelnet's focus on the linguistic changes that occur in translation led them to classify the different procedures and strategies to which translators have recourse. However, many translation theorists see this type of approach as far too reductive and prescriptive. Criticism of linguistic approaches to translation has been prevalent since the 1980s, when a shift from linguistically oriented approaches to culturally oriented ones occurred (translation studies was then characterised by the "cultural turn"). The prescriptive orientation of many early linguistic approaches to translation was challenged by scholars who argued that it did not serve the interest of translation studies. As an empirical discipline, its aim ought to explain what translation is, rather than what it should be. Additionally, the earlier theories were criticised for being simplistic, seen as divorced from context and presenting a deceptive façade of scientificity. As Mona Baker points out, in linguistics-oriented studies, translation difficulties were perceived "as essentially formal in nature" (Baker, 2011: 21).

In spite of the criticism it has received, it is our contention that the linguistic approach can help us develop our awareness of linguistic norms; of the interconnection between style and genres (or text types); of the idiosyncrasies of a particular author or narrator, and of the writing norms of a particular time period. The linguistic approach also helps us understand the translation process which oscillates constantly between literal and free translation. At both ends of the translation spectrum can be found *literal* (or word-for-word) translation on the one hand (which is sometimes referred to in the translation theory literature as *direct translation*) and *free translation* on the other hand. With free translation, the correspondence between the source utterance and the target utterance is not linked to a correspondence between the individual parts of the utterance but rather with the utterance taken as a whole. It can also be useful to distinguish between *literal* and *interlinear* translation. Roughly speaking, a *literal translation* might be clumsy but respects the grammar of the TT; *interlinear translation* on the other hand shows a bias towards the SL and does not aim at being grammatical.

For the sentence "Je persiste à croire qu'elle n'avait pas tort de le dire", Hervey and Higgins (1992: 16) give the following example of literal and free translations, as well as intermediate levels (based on Newmark's typology). These provide a good overview of the different levels of literality that can be envisaged:

> INTERLINEAR I persist to think that she not had no wrong to it say.
> LITERAL I persist in thinking that she wasn't wrong to say it.
> FAITHFUL I still think she wasn't wrong to say it.
> BALANCED I still don't think she was wrong to say it.
> IDIOMISING I still think she hit the nail on the head.
> FREE No way should she retract.

As the example demonstrates, *free translation* relies heavily on context and focuses on the functional and pragmatic value of the text or utterance. The TT might appear semantically quite distinct from the ST, but nevertheless it retains its pragmatic function and its effect on the TT reader is similar to the effect of the ST in the SL. Free translation is, for instance, frequently used when translating songs or poems where the sounds and prosody of the original text are key features of the text. In Malmkjær and Windle (2011), Charlotte Bosseaux gives the following example as an illustration of free translation; the text is taken from a song that appears in the musical *The Fantasticks*, which was translated into Canadian French:

I'd *like* to swim in a *clear* blue stream,
Where the *wa*ter is icy *cold;*
Then *go* to town in a *gol*den gown,
And *have* my fortune *told.*

Je *veux* nager dans une *onde* pure
Vêtue de soie et de *velours*
Pour *con*naître la grande *a*venture
Au *pays* de l'a*mour.*

A different point of view is adopted, "a clear blue stream" becomes "une onde pure" – the blue colour and clarity of the water have given way to the more abstract notion of purity. The second line of the song is even more striking, as being entirely made-up ("Vêtue de soie et de *velours*") since there is no reference to how the narrator is dressed in the English original.

Semantically there is an obvious difference between the ST and TT; they conjure up different images and evoke different sensations. However, the spirit and musicality of the song are retained via the use of assonances, alliterations and rhymes (these devices will be discussed in more detail in Chapter 6).

In this chapter, we will review some of the most common linguistic procedures translators have recourse to in order to avoid translating literally. The chapter will also aim at presenting some of the basic tenets of what is referred to as the *linguistic approach* mentioned above. These procedures correspond to strategies translators use (more or less consciously). Developing awareness of these processes should be of use to anyone who is keen to develop their translation skills and their knowledge of both the SL and TL.

1 Transposition

Unsurprisingly, the main and most common procedure presented by Vinay and Darbelnet is *transposition*, the process whereby an item in the ST is replaced by an item in the TT that belongs to a different grammatical category – that is, a part of speech is substituted for another without a change of meaning of the overall utterance (e.g. a verb is used in the TT, an adjective in the ST).

Example: People are <u>suspicious</u>: les gens <u>se méfient</u> (Chuquet and Paillard, 1987: 12)
Adjective → verb

Here are further examples of other types of grammatical transpositions that often occur when translating from English into French:

Adjective → noun
There are three times as many people in the world as there were <u>when I was born</u>.
*Il y a trois fois plus de gens dans le monde aujourd'hui qu'<u>au jour de ma
naissance.</u>*

Noun → verb
I want no <u>part</u> in spreading such a message.
Je ne veux pas <u>contribuer à</u> propager un tel message.

Adverb → verb
The Conservatives <u>simply</u> want to win votes.
Les conservateurs <u>ne cherchent qu</u>'à gagner des votes.

Adverb → adjective
He paused <u>uncertainly</u> and said: "you could perhaps change your mind".
Il s'arrêta <u>incertain</u> et dit: "vous pourriez peut-être changer d'avis".

Adjective → relative clause
The Very <u>Greedy</u> Bee (title of a children's book).
L'abeille <u>qui aimait trop</u> le miel.

Transpositions of this kind are obligatory to varying degrees. For instance, in the first sentence, *when I was born* could have been translated literally, *quand je suis né(e)*, using the same grammatical form (a verb) in both the ST and the TT. However, translating the second one literally would be misleading – *Les conservateurs cherchaient simplement à gagner des votes* would put a positive spin on what the Conservatives are doing. Transposition is generally required in order to produce an idiomatic TT, that is, when the translator seeks to produce an utterance that might give the reader the impression that the text was originally written in the TL and not in the SL. There are a lot of cases of obligatory transpositions where modifications might occur purely for grammatical reasons. For instance, there are cases where the English articles in the ST disappear in the TT, as in the following examples: *she is a great doctor*: elle est Ø très bon médecin; *what sort of a father are you?*: quel genre de Ø père êtes-vous?; or in structures such as "an attempted + noun" where the participial adjective will systematically have to be translated by a noun "*une tentative de* + noun".

1.1 Chassé-croisé and the translation of phrasal verbs

A particularly useful type of transposition when translating from English into French is what is called in French *chassé-croisé* (a term normally used to refer to an "échange réciproque et simultané de place, de situation" according to the Robert dictionary). Every summer, at the end of July, French radio and TV commentators talk about the *chassé-croisé des juilletistes et des aoûtiens* (when holidaymakers who take their holiday in July are replaced by those who take their holidays in August; this always causes a lot of traffic jams and delays on French roads).

In the English edition of Vinay and Darbelnet's book, *chassé-croisé* is referred to as an *interchange* (Vinay and Darbelnet, 1995: 103–104). This is a particular type of transposition mostly used to translate *phrasal verbs* – idiomatic verbs such as *get in*, *take out* and *walk down* consisting of a verb followed by an adverb or a preposition. Phrasal verbs are an important feature of the English language that has no equivalent structural counterpart in French. The two examples below are taken from Vinay and Darbelnet (1958: Chapter 3):

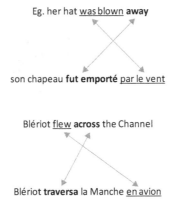

This type of transposition is described by Chuquet and Paillard as a "double transposition où l'on a à la fois un changement de catégorie grammaticale et une permutation syntaxique des éléments sur lesquels est réparti le sémantisme".[2] Firstly, each of the two elements that form the phrasal verb is transposed (i.e. a different part of speech is selected). Secondly, the information is presented in reverse order. If we look at the first sentence, the information that appeared in first position (*blown*) in the ST appears in second position in the TT (*par le vent*). Conversely, the information presented in second position (*away*) in the ST appears in first position in the TT (*fut emporté*). This is what Chuquet and Paillard mean by a "permutation syntaxique des éléments sur lesquels est réparti le sémantisme". Methodologically, the first thing to do when translating phrasal verbs is, therefore, to transpose the preposition or adverb that appears in the English phrasal verb into a French verb and then consider what other part of speech might be used to translate the verb.

The *chassé-croisé* is used almost systematically when translating transitive verbs that take a preposition – such as *run across* and *sail across*:

He <u>ran</u> **across** the street.
*Il **a traversé** la rue <u>en courant.</u>*

Francis Drake <u>sailed</u> **across** the Cape Horn in 1578.
*Francis Drake **a franchi** le cap Horn <u>à la voile</u> en 1578.*

It therefore constitutes a very useful and powerful way of approaching these types of phrasal verbs. Note, however, that there are cases where the *chassé-croisé* is not the only possibility:

He <u>hurried</u> **across** the road.
*Il **traversa** la rue <u>à la hâte.</u>*
Il se dépêcha de traverser la rue.

1.2 Chassé-croisé and motion verbs (verbes de mouvement)

With this specific subset of phrasal verbs – verb of motion + adverb/preposition, such as *walk out*, *drive into* and *ride into* – the *chassé-croisé* is not always complete. The information provided by the adverb or preposition is systematically translated and transposed into a verb; however, the information provided by the verb in the ST is left untranslated. This information has invariably to do with the type of motion involved (the first example is from Chuquet and Paillard, 1987: 14, the second from Vinay and Darbelnet, 1958: 106):

Then he <u>walked</u> **out** of the office.
*Puis il est **sorti** du bureau.*

The horsemen *rode **into*** the yard.
*Les cavaliers sont **entrés** dans la cour.*

With utterances of this type, the information given by the English verb in the ST is better left implied in the TT. The context is clear enough and making that information explicit could be misleading. If we consider the first sentence above, the person leaving the room is in a prototypical situation and is expected to walk out of the room. Underlining the type of motion involved in the TT (*en marchant*) will place a particular emphasis on that piece of information and grant it special status. It signals surprise and the fact that the action was unanticipated. Indeed, *Il est sorti du bureau en marchant* would imply that the fact the person is walking was not expected. We might be in a context where the person in question was not previously able to walk or was pretending not to be able to walk prior to the event (maybe this person was lying or maybe a miracle has just taken place). If we are dealing with a situation where the person was expected to *walk* out of the room, specifying that the person left the room *en marchant* will be redundant or even misleading. The key information here is that the person left the room, not how they left. Similarly, with the second sentence, one would, in most prototypical situations, expect *horsemen* to be entering a courtyard on *horseback*. What matters is that the horsemen entered the courtyard, and specifying how they did it is irrelevant or redundant.

1.3 Prepositions and étoffement (amplification)

Another procedure worth bearing in mind when translating from English into French is what is called in French *étoffement*. As Hervey and Higgins (1992: 236) note: "in translating from English into French [. . .] the translator is seen to be forced into grammatical transposition, usually in the form of adding reinforcing elements to the TT". This "adding reinforcing elements" (or *étoffement* in French, also called *amplification* in English) is a procedure the translator is most likely to use when translating prepositions because, as Hervey and Higgins (1992: 238) point out, "a normal English text is liable to contain prepositional structures that have no structural counterparts in French".

The term *étoffement* comes from the noun *étoffe* (i.e. cloth, material), or *estoffe* in Old French, from which the term *stuff* in English originates. It is here used metaphorically; *étoffer* in this context means to give more importance, strength, body (i.e. a *stuffing up*, which is in fact a *fleshing out*). This procedure is primarily (but not solely) associated with the translation of English prepositions because of the economical and dynamic power of English prepositions. These cannot be translated into French without grammatical transposition, as the examples later will show.

English preposition → French prepositional phrase or French preposition reinforced with a noun

There are a lot of cases where a simple English preposition is rendered in French through a *prepositional phrase*:

If you redeem **through** your dealer, they will advise you what documents they require.
*Si vous effectuez le rachat **par l'intermédiaire de** votre courtier, ce dernier vous avisera des documents que vous devez fournir.*

I have heard worse **from** better people, Mr. Speaker.
*J'ai déjà entendu pire **de la part de** meilleures personnes, monsieur le Président.*

In some cases, as in the two examples here, using the prepositional phrase instead of the corresponding simple form (*par* instead of *par l'intermédiaire de*, *de* instead of *de la part de*) is obligatory in order to make the utterance explicit enough or to avoid ambiguity: *J'ai déjà entendu pire **de** meilleures personnes* could easily be understood as *J'ai déjà entendu pire à propos de meilleures personnes* (*I have heard worse about other people* instead of *I have heard worse from other people*). There are also cases where the use of the compound preposition is motivated by register:

> **Like** many artists of the time, he had to work hard and even fight to get his new ideas across.
> *À l'instar de plusieurs artistes de l'époque, il doit travailler fort et même se battre pour imposer ses idées nouvelles.*

> Discrimination **against** women
> *La discrimination à l'encontre des femmes*

In the two sentences given earlier, *comme* could easily be used in the first one and *contre* in the second one without the sentence semantically lacking something and appearing underdetermined. What motivates the use of the prepositional phrases in these instances is the need to produce an utterance that appears more formal, learned or sophisticated. Register is therefore the driving force. Some prepositional phrases combine a higher register value with a higher degree of specificity, as is the case with *prepositions of space and movement* which very often require an *étoffement* of this type:

> The passenger, a U.K. national and resident of Hong Kong, was arriving on a flight **from** India.
> *Le passager, un citoyen du Royaume-Uni et résident de Hong Kong, arrivait par un vol en provenance de l'Inde.*

> Exports **to** France were the third largest, books accounting for 60% of them.
> *Les exportations à destination de la France étaient les troisièmes plus élevées, et 60 % d'entre elles étaient constituées de livres.*

English preposition → French verb or preposition reinforced by a verb

> What's the quickest way **to** the university please?
> *Quel est le chemin le plus court pour se rendre à l'université?*

> They help me **with** the housework, the cleaning and the cooking.
> *Ils m'aident à faire les travaux ménagers, à nettoyer l'appartement et à faire la cuisine.*

English preposition → preposition reinforced by an adjective or past participle

> The children, **in** the driveway **outside** the hotel, were dragging a large box.
> *Les enfants, regroupés dans l'allée située devant l'hôtel, traînaient une grosse boîte.*

English preposition → French relative clause or present participle

> He pulled out an envelope from the folder **on** his desk.
> *Il sortit une enveloppe du dossier **qui se trouvait** sur son bureau.*
> *Il sortit une enveloppe du dossier **se trouvant** sur son bureau.*

This type of *étoffement* is frequently used in descriptions introduced by *with* (and rarely corresponds to *avec* in French):

> She has decided to marry the man **with** the best-looking moustache in town.
> *Elle a décidé de se marier avec l'homme **qui porterait/aurait** la plus belle*
> *paire de moustache.*

> Nothing can stop the person **with** the right mental attitude.
> *Rien ne peut arrêter une personne **qui a** la bonne attitude mentale.*

What we have observed with *étoffement* is largely due to the fact that French tends to make the connection between the different semantic elements that make up a proposition more explicit than English does. Generally speaking, English favours juxtaposition and tolerates a higher degree of ambiguity than does French. Is a *French student* somebody who studies French or someone who is actually French? Consider translating the following into French:

> The United States Second World war nationwide effort

It would be simply impossible to render this clause into French without introducing a verb and prepositions:

> *L'effort de guerre national **mis en oeuvre** aux Etats-unis **au cours de** la*
> *deuxième guerre mondiale*
> Or even:
> *L'effort de guerre national mis en oeuvre à l'échelle nationale aux Etats-*
> *unis **au cours de** la deuxième guerre mondiale*

The fact that English allows a greater level of underdeterminacy also correlates with the fact that English tends to use more concrete forms where French will select more abstract ones. In French, the relations between the elements that form a sentence are more explicitly marked.

1.4 Adverbials

Adverbials are another type of structure for which there is no systematic one-to-one correspondence across English and French. Morphologically, most adverbs are formed in English by the addition of *-ly* to an adjectival root. Similarly, in

French, adverbs are created by adding *-ment* to an adjectival root (see Battye and Hintze, 1992: 192 for a presentation of this derivational process). Morphologically, there seems to be a perfect fit between the two types of structures. However, as others have pointed out (Astington, 1983: 10–13; Hervey and Higgins, 1992: 99; Armstrong, 2005: 120–121), there are a lot of cases where *-ment* adverbs are best avoided when translating *-ly* adverbs.

Very often the *-ly* adverb will correspond to an NP after the "avec + noun" type:

> I would do it **happily**: *je le ferais <u>avec joie</u>*
> She responded **angrily**: *elle a réagi <u>avec colère</u>*

Or to NPs after the "d'un(e) + noun + adjective" type: "d'un geste x", "d'une façon x", "d'un air x", and so on:

> She spoke **solemnly**: *elle s'est exprimée <u>de façon solennelle</u>*
> The figures have been **wrongly** used: *les chiffres ont été utilisés <u>de façon erronée</u>*

The English structure: "*-ly* adverb + adjective" is often translated as "d'un/une + noun + adjective" in French:

> he was **repulsively ugly**: *il était <u>d'une laideur répugnante</u>*
> she was **intimidatingly smart**: *elle était <u>d'une intelligence désarmante</u>*

Figure 2.1

Generally speaking, as we can see from these examples, the translation of English adverbs often give rise to a noun form in French; nominalisation should therefore be considered as a strong option when translating these forms.

2 Modulation

Alongside *transposition*, the other procedure commonly used by translators in order to avoid translating too literally is *modulation*. While *transposition* involves grammatical categories and syntax, *modulation* concerns mostly the semantic and pragmatic levels. It is defined in broad terms as a change of point of view (Chuquet and Paillard, 1987: 26). Vinay and Darbelnet (1995: 36) define it in the following terms: "variation of the form of the message, obtained by a change in the point of view [. . .] justified when, although a literal, or even transposed, translation results in a grammatically correct utterance". The term *modulation* comes from the French verb *moduler*, which comes from the noun *un mode*, and broadly involves the way or manner in which something occurs or is experienced. Although modulation and transposition are of a different nature, they are intertwined, as modulation will often trigger transposition and vice versa.

One of the most frequently used type of modulations is the *point of view reversal*, or "négation du contraire" following Chuquet and Paillard (1987: 34) who use the correspondence between the utterances below to illustrate this procedure. Somebody visiting a hotel might come across the following sign:

No vacancies: *Complet*

While the utterance is negative in the ST, it is affirmative in the TT – we can note, in passing, that in the first example the translation process correlates with transposing the noun *vacancy* into and adjective *complet*.

Other examples of this phenomenon:

And he may be right: *Et il n'a peut-être pas tort*
It is not difficult to show . . . : *Il est facile de démontrer . . .*

As we can see from this, the translation process involves looking for an *antonym* of the term appearing in the utterance and reversing its polarity (negative to positive, and vice versa). Recently, the title of the novel *Never Let Me Go* by Nobel Prize winner Kazuo Ishiguro was translated as *Auprès de moi toujours* in the Gallimard edition of the novel.

2.1 Injunction and orders

Chuquet and Paillard (1987) also mention the type of utterances encountered in situations where instructions are given and point out that English will use the imperative where French will tend to use the infinitive of a nominal form (French

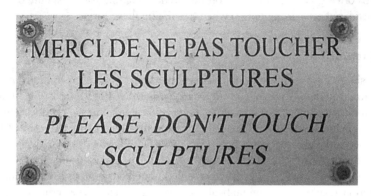

Figure 2.2

tends to use an assertion where English favours an injunction). In cookery books for instance, English uses the imperative in utterances such as *fill the plan with water* and *rinse the vegetables*, using the imperative where French will tend to have *remplir le récipient d'eau*, and *rinser les légumes*, using the infinitive. Similarly, the signs displayed in public places will show the preference in English for the imperative, *keep off the grass*, against the French preference for nominal forms, *pelouse interdite*. Whether English and French speakers approach the production of utterances of this kind differently, as the different formulations seem to suggest, can only be speculated upon. However, Vinay and Darbelnet's approach, which places a lot of emphasis on *démarche de langue*, seems to suggest that these are not mere linguistic habits but are indicative of a certain way of being in the world. This is reminiscent of the Sapir and Whorf hypothesis, according to which our language largely shapes our relationship to the world around us.

2.2 Modulation and lexis

Although modulation can occur at the level of a whole utterance, it can also be limited to a single lexical item or idiom. Metonymic modulations, where a part of something that refers to the whole of something (i.e. *synecdoche*) in the ST corresponds to a different part in the TT, are frequent when translating:

> He shut the door in my <u>face</u>: *il m'a fermé la porte au <u>nez</u>*
> She was up to her <u>eyes</u> in debt: *elle était endettée jusqu'au <u>cou</u>*

The change of point of view can occur at different levels:

- **Spatial**:
  outside the town hall: *devant la mairie* (not *à l'extérieur de*)

- **Temporal**:
  A quarterly magazine: *un magazine trimestriel*
  Every other week: *une semaine sur deux*
- **Spatial to temporal**:
  le moment où: *the time when*

The examples here are taken and adapted from Chuquet and Paillard's section on "modulation métonymique" (Chuquet and Paillard, 1987: 30–32). For a more exhaustive presentation of the various types of modulation, see (Chuquet and Paillard, 1987; Astington, 1983; Vinay and Darbelnet, 1958: 235–241); other types of oppositions include *abstract* vs. *concrete*, *cause* vs. *effect* and *active* vs. *passive*.

Modulation is often the prime procedure used to translate idioms, proverbs and metaphorical expressions:

To have other <u>fish</u> to fry
Avoir d'autres <u>chats</u> à fouetter

To have a <u>frog</u> in one's throat
Avoir un <u>chat</u> dans la gorge

Obviously, the best approach when dealing with idioms and fixed expressions is to look for an equivalent idiom in the TT and avoid a literal translation. In most contexts, *to have a cat in one's throat* would be nonsensical and would not be an adequate translation of the French idiom (*avoir un chat dans la gorge*)! Of course, there might be cases where there is no equivalent counterpart to the SL idiom in the TL, there might be a semantically similar idiom in the TL but used in different contexts, or the idiom might also not match in terms frequency. Note that there might be translation contexts where the meaning of the idiom might need to be retained. Imagine for instance the following: " 'well, I have other fish to fry', said the chef jokingly", where a fictitious chef makes a play on words based on his actually having fish to fry. It would be difficult in such a context to do with away the reference to fish.

Vinay and Darbelnet (1958: 88) introduce a distinction between *modulation libre* and *modulation figée*. When dealing with *modulation figée*, the translator has no choice and must seek the right equivalence. Translating an utterance such as *I will drop you a line* by *je t'enverrai une ligne* might not be far off the mark and might well be understood by the addressee, but it is nevertheless awkward since it is not transparent enough and not immediately recognisable (contrary to *envoyer un mot*, which can be found in the French dictionary and is part of a French speaker's lexicon). The translation process that underpins the production of *envoyer un mot* is therefore a *modulation figée* as it is the only metonymic expression available. A free modulation could also be used to translate the utterance such *I'll drop you a line*: *je te contacterai*. The metaphorical element present in the ST would, however, be lost, which depending on the translation context might not be welcome.

3 Cultural transposition

When no equivalence can be found in the TL culture, *adaptation* is needed. According to Vinay and Darbelnet (1958: 52–54), adaptation, which they view as the extreme limit of translation, is needed when an element or a situation the ST refers to does not exist in the TL or does not carry the same connotations. As an illustration of this phenomenon, Vinay and Darbelnet consider the translation of an utterance such as *he kissed his daughter on the mouth*, which refers to a situation that is not uncommon in a British context. This situation might not obviously be transferrable to another culture without the same meaning being attributed to the kiss. In a French context, for instance, this innocent familial gesture might be perceived as incestuous and deviant. It would therefore be problematic to translate the TT by *il a embrassé sa fille sur la bouche*; this would imply behaviour of a totally different nature and would thus constitute a definite *contresens* (misinterpretation). For this reason, Vinay and Darbelnet suggest something along the lines of *il serra tendrement sa fille dans ses bras*.

An adaptation of this kind might not always be possible or necessary. Chuquet and Paillard (1987) suggest for the translation of the title of a newspaper article, "*Cycling through Coronation Street*", in which the merits of using an exercise bike are discussed, "*Entrainez-vous en regardant la télévision*". The ST obviously refers to a very specific element of British culture, *Coronation Street*, one of the longest lasting TV sitcoms broadcast in the United Kingdom. *Coronation Street* has never been broadcast in France or in other Francophone countries and is unknown to French-speaking audiences; such a specific reference can therefore not be retained. Consequently, something less specific to British culture, or universally known, needs to be used in the TT. It is also useful to probe the function of the *Coronation Street* reference. Even though the reference brings humour to the text, it does not add much to the overall message of the ST (i.e. the fact that it is now possible to exercise in one's living room). A good strategy in this context is therefore to propose something less specific in the TT (*regarder la télévision*), with no mention of an actual programme. This strategy obviously has the advantage of making the TT absolutely transparent; the reference to the SL culture however is lost. Another strategy would be to try to find an equivalence and propose a popular French programme, *Des Chiffres et des lettres*, *Plus belle la vie*, for instance (i.e. well-known popular programmes that also convey a certain sense of homeliness). It is key, of course, to take into account the target audience – these examples would work well in France but not necessarily in other French-speaking countries (*la Petite Vie* might work better in Québec and *A nous la vie* in Burkina Faso and West Africa).

Cultural adaptation is needed when associative and connotational meanings differ in the ST and TT cultures, even when the referent exists in both cultures. Armstrong (2005: 71) discusses the translation of the French term *banlieue*, which is understandably often translated as *suburb* in English texts. Although *suburb* is an appropriate translation in terms of denotation, a place not too distant from the centre of a city, it does not have the same connotations: "the English term 'inner city', therefore, while less accurate in terms of denotation, captures better the connotation of *banlieue*." Obviously, the selection of *inner city* over *suburb* will depend on the context in which *banlieue* is used and whether the connotative meaning mentioned by Armstrong is actually activated in the text in question.

Concluding remarks and evaluation of the linguistic approach

Vinay and Darbelnet (1958) see transposition and modulation as central to the translation process (alongside explicitation and implicitation, omission and addition, equivalence and adaptation). In their view, these procedures are to be used profusely if idiomaticity is required. There are, however, a number of difficulties in applying the type of linguistic approach advocated by Vinay and Darbelnet (1958). Firstly, there are internal difficulties linked to the use of their taxonomy. Some of the procedures identified, such as transposition and modulation, show a high degree of overlap, and it is not always easy to distinguish one from the other. Besides, these procedures are often intertwined, one triggering the other, and it is not always easy to identify the trigger and/or to know whether a modification for instance is necessary for lexical, grammatical or cultural reasons.

Furthermore, the commonly held idea that a translated text should be transparent and give the impression of having been written in the TL has been discussed and vehemently criticised by translation theorists such as Venuti, one of the most strident detractors of the linguistic approach:

> A translated text, whether prose or poetry, fiction or nonfiction, is judged acceptable by most publishers, reviewers and readers when it reads fluently, when the absence of any linguistic or stylistic peculiarities makes it seem transparent, giving the appearance that it reflects the foreign writer's personality or intention or the essential meaning of the foreign text – the appearance, in other words, that the translation is not in fact a translation, but the "original." The illusion of transparency is an effect of a fluent translation strategy, of the translator's effort to insure easy readability by adhering to current usage, maintaining continuous syntax, fixing a precise meaning.
>
> (Venuti, 1995: 1)

This type of approach creates in Venuti's view an ethnocentric bias towards the culture of the English-speaking world (when applied to the translation of foreign texts into English), losing all trace of foreignness in the process, which is exactly what translation is not supposed to do:

> By producing the illusion of transparency, a fluent translation masquerades as a true semantic equivalence when it in fact inscribes the foreign text with a partial interpretation, partial to English-language values, reducing if not simply excluding the very differences that translation is called on to convey.
>
> (Venuti, 1995: 16)

Hatim and Mason, who view translation as a communicative process and stress the importance of the social context in which translation occurs, make observations that echo Venuti's criticism and lead them to reject the terminology used by advocates of the linguistic approach:

> The use in linguistics and translation theory of the terms "message", "encode" and "decode" has not helped the situation . . . the impression has been fostered that the process of transferring meaning into text is a mechanical one, in which lexical entries and syntactic patterns are "mapped onto" a semantic core in the manner of a primitive machine-translation system. The inference is allowed that the "message" is an invariant construct, a concrete entity which is conveyed intact from speaker/writer to hearer/reader as if by semaphore or Morse code.
>
> (Hatim and Mason, 1990: 192/193)

These issues will be revisited in subsequent chapters, and it is important not to underestimate their importance – translation should not be approached as a search of allegedly existing equivalences nor should the translation process necessarily be made invisible. Having said that, it must also be pointed out that the notion of meaning on which criticisms of the linguistic approach are based can in some cases be extremely elusive and hold a very narrow and reductive view of what the linguistic approach involves and condones. In our view, especially given the practical orientation of this book, the contrastive approach presented in this chapter helps raise awareness of the linguistic procedures involved in the translation process and is a good starting place for the novice translator. Obviously there are limits to an approach of this kind, and its predicting power is partial, but it is our view that the linguistic focus does not necessary prevent the approach from being integrated into a wider framework. Ultimately, there is something empowering and illuminating in developing a sharp sense of what happens when transferring meaning from one language to another, paying attention to what happens at a close linguistic level, and realising in the process that translation is not something some people are simply very good at and others not. One can, in this respect, draw a parallel with musicianship. The talent of a good performer goes well beyond the purely technical level, or in the words of jazz supremo Charlie Parker – "master your instrument, master the music & then *forget* all that and just play". Similarly, a good translator needs to know the tricks of the trade, learn the scales, so to speak. However, the translator's work cannot be reduced to simply applying a set of predefined processes. The translator also needs to *play* and call on his/her creativity and feel for the language.

4 Activités de mise en pratique

I Identification des procédés de traduction

Observer ces citations célèbres, essayer de les traduire, puis se reporter aux traductions proposées afin d'identifier toutes les modifications survenues lors du passage de l'anglais au français (changements grammaticaux; procédés de traduction: transposition, étoffement, modulation libre, modulation par le contraire, etc.).

1   The telling of beautiful untrue things is the proper aim of Art. —Oscar Wilde

2   To love oneself is the beginning of a life-long romance. —Oscar Wilde

3   Honest criticism is hard to take, particularly from a relative, a friend, an acquaintance, or a stranger. —Franklin P. Jones

4   There is no remedy for love but to love more. —Henry David Thoreau

5   I don't want to achieve immortality through my work. I want to achieve immortality by living forever. —Woody Allen

6   Life is like riding a bicycle. In order to keep your balance, you must keep moving. —Albert Einstein

7   Money is better than poverty, if only for financial reasons. —Woody Allen

8   If you would be loved, love and be lovable. —Benjamin Franklin

9   A kiss is a lovely trick designed by nature to stop speech when words become superfluous. —Ingrid Bergman

10   At the touch of love everyone becomes a poet. —Plato

11   The ultimate measure of a man is not where he stands in moments of comfort and convenience, but where he stands at times of challenge and controversy. —Martin Luther King

12   The course of true love never did run smooth. —William Shakespeare

II   Traduction d'extraits tirés du magazine bilingue Metropolitan

Extrait 1

COSY UP TO THESE WINTER WARMERS

Forget about the winter chill with our selection of warming dishes, from hearty mushroom stroganoff to comforting penne alla bolognese. Bon appétit.

UN PEU DE RÉCONFORT

L'hiver vous donne des envies de cocooning? Champignons Stroganoff ou pennes à la bolognaise, essayez nos plats anti-coup de froid. Bon appétit.

(Metropolitan, février 2017, p. 60)

Pensez-vous que ce texte a d'abord été écrit en français puis traduit en anglais ou bien d'abord écrit en anglais puis traduit en français? Que pensez-vous de l'utilisation du terme cocooning dans le texte français?

Extrait 2

RAMPAGE

Billed as the 'biggest drum'n' bass and dubstep party in the world', Rampage – which isn't half as disorderly as its name suggests – sees acts such as Bristol dubstep duo Loadstar head an all-night line-up./La *"plus grosse fête dubstep et drum'n'bass du monde", bien plus organisée que son nom (déchainement) l'indique, accueillera les meilleurs, tels que le duo dubstep Loadstar, venu de Bristol, pour une affiche de qualité qui se produira toute la nuit.*

(Metropolitan, février 2017, p. 60)

Auriez-vous traduit "Bristol dubstep duo" de la même manière? Que pensez-vous de la traduction proposée pour "all-night line-up"?

Extrait 3

NOUVELLE VAGUE

Parisian duo Marc Collin and Olivier Libaux cover new wave and punk hits in a bossa nova style; imagine Joy Division at a 50s cocktail party. Their concerts are a blast – what's more fun than singing "Teenage Kicks" at third of its original speed?

Les Parisiens Marc Collin et Olivier Libaux reprennent des tubes punk et new wave façon bossa nova (Joy Division à un cocktail des fifties). Leurs concerts sont géniaux. Quel pied de chanter Teenage Kicks trois fois plus lentement que l'original!

(Metropolitan, février 2017, p. 60)

A quoi correspond "what's more fun dans le texte français? A quoi correspond "a blast" dans texte anglais?

Extrait 4

La princesse des podiums
  For the love of Di

A style heroine for generation X. Reclaimed by millennials, "Lady Di" knew how to wear a frock. As some of the standouts of her wardrobe go on show in London, we look at the enduring legacy of the people's princess./*Egérie du style pour la génération X, puis la suivante, Lady Di savait porter le tailleur. A l'heure où une selection de sa garde-robe est exposée à Londres, retour sur le legs de la princess du people.*
(Metropolitan, février 2017, p. 60)

A quoi correspond le terme "millennials" dans le texte français? A quel terme français "le legs" correspond-il dans le texte anglais?

III Transposition

Traduire les phrases suivantes en remplaçant les mots soulignés par la catégorie grammaticale suggérée sans changer le sens du message.

Verbe → nom

1   When I was in Germany, I saw a lot of . . .

2   Once he has left, she makes bread and continues her housework.

3   A year after retiring, she divorces Pierre.

4   When he died in 1896, Alfred Nobel left practically nothing to his direct heirs.

Adjectif → nom

5   She is often seasick.

6   When I was in law school in the late sixties and early seventies . . .

Nom → verbe

7   The wife wanted to be kept alive by all possible means, and the husband wanted no resuscitation.

8   I wanted no witness of poor Lucy's condition. (Bram Stoker, *Dracula*)

Adverbe → nom

Comme nous l'avons signalé précédemment, la traduction des adverbes en *-ly* appelle très souvent une nominalisation:

9   The defenders fought **bravely** before being forced to surrender.

10   He raced **bravely** but finished last.

11   I am totally amazed by how **quickly and capably** they act.

12   Exposure to media violence causes children to behave more **aggressively**.

13   Donald raised his children **firmly and lovingly**.

14   She nodded **knowingly**.

15   When asked what she does in her free time, **Dina sheepishly says**, "I won't lie; I don't do much".

16   I like to laugh, he said **cheerfully**.

17   He laughed **amusedly** at the tall stories we told.

18   By joining, you've made an **extraordinarily generous** commitment.

IV Transposition et phrasal verbs

Utiliser le chassé-croisé pour traduire les phrases suivantes:

1   He <u>ran into</u> the house.

Notez que d'autres traductions sont possibles:

Il s'est précipité dans la maison.

Dans cette traduction, l'action concrète de courir reçoit une interprétation: il s'agit de précipitation. L'énoncé ne fait pas que décrire ce qui est vu par l'observateur. Autres possibilités:

Il s'est dépêché d'entrer dans la maison.
Il a fait irruption dans la maison.

2   She <u>stormed out</u> of the house.

3   He <u>felt</u> his way <u>across</u> the room.

4   As she could not walk she had to <u>crawl down</u> the stairs.

Avec les verbes transitifs de mouvement de ce type, le chassé-croisé est quasi-systématique.

On rencontre parfois en anglais des verbes de mouvement accompagnés de deux prépositions:

5   The lady <u>went up</u> the steps and <u>into</u> the house.

Dans l'énoncé français, chaque préposition correspond alors à un verbe.

Comme nous l'avons vu précédemment, le chassé-croisé n'est pas toujours complet avec les verbes de mouvement:

6   A cyclist <u>rode into</u> a pedestrian and tried to steal a handbag.

7   She entered the car and <u>drove out</u> of the garage.

On rencontre le chassé-croisé avec les structures de type résultatif:

8   I <u>kicked</u> the door <u>open</u>:

9   A police officer tried <u>to slap</u> a man <u>awake</u> as he lay unconscious.

10   He had been <u>kicked to death</u>.

Il faut distinguer le type de verbes ci-dessus, dont le complément est introduit par une préposition, des verbes qui sont accompagnés d'une particule adverbiale, et qui sont généralement traduits par un seul verbe et pour lesquels on n'applique pas le chassé-croisé:

11   The racing car <u>blew up</u> after it crashed into the fence.

12   Can you <u>take</u> the garbage <u>out</u>?

13   When I <u>think back</u> on my youth, I wish I had studied harder.

14   He <u>ran away</u> when he was 15.

V   Transposition et étoffement – traduction des prépositions

Préposition simple en anglais → locution prépositionnelle en français

1   In order to combat piracy <u>off</u> Somalia, the government decided to . . .

2   Seat reservations are obligatory for all trains <u>to</u> Italy.

3   A stewardess on a flight <u>from</u> Chicago found a suspicious package left in the toilet.

4   <u>Off to</u> Peru next month, surveying some new ruins.

5   We're looking for money to come in <u>from</u> international partners.

6   A complaint must be made <u>within</u> two years of the date when you became aware of the facts.

7   As a result, many of these companies collapsed <u>within</u> a few months.

Préposition en anglais → verbe ou préposition renforcée *par* un verbe en français

8   There were accusations <u>against</u> him.

9   The woman <u>in</u> a yellow dress.

10   They cannot leave their homes without a male relative.

11   Send your application form <u>along with</u> a letter to your tax centre.

Préposition en anglais→subordonnée relative ou participe présent en français

12   Their insightful outlook on the world <u>around</u> them deserves to be shared.

13   He was the only man married <u>with</u> children.

14   "I know I'm right", she said <u>with</u> a smile.

VI Modulation

Traduire les phrases ci-dessous en introduisant une modulation par le contraire pour traduire la partie de la phrase soulignée:

1   Did she know that I was sad and that <u>I kept weeping</u>?

2   Well, she is <u>always</u> having headaches and missing school.

3   The two boys <u>kept giggling</u>.

4   <u>Remember</u> to smile and thank the fans [coach giving advice to football players].

5   This product is not a <u>safe</u> alternative to cigarettes.

6   It would <u>certainly</u> have surprised him.

7   What this stuntman does is <u>not safe</u>.

8   <u>The things we do</u> for our readers!

VII Modulation métonymique

PROVERBES ET EXPRESSIONS IMAGÉES METTANT EN SCÈNE DES ANIMAUX

Traduire les phrases ci-dessous.

Les animaux occupent une place privilégiée dans les proverbes et expressions imagées, mais attention, il ne s'agit pas toujours du même animal dans les deux langues:

1   He's taken to his new school like <u>a duck</u> to water.

Il s'est très vite habitué à son école, il y est . . .

2   Why do humans get <u>goose bumps</u>?

Pourquoi . . .

3   I didn't have breakfast this morning, and now <u>I could eat a horse</u>.

    Je n'ai pas pris . . .

4   Let sleeping <u>dogs</u> lie.

    On ne réveille pas . . .

5   The president cannot behave like a <u>bull in a china shop</u>.

    Il est inconcevable que le président . . .

Dans de nombreux cas on a affaire à une double modulation:

6   She is very kind but she is as <u>blind</u> as a <u>bat.</u>

    Elle est . . .

7   One can't teach an old <u>dog new tricks.</u>

    On n'apprend pas . . .

8   <u>Walk into</u> the <u>lion</u>'s den.

    Se . . .

9   When <u>pigs fly.</u>

    Quand . . .

Bien qu'on ait affaire à une expression en apparence équivalente dans les deux langues, il y a parfois des nuances au niveau du sens de l'expression:

10   To be <u>as happy as a lark</u>.

    Etre . . .

On a presque affaire au même oiseau (*a lark*: une alouette; *un pinson*: a finch), néanmoins l'expression française ne décrit pas un trait de caractère aussi permanent de la personne en question que l'expression anglaise, l'expression française est en fait synonyme *d'être très joyeux*, de façon spontanée et momentanée, tandis que l'expression anglaise indique un sentiment de bonheur d'une plus grande permanence. Pour cette raison, on va selon le contexte préférer une des trois expressions suivantes:

Être heureux comme un poisson dans l'eau
Être heureux comme un pape
Être heureux comme un roi

Expressions construites sur le même modèle (to be x as a x → être x comme un x). Cette structure est relativement productive en anglais puisqu'on rencontre également: *to be as happy as a clam/a pig in mud*.

Il y aussi des cas où il s'agit de la même image et du même animal dans les deux langues, ce qui n'empêche pas les modulations d'un autre type (grammatical ou syntaxique):

11   When the cat is away the mice will play.

   Le chat . . .

12   Get off your high horse.

   Ne monte pas sur . . .

Et il y a bien sûr certaines expressions pour lesquelles on retrouve le même animal, et qui peuvent en outre être traduites littéralement sans modulation:

13   One swallow doesn't make a spring.

Notons cependant qu'en anglais il est possible de rencontrer "one swallow doesn't make a *summer*", alors qu'il est tout à fait impossible d'avoir "une hirondelle ne fait pas *l'été*" en français!

   Il existe bien sûr des expressions figées mettant en scène des animaux dans une langue mais pas dans l'autre:

   Poser un lapin à quelqu'un

   To stand somebody up

VIII   Traduction d'un extrait de roman: Americanah, *Chimamanda Ngozi Adichie*

Analyse avant de traduire le texte

- Narrateur 3ème personne, focalisation interne (immersion dans le point de vue du personnage).
- Situation de rupture: fin d'un long processus, fin qui annonce un nouveau début. Le texte est une justification de la décision du personnage de quitter son conjoint. Même si sa décision comporte de l'incertitude, sa résolution est forte et la rupture inévitable.
- Tonalité et registre du texte: ton conversationnel et poétique, caractère poignant du texte (conflit interne de la protagoniste: elle est résolue mais ne veut pas heurter son conjoint qu'elle semble aimer encore).

- Dimension grammaticale et temporelle: présence du "pluperfect" (lignes 12, 15, 23); traduction de "would" (lignes 5 et 7).

  - Deux séquences temporelles: 1) le moment de la rupture (séquence principale); 2) séquence antérieure: évènements qui ont précédé la rupture.
  - Traduction de la forme en – *ing* (*she was telling* 19, *he was asking* 21).
  - Participe présent dans la dernière phrase (27, 28).

Extrait à traduire

She began to plan and to dream, to apply for jobs in Lagos. She did not tell Blaine at first, because she wanted to finish her fellowship at Princeton, and then after her fellowship ended, she did not tell him because she wanted to give herself time to be sure. But as the weeks passed, she knew she would never be
15 sure. So she told him that she was moving back home, and she added, "I have to," knowing he would hear in her words the sound of an ending.
"Why?" Blaine asked, almost automatically, stunned by her announcement. There they were, in his living room in New Haven, awash in soft jazz and daylight, and she looked at him, her good, bewildered man, and felt the day
10 take on a sad, epic quality. They had lived together for three years, three years free of crease, like a smoothly ironed sheet, until their only fight, months ago, when Blaine's eyes froze with blame and he refused to speak to her. But they had survived that fight, mostly because of Barack Obama, bonding anew over their shared passion. On election night, before Blaine kissed her, his face wet
15 with tears, he held her tightly as though Obama's victory was also their personal victory. And now here she was telling him it was over.
"Why?" he asked. He taught ideas of nuance and complexity in his classes and yet he was asking her for a single reason, the cause. But she had not had a bold epiphany and there was no cause; it was simply that layer after layer of
20 discontent had settled in her, and formed a mass that now propelled her. She did not tell him this, because it would hurt him to know she had felt that way for a while, that her relationship with him was like being content in a house but always sitting by the window and looking out.
Americanah, Chimamanda Ngozi Adichie
(London: Fourth Estate, 2013)

Traduction proposée

Elle se mit à faire des projets, à caresser des rêves, à répondre à des propositions de travail à Lagos. Elle n'en dit rien à Blaine au début, car elle voulait poursuivre ses études à Princeton jusqu'à la fin de sa bourse, et ensuite elle resta silencieuse parce qu'elle voulait se donner le temps d'être sûre d'elle.
5 Mais, les semaines passant, elle se rendit compte qu'elle ne serait jamais sûre.

Aussi lui annonça-t-elle qu'elle retournait chez elle, en ajoutant: "Il le faut", sans ignorer qu'il percevrait dans ces mots le ton d'une rupture.

"Pourquoi?" demanda Blaine presque machinalement, stupéfié par ce qu'elle venait de lui annoncer. Ils étaient là tous les deux, dans son salon de
10 New Haven baigné de lumière et d'un fond de jazz, et elle le regarda, cet homme bon, interloqué, et sut que la journée allait prendre un tour épique et triste. Ils avaient vécu ensemble pendant trois ans, trois années sans heurts, lisses comme des draps fraîchement repassés, jusqu'à leur unique dispute, quelques mois plus tôt, lorsque le regard de Blaine s'était empli de reproches
15 et qu'il avait refusé de lui parler. Mais ils avaient survécu à cette dispute, en grande partie grâce à Barack Obama, scellant à nouveau leur passion commune. Le soir de l'élection, avant de l'embrasser, le visage mouillé de larmes, Blaine l'avait serrée contre lui comme si la victoire d'Obama était aussi leur victoire personnelle. Et maintenant elle lui disait que c'était fini. "Pourquoi?"
20 demanda-t-il. Il enseignait les notions de subtilité et de complexité dans ses cours et malgré tout lui demandait de fournir une seule raison, la *cause*. Mais elle n'avait pas eu de révélation soudaine et il n'y avait pas de cause; c'était simplement que, peu à peu, l'insatisfaction s'était installée en elle jusqu'à former une masse qui aujourd'hui la poussait irrésistiblement à aller de l'avant.
25 Elle ne le lui dit pas, car il aurait été blessé en apprenant que cette impression durait depuis un certain temps, que sa relation avec lui consistait seulement à vivre heureuse dans une maison, où elle restait assise à la fenêtre à regarder au-dehors.

Traduit de l'anglais par Anne Damour
(Paris: Gallimard, 2016)

Commentaire linéaire de la traduction proposée

Modulations:

she wanted to <u>finish her fellowship</u> at Princeton, and then after her fellowship ended, <u>she did not tell him</u> 2/3
    elle voulait <u>poursuivre ses études</u> à Princeton jusqu'à la fin de sa bourse, et ensuite <u>elle resta silencieuse</u> 3/4

Transposition:

Participe passé en anglais/participe présent en français:
    as the weeks passed/les semaines passant

Lexique: terme générique en anglais/terme plus spécifique en français

she <u>knew</u> she would never be sure/elle <u>se rendit compte</u> qu'elle ne serait. . .

Inversion verbe-sujet déclenchée par "aussi" en position frontale:

So she told him that she was moving back home 5
Aussi lui annonça-t-elle qu'elle retournait chez elle 6

Noter au niveau lexical l'utilisation du verbe "annoncer" plus spécifique que "tell".

Modulations et transposition (négation: "sans" dans le TC; lexique: hear/ percevoir, the sound/le ton):

knowing he would hear in her words the sound of an ending 7
sans ignorer qu'il percevrait dans ces mots le ton d'une rupture. 9

Inversion verbe-sujet, transposition du nom en verbe:

"Why?" Blaine asked, almost automatically, stunned by her announcement. 9
"Pourquoi?" demanda Blaine presque machinalement, stupéfié par ce qu'elle venait de lui annoncer. 11

Utilisation des temps: noter l'emploi du plus-que-parfait (en particulier pour la troisième et cinquième formes verbales qui correspondent à des formes simples dans le TS: he refused 15; he held her 18):

Ils avaient vécu ensemble pendant trois ans [. . .] jusqu'à leur unique dispute, quelques mois plus tôt, lorsque le regard de Blaine s'était empli de reproches et qu'il avait refusé de lui parler. Mais ils avaient survécu à cette dispute [. . .] Le soir de l'élection, avant de l'embrasser, le visage mouillé de larmes, Blaine l'avait serrée contre lui [. . .]

Noter la transposition de "eyes" en "regard" (concret/abstrait).
Modulation:

it was simply that layer after layer of discontent had settled in her, and formed a mass 23
c'était simplement que, peu à peu, l'insatisfaction s'était installée en elle jusqu'à former une masse 27

Noter ci-dessous l'utilisation de la construction "jusqu'à + infinitif".
Transposition: participe présent en anglais/infinitif en français:

that her relationship with him was like being content in a house but always sitting by the window and looking out. 26

sa relation avec lui consistait seulement <u>à vivre</u> heureuse dans une maison, où elle restait assise à la fenêtre <u>à regarder</u> au-dehors. 32

Notes

1 In the glossary to the English edition, *démarche* is translated as *nature*: "property of language which indicates preference for certain forms and structures, where others are possible" (Vinay and Darbelnet, 1995: 346).
2 "a double transposition that combines a change of grammatical category and a syntactical rearrangement of the elements on which meaning is inscribed" (Chuquet and Paillard, 1987: 13, our translation).

References

Armstrong, N. (2005). *Translation, Linguistics, Culture: A French-English Handbook.* Bristol: Multilingual Matters.

Astington, E. (1983). *Equivalences: Translation Difficulties and Devices French-English, English-French.* Cambridge: Cambridge University Press.

Baker, M. (2011). *In Other Words: Coursebook on Translation.* London: Routledge.

Battye, A. and Hintze, M.A. (1992). *The French Language Today.* London: Routledge.

Chuquet, H. and Paillard, M. (1987). *Approche linguistique des problèmes de traduction anglais – français.* Paris: Ophrys.

Hatim, B. and Mason, I. (1990). *Discourse and the Translator.* London and New York: Longman.

Hervey, S.G.J. and Higgins, I. (1992). *Thinking French Translation: A Course in Translation Method French to English.* London and New York: Routledge.

Malmkjær, K. and Windle, K., eds. (2011). *The Oxford Handbook of Translation Studies.* Oxford and New York: Oxford University Press.

Venuti, L. (1995). *The Translator's Invisibility: A History of Translation.* London and New York: Routledge.

Vinay, J.-P. and Darbelnet, J. (1958). *Stylistique comparée du francais et de l'anglais.* Paris: Didier.

Vinay, J.P. and Darbelnet, J. (1995). *Comparative Stylistics of French and English: A Methodology for Translation,* trans. J.C. Sager and M.J. Hamel. Amsterdam: J. Benjamins.

Chapter 3

Translating sentences
Word order and syntax

Introduction

Broadly speaking, syntax deals with how sentences are formed and how words are ordered within a sentence. We discussed word formation in Chapter 1 and focused on the translation procedures used to remedy some of the difficulties linked to certain constructions. In this chapter, we will pursue this exploration by looking at syntactical arrangements (i.e. the linear arrangements of words to form phrases, clauses and sentences). We will try to identify the type of arrangements preferred in both English and French. We will consider canonical structures in English and French and try to understand why speakers sometimes prefer non-canonical structures, answering questions such as why elements of the sentence are not always ordered in a linear fashion. This chapter will focus mostly on the areas of syntax that show significant differences and incommensurabilities across French and English.

Because there are intrinsic differences in the syntax between the two languages, the translator often has to introduce structural changes at the syntactical level. Some structures (English question tags for instance, i.e. adding an interrogative phrase after a declarative sentence: *It's beautiful, isn't it?*) often cannot be translated by an equivalent structure in the SL, or using an equivalent structure might result in producing a sentence that has different connotations. For instance, using an interrogative phrase in French (. . . *n'est-ce pas*) to translate an English question tag might produce an utterance that's more formal than the original. Conversely, a construction like dislocation (*Il est bon, ce pain!*), which is very common in French, especially in speech, is almost inexistent in English. Translating a sentence such as *Il est bon, ce pain* means that the syntactical structure of the source sentence cannot be simply replicated (*It is good, that bread*), and that another way of saying the same thing through other means needs to be found. *That bread is really nice*, with intonation signalling the emphasis present in the French construction would, for instance, be one way of doing this.

This chapter will also address how syntax is linked to text types and register and, more marginally, to social or geographical variation. It will also look at differences between speech and writing. The issue of information presentation at a sentence level will also be considered: what information is presented when, why parts of a sentence might have to be moved when translating, and/or why some parts of a sentence or phrase might have to be added or removed. The strategies that need to be implemented to tackle the syntactical issues encountered will be reviewed. These include elements of a sentence that are conveyed through syntax in the ST that might be conveyed through other means in the TT: lexis, prosody, reduction or expansion, and make an utterance more or less explicit or salient.

This chapter will discuss what motivates speakers' or authors' choices when it comes to sentence structure. It will look at balancing linguistic constraints inherent to English and French against authors' choice and style.

1 Definitions: What's in a sentence?

Although expert knowledge of linguistics or grammar is not a prerequisite for this chapter, understanding basic notions of syntax will be useful. For this reason, we will provide a brief overview before analysing specific constructions. A sentence is characterised by formal autonomy and must contain a verb. A sentence forms one whole entity, unlike clauses and phrases that rely on other parts of a sentence.

Sentences are made up of words that belong to different *word categories*, or different *parts of speech*: nouns, pronouns, verbs, adjectives, adverbs, prepositions, determiners, conjunctions and interjections. A *word category* includes words that can have the same place within a sentence. However, word categories need to be distinguished from the way a given word functions within a sentence. Indeed, the function of a word cannot be listed in a dictionary, as it is entirely dependent on the place an item occupies within a sentence. To put this another way, it is relative to the syntax of the clause containing the item and cannot therefore be fully anticipated. For instance, if we consider functions such as subject and object, a word that is formally identical (and therefore belongs to the same word category) might not have the same function:

John loves Nina.
Nina loves John.

Although the proper noun *Nina* appears in both sentences, it is the object of the first sentence but the subject of the second one. If we replaced *Nina* by a pronoun, we would then have two different forms (*her*, the object pronoun in the first sentence, and *she*, the subject pronoun in the second one):

John loves *her*.
She loves John.

1.1 Complex and compound sentence, main and subordinate clause

Every sentence contains at least one *main clause*. A main clause may form part of a *compound sentence*, but it also makes sense on its own. If the clause can stand by itself and become a complete sentence, the clause is an *independent clause*. Compound sentences are made up of two or more main clauses linked in English by a conjunction such as *and*, *but* or *so* (or *mais, ou, et, donc, or, ni* or *car* in French):

> Elle est partie ce matin = simple sentence (i.e. one main clause)
> <u>Elle est partie ce matin mais je ne l'ai pas vue</u> = compound sentence made up of two clauses

A *subordinate clause* depends on a main clause for its meaning (it is therefore a dependent clause). Together with a main clause, a subordinate clause forms part of a *complex sentence*. Subordinate clauses have a subject doing a verb, and they have a *subordinate conjunction* placed in front of the clause (*comme, lorsque, puisque, quand, si, etc.*):

> <u>Comme il faisait très chaud</u>, elle n'avait pas quitté son bureau.
> *As it was very hot, she was still in her room.*

The underlined clause is the subordinate clause; *elle n'avait pas quitté son bureau* is the main clause.

1.2 Clause vs. phrase

It is important to distinguish a *phrase* from a *clause*. A phrase is a group of words that functions as one constituent in the syntax of a sentence, a single unit within a grammatical hierarchy. It is a collection of words that may involve nouns or verbals (i.e. participles, gerunds and infinitives), but unlike a clause, it does not have a subject doing a verb. The head word identifies the type of phrase[1]:

> Le train avance <u>très rapidement</u> = adverbial phrase
> <u>Le Petit Chaperon rouge</u> marche à grands pas = noun phrase
> Cendrillon dort toujours <u>dans la cuisine</u> = prepositional phrase
> Les trois petits cochons <u>ont refusé de laisser entrer</u> le loup = verb phrase

1.3 Sentence types

From the point of view of their meaning, a link can be established among four types of sentences and the kind of speech acts they allow to perform: (1) declaratives are typically used to make a statement, relay information or present an idea (*Elle est venue ce matin*); (2) interrogatives to ask a question (*Quand est-elle venue?*); (3) imperatives to issue a command, an order or a request (*Viens*); and (4) exclamatives to express a strong emotion (*Quelle belle surprise!*).

1.4 Sentence vs. utterance

It is also useful to distinguish *sentences* from *utterances*. An *utterance* is what a sentence means in context. Depending on the context, a sentence such as *Can you open the window*, which is formally a question, might mean: *Open the window please* (and therefore be a request) or be a real question: *Are you able to open the window that is stuck?* It is also useful to note that an utterance does not necessarily have to be a fully formed sentence. In a conversation, a simple interjection might constitute an utterance:

> A: Did you buy some bread?
> B: Damn!

Although B's intervention is made up of one single word, its meaning in context is clear (*No, I didn't but I wish I had*) and fully appropriate from the point of view of providing an answer to A's query. From a translation point of view, it is key to take into account the meaning of an utterance in context rather than focusing on the literal meaning of the words that form the sentence. The translation of *damn*, in the example above, is likely to have more to do with expressing disappointment through the use of a familiar interjection (*Mince!* in French, for instance), rather than a statement involving damnation or being damned. That said, you might see *Que je sois damné*, for example, but this would be far less usual and is stylistically marked as archaic and is, in fact, much more hyperbolic than *Damn*. Besides, French has a set phrase to invoke damnation upon oneself: *Que le diable m'emporte*, which would be preferable to *Que je sois damné* in most contexts.

The translation of the following sentence is often given as an illustration of the distinction between utterance and sentence:

> Zoé ma grande fille veut que je boive ce whisky dont je ne veux pas.

Usually translated in English as:

> *The quick brown fox jumps over the lazy dog.*

Although the English translation is semantically very distinct form the source sentence, it is nonetheless a very good translation. As a matter of fact, this sentence used to be commonly used for touch-typing practice as it contains all the letters of the alphabet, a feature which the English sentence also displays.

2 Comparing French and English syntax

From a contrastive point of view (English-French), it is important to note that word order follows the same pattern in the two languages: subject-verb-object (SVO, henceforth). In linguistic typology, languages are classified according to the order in which the three basic components of a declarative sentence appear (subject, verb, object). From this point of view, French and English belong to the same category and the types of constructions that are used in interrogative, imperative and exclamative sentences do show many similarities.

2.1 Interrogatives and inversion

Both in French and English, inversion is prototypically associated with interrogation. In both English and French, the syntax of yes-no questions (also called *complete questions*) is characterised by verb-subject inversion (*Are you happy? Es-tu content?*). To put it differently, having recourse to an inversion of the subject-verb structure found in declarative sentences (*You are happy, Tu es content*) produces an interrogative (*Are you happy?, Es-tu content?*). Note, however, that subject-verb inversion in French is only possible with a pronoun. So, how can we translate the question, *Is John happy?* A calque of the English structure (*Est Jean heureux?**) will not work, and we will have to use a *complex inversion* instead (*Jean est-il heureux?*: proper noun + verb+ clitic pronoun). The use of the interrogative phrase, *est-ce que* at the beginning of the sentence (*Est-ce que Jean est heureux?*), which is a standard and stylistically neutral way of asking a question, is also possible. It is, in fact, a good alternative to complex inversion. In speech, it is very common for yes-no questions to take the form of a declarative sentence with a rising intonation such as *Tu vas venir?* In an utterance, such as this one, intonation is the only interrogative marker in the utterance.

Partial or *open questions* (i.e. questions with a wh- or qu- word at the beginning of the sentence) are also characterised by inversion. Similar to complete questions, partial questions in speech often take the form of a subject + verb, a structure normally associated with declarative sentences, followed by a qu- word at the end of the sentence: *Tu viens quand, Il parle à qui?, Ils vont où?* The French tendency to avoid subject-verb inversion means that a question whose subject is a proper noun (as in the English question *Is John happy?*), which, as we saw, would call in French for a complex inversion *(Jean est-il heureux?)*, will, in many contexts, take the following form: *Il est heureux, Jean?* In this sentence, comprising both a pronoun and a noun that refer to the same referent, there is a *detachment* (or dislocation) of the noun-subject (Jean) to the right of the sentence. In French, this type of construction, which avoids subject-verb inversion, is very common.

2.2 Making sense of sentence structure in French interrogatives

Although questions are structurally similar in the two languages, when you compare French and English interrogatives, you can observe a wider array of interrogative constructions available in French than in English (Armstrong, 2005). There is indeed a lot more interspeaker and intraspeaker variation at this level in French. Consider, as an example, the following illustration provided by Gadet (1997: 7–8). Here are different options for a simple question such as *When are you coming?*:

1   Quand venez-vous?
2   Quand est-ce que vous venez?
3   Vous venez quand?
4   Quand vous venez?
5   Quand que vous venez?
6   Quand que c'est que vous venez?
7   Quand c'est que vous venez?
8   Quand c'est que c'est que vous venez?
9   Quand que c'est que c'est que vous venez?
10   Vous venez quand est-ce?
11   Vous venez quand ça?

French interrogative forms depend much more than English interrogatives on external factors, such as the age of the speaker, the social group they belong to, where they are from, and with whom they identify. The formality of the situation in which these forms are used is also a factor. In other words, in French, there is a strong correlation between the type of question used and the social identity of a speaker and/or the situation and social setting in which the question appears. English, on the other hand, shows a lot more stability and regularity at this level. The same forms are used in different contexts, regardless of a speaker's social identity. The high level of variability regarding interrogative structures in French correlates with the fact that the different variables are invested with different values and the translator needs to be able to identify this. For instance, Armstrong (2005: 20) contrasts the following example: *Tu es de quelle origine?* with the less standard form: *Tu es d'origine quoi?* The choice might be determined by the social identity of the speaker. Some speakers might see the latter form as erroneous and want to avoid it at all cost, others might use it readily and even find it positively connoted. Note that the speaker might not belong to a social group that normally uses this form but might use it in order to accommodate towards the way his/her interlocutor speaks. As the interrogative system of English shows little variability, it is difficult to translate the extra connotative information that the use of such a form provides. Armstong notes: "an attempt to render into English the very informal nature of *Tu es d'origine quoi?* would probably have to use resources from a linguistic level other than syntax" (2005: 21).

    Contrary to what prescriptive grammars would have us believe, sociolinguists have shown that, in speech, verb-subject inversion is the exception, not the rule. Blanche-Benveniste (1997), for instance, considers inversion as conveying prestige, while Coveney (2002) notes an absence of total interrogatives with inversion in his corpora of spoken French data. In terms of geographical variation, inversion seems more common in Canada than in other parts of the French-speaking world.

Complex inversion (e.g *Jean est-il heureux? Ta mère viendra-t-elle?*) tends to be completely absent from corpora in most varieties of spoken French. Since inversion is marked (i.e. not the default way of asking a question), it can be used to make a particular question salient: *As-tu vu le nouveau film de Godard? C'est un véritable chef d'oeuvre.* In this example, inversion correlates with the speaker's subjectivity and involvement with the subject matter (i.e. the speaker believes the film in question to be exceptional or, on the contrary, the speaker is exaggerating and being ironic and actually believes the film to be particularly bad). Inversion also appears in the formulaic self-addressed question, *Comment dirais-je?* This is used by speakers in debates when they hesitate and cannot find the right word (the equivalent of *How shall I put it?* in English).

Inversion in speech is associated with a formal register. It is absent from vernacular varieties of metropolitan French, and interrogative forms that avoid having recourse to inversion are preferred. According to some linguists, inversion of subject pronoun and verb is not part of the grammar of speakers of vernacular French (Meisel Elsig and Bonnesen, 2011), but it remains the standard construction in formal writing. A clear distinction between speech and writing therefore needs to be drawn.

In speech, in contemporary French, *Quand est-ce que vous venez?* or *Vous venez quand?*, as variants of the more formal *Quand venez-vous*, are neutral in their sociostylistic value (Armstrong, 2005). Inversion is still current in conversation in contexts where formal connotations are called for, especially with qu- questions (the case is slightly different with yes-no questions). The formula *est-ce que* is used widely these days and has become the obligatory formulation for first-person interrogatives (*Est-ce que j'écris?* not *Ecris-je?*). According to linguists, the growing tendency towards using *est-ce que* and intonation interrogatives signals a move away from inversion – although *est-ce que* contains an inversion within itself, its presence "makes further inversion unnecessary" (Ball, 2000: 27).

A yes-no question, *Où vas-tu?*, will be generally perceived as formal, *Où est-ce que tu vas?* as neutral, and *Où tu vas?* as more colloquial (Ball, 2000: 30). Speakers do not, however, systematically use *est-ce que*, and it is common nowadays to hear: *Où c'est que tu vas?* or *C'est où que tu vas?* (with more emphasis on *où*), or even a combination of *c'est* and *est-ce que* when saying *Où est-ce que c'est que tu vas?* In so-called indirect questions, as in *Je te demande pourquoi tu ris*, which do not normally take an inversion, the grammatically "faulty" *Je te demande pourquoi est-ce que tu ris?* has become increasingly common. Similarly, *Je te demande pourquoi c'est que tu ris* (perceived as more colloquial) or even *Je te demande pourquoi que tu ris* (which is distinctly marked as *populaire*, according to Ball, 2000: 34) are now more frequent.

3 Information management in sentences

Although SVO remains the canonical order for declarative sentences in written standard French, there are sentence structures that are widely used in less formal registers, especially in conversation, and these clearly challenge the SVO order.

The use of these structures is often linked with the presentation and management of information. In most cases, an utterance will contain a *topic*, or theme (i.e. what is being talked about), and a *comment* (*rheme* or *focus*, i.e. what is being said about the topic). In French, the topic of a sentence appears at the beginning of the sentence. Prototypically, there is a match between topic and subject – what is being talked about corresponds in principle to the grammatical subject. In terms of information management, when the topic is placed in the subject position, it tends already to be familiar to the hearer/reader. If I say *Le petit chien descend la rue*, I assume that my interlocutor knows what *petit chien* I am talking about. If I am recounting an anecdote to a friend and want to introduce a new referent such as *le petit chien*, I might say something like: *Je me promène dans la rue lorsque tout à coup je vois un petit chien*, placing the *petit chien* in object position before making it the subject of the next sentence. As Hansen (2016: 358) points out, "grammatically indefinite subjects [. . .] tend to be dispreferred in French" precisely because of the drive towards placing topical referents before less topical ones in the utterance (topical being synonymous here with already being known).

3.1 Left-dislocation

Let's imagine that I am talking about a friend with annoying idiosyncrasies and want to say something along the lines of *We all know her/his annoying ways*. I can say, *Nous connaissons bien ses petites manies*, which matches the syntax of the English sentence, or something more likely in an informal conversation: *Ses petites manies, nous les connaissons bien* (note the reprise of the object in the main clause via the use of the resumptive pronoun *les*). This type of structure is called *detachment* or *dislocation* (the present example is a case of *left-dislocation*). If we compare the first sentence (*Nous connaissons bien ses petites manies*) with the dislocated one (*Ses petites manies, nous les connaissons bien*), we can see that by moving the object to the left of the sentence, the speaker makes it clear that the object *ses petites manies* is the topic of the utterance, and, consequently, places the focus of the sentence on the fact that we know, all too well, about our friend's irritating behaviour.

If we compare the two following sentences taken from Jones (1996: 33):

(1) Pierrre a donné une voiture à son fils.
(2) A son fils, Pierre a donné une voiture.

In (2), *à son fils* is the topicalised element. As Jones rightly points out, the "topicalised element has a scene-setting function" (1996: 33). By placing *à son fils* at the beginning of the sentence, the speaker provides the background information necessary to understand the main information. The construction acts as a frame, pointing to the focal point of the sentence. One of the consequences of placing *à son fils* at the beginning of the sentence is to move the focus which would normally be placed on *à son fils* (as in sentence (1)) to *donné une voiture*. As with the previous set of sentences, the topicalisation of one phrase correlates with the focalisation of another.

The tendency to place old or background information at the beginning of a sentence is not absolute in French (Jones, 1996: 33), but it is much more prevalent than in English. In English, prosody can be used to present an item as the focus of the sentence; even if it does not appear in final position, contrastive stress is used to highlight the item: *Pierre gave a car to his son* (Jones, 1996: 33). In French, this tendency, which affects declarative sentences, can also affect interrogatives, especially in speech. If we consider a question such as *Où est le trésor que tu as trouvé?*, the topic of the sentence is *le trésor que tu as trouvé*. Therefore, rather than formulating it as: *Où est le trésor que tu as trouvé?*, which would be fairly standard in writing, there will be a preference in spoken French for something like: *Le trésor que tu as trouvé, où est-il?* What appears first in the sentence is the topic (*le trésor que tu as trouvé*). The verb-subject inversion is marked, but in an informal setting the speaker might avoid the inversion and instead suggest: *Le trésor que tu as trouvé, où il est?* The speaker might even adopt the topic-first preference and move the interrogative to the right resulting in the following: *Le trésor que tu as trouvé, il est où?*

As Hansen (2016: 360) points out, left-dislocation is often used to contrast the topics of two sentences: *Toi, tu peux y aller. Moi, je n'ai pas envie.* This emphasises the subject pronoun (note, also the use of the so-called disjunctive pronouns: *toi, moi*). Both contrasted sentences do not necessarily have to appear in the interaction for the contrast to be activated – *Toi, tu peux y aller* might be enough to imply to one's interlocutors that one is not moving (*Moi, je vais rester*). During the 2012 French presidential campaign, in a televised debate with Nicolas Sarkozy, the then presidential candidate, François Hollande, when asked by the journalist Laurence Ferrari the following question: *Quel président comptez-vous être?* (*What sort of a president are you planning to be?*), answered with a long tirade in which he used the following anaphora: *Moi président de la République, je . . .* 15 times.[2] Hollande's response attracted significant attention from political commentators in the media. Most agreed that through the repeated use of this particular structure, Hollande had scored points over his opponent. The use of dislocation was unquestionably part of Hollande's strategy to categorically distinguish himself from his adversary, using a fairly theatrical device in a way that seemed spontaneous and off-the-cuff. Since then, this construction has kept cropping up in French popular culture, in countless rap songs, TV series, and radio shows. For instance, the title of the 2012 American film *The Campaign*, a political satire comedy starring Will Ferrell and Zach Galifianakis, who play two candidates who run for Congress, was translated in French as *Moi, député* in reference to Hollande's famous anaphora.

3.2 Right-dislocation

(1) Le vin est excellent.
Il est excellent, <u>le vin.</u>

(2) Ton père vit-il à Paris?
Il vit à Paris, <u>ton père?</u>

Functionally, right-dislocation is also linked to information management. By using right dislocation, the speaker seems initially to assume that the hearer knows what he or she is referring to. The element in question might have been previously mentioned (the two interlocutors might have been talking about the hearer's father) or might be present in their shared field of perception. In (2), the two interlocutors might have been drinking the wine in (1), before re-identifying what the pronoun in the main clause refers to in the dislocated element (*le vin, ton père*).

Ball (2000) provides the following example: *C'est pour Madame, le café au lait?* where, dislocation has the effect of highlighting the comment (*c'est pour Madame*), the right-dislocated NP only acts as a reminder of what the utterance refers to (*le café au lait*) in case the hearer did not know. The famous catch-phrase: *Ils sont fous, ces Romains (These Romans are crazy)*, uttered by the famous cartoon character Obélix, is a famous example of right-dislocation. By highlighting the comment *ils sont fous* and placing the NP (*ces Romains*) outside the core of the sentence, the exclamatory force of the utterance is enhanced (contrast with the following: *Ces Romains sont fous*). We can note that this type of structure has become very productive in French and can be used in any context where the quality of a particular subject needs to be highlighted: *Ils sont nuls, ces héros* is the title of a children's novel that parodies traditional fairy tales; Obélix himself uses this formula to describe various peoples: *Ils sont fous, ces Goths/Egyptiens/Bretons*, and so on. One could also easily envisage a variation based on the change of adjective: *Ils sont timbrés, ces Gaulois*. The almost identical construction "il est à + infinitif, ce x" is also very common in casual French: *Il est à pleurer, ce film; Il est à vomir, ce mec. Il est à mourir d'ennui, ce livre etc.*

Right-dislocation also appears in the title of a book written by Marion Lagardère and published by Grasset in 2017: *Il est comment, Mélenchon en vrai?* The book is a biography of the French politician Jean-Luc Mélenchon. When used in the title of a biography, as in this example, dislocation creates a false sense of familiarity with the topic, as it presupposes that the reader knows who is being talked about (and therefore implies that there is nobody else we should currently be talking about). It also places emphasis on questioning what the person is really like (*il est comment*), creating a sense of suspense and implying that if you want to find out, you need to read the book!

CONCLUSION ON DISLOCATION

Linguists are unanimous in their assessment of the prevalence of dislocation in casual contemporary French. As Planchenault points out (2017: 136), left-dislocation with resumptive pronoun is one of the strategies used by Agatha Christie to make the French-speaking Hercule Poirot sound foreign and bring a distinctive French flavour to his speech ("Your wife she made no will. . . . Your wife she dies. The money it is yours", etc.). Leonarduzzi and Herry (2005: 9) also signal that the play *En attendant Godot* by Samuel Beckett, which the author translated into English himself, comprises over 20 dislocations in the French original, against five in the English translation.

It should be noted that left-dislocation is not impossible in English. The sentences below are taken from Gardelle (2010: 6):

> We went to Florida last summer, and we went to Disney World. The best ride the whole time was Jurassic Park. *My sister Chrissie, her* eyes were poppin' out.

The sentence above might be preferred over:

> *My sister Chrissie's* eyes were poppin' out.

The former allows for a clearer distinction between the topic and the comment: the reference to *my sister* (topic) appears first, before the important information is introduced in the second part of the sentence (see Gardelle, 2010: 8 for an extensive analysis of left-dislocation in English). According to Gardelle, the fact we are dealing with a particularly long and complex referent (*My sister Chrissie's eyes*) in topic position triggers left-dislocation.

Left-dislocation also appears when stress is placed on the resumptive pronoun (example taken from Gardelle, 2010):

> Students who say oh well I might as well just take, Honors Math because I need another honors course, *those* are the students who probably shouldn't be taking Honors Math.

In English, left-dislocation is mostly encountered through sentences that belong to categories of this type. Left-dislocation is encountered constructions with double pronouns (such as "him, he . . .", "them, they . . ."), which are extremely common in French, never occur in English, nor do multiple dislocations of the "me, my mother, she thinks . . ." type (Gardelle, 2010).

In English, right-dislocation is mostly used to re-identify or remind one's interlocutor of what one is referring to (*Does she live on her own, your mother?*) Left-dislocation in particular, tends to be associated with unplanned, oral discourse. Leonarduzzi and Herry (2005) show that left-dislocation can be used in televised debates (to introduce new or previously mentioned topics) but this is rather rare. They also note that they are very seldom used in film dialogues. Interestingly, they find that right-dislocation tends to be as frequent in writing as in speech. It should be noted that right-dislocation is far from being associated with a low register. Oscar Wilde uses them to give some of his characters a definite air of sophistication. Colin Dexter also peppers the speech of his main character, the Oxford-educated inspector Morse, with right-dislocations. The sociostylistic value of these forms is therefore diametrically different in French and English.

3.3 Cleft constructions

As we saw in the preceding section, although contrastive stress is not impossible in French, it is far less used than in English. This means that when it comes to expressing contrast and/or focus, syntactical means tend to be preferred over prosodic ones. Dislocation falls into this category, as do *clefts*. It is indeed very common in French to use a special construction such as the following: "c'est + X + relative pronoun qui/que + Y" in which the focus is introduced by *c'est*: *C'est lui qui m'a dit ton secret* (which could be translated as: *It was him who told me your secret*, or: *HE told me your secret*).

While clefts are typically associated with declarative sentences, they can also appear in interrogative sentences, highlighting the constituent in X (i.e. the interrogative). Note the absence of subject-verb inversion with that interrogative construction:

> C'est comment qu'elle s'appelle *(What's her name?)*
> C'est comment qu'on freine? [title of a popular song by Alain Bashung]
> *How on earth does one brake?*

Sentences of this type are stylistically marked as colloquial.

Clefts can be used to place the focus on the subject of the dependent clause (which is presented as the object of the main clause, *c'est X*: *c'est moi qui l'ai fait (I did it)*). In the late 1980s, following a popular TV advert with comedian Valérie Lemercier, *C'est moi qui l'ai fait* became a leitmotiv in France.

Note that clefts can be used to place the focus on the object:

> Ce sont <u>vos empreintes</u> qu'on a retrouvées sur l'arme du crime.

Contrary to English, clefts do not always have a contrastive meaning as they do not imply "a contrast between the X element and any other entity" (Hansen, 2016: 363).

If we consider the following example:

C'est mon accent qui vous fait rire?
You find my accent funny (don't you?)

This sentence presupposes that the speaker's interlocutor finds something funny about the speaker. The cleft expresses what that something is and draws attention to it.

3.4 Presentative constructions

There are also clefts which are often labelled as *presentative constructions* (see Ayres-Bennett Carruthers and Temple, 2001: 267; Hansen, 2016: 365):

(II) y a + X + relative pronoun qui/que + Y
Il y a Jean qui a telephoné.
Jean phoned.

This type of construction often has an event-reporting function. It announces an event as particularly worthy of notice, presenting the non-topical element (here, the fact that Jean phoned) as unexpected or surprising.

This construction can appear in the first person as well:

J'ai ma sœur qui habite Paris.
My sister lives in Paris.

Il y a mon frère qui s'est endormi.
My brother has fallen asleep.

The first clause presents the topic as part of a shared frame of reference. It is assumed that the hearer already knows that the speaker has a house, a sister or a dog, for instance, while the main information provided by the sentence appears in the second clause.

Indefinite nouns are ideal candidates for presentational clefts. Once the referent in question has appeared as the focus of a presentative cleft, it can then be the topic of a subsequent sentence as a definite noun:

Il y a mon chien qui a attrapé <u>une</u> tique. <u>La</u> tique lui a donné un virus.
My dog got a tick. The tick gave it a virus.

Indefinite nouns cannot normally be used in detached structures. In order to be detached, an item has to be inferable or known by the hearer/reader, which is why dislocation is impossible with indefinite NPs:

> Une personne elle est venue ce matin*
> Quelqu'un il est venu ce matin*

> Une personne est venue
> Quelqu'un est venu

For many observers, clefts are a strong indication of a trend towards placing non-topic subjects at the beginning of the sentence and are particularly prevalent in colloquial French. There seems to be evidence to show that, from a cognitive point of view, focus-marking facilitates processing.

It is, in any case, important for non-native speakers of French to bear in mind that when introducing a new referent in an interaction or a text, there is a strong tendency in French to avoid placing the new referent in topic position. Many observers point to a grammaticalisation of the forms in question (see the discussion in Ayres-Bennett, Carruthers and Temple, 2001: 267 on this). This means that *Il y a mon frère qui a acheté une voiture* might, in certain contexts, be a more neutral and unmarked form than *Mon frère a acheté une nouvelle voiture*. From a translation point of view, it means that a sentence such as *My brother has a new car*, that you would most likely find in a dialogue, might be more appropriately translated as *Il y a mon frère qui a acheté une voiture* rather than *Mon frère a acheté une nouvelle voiture*.[3]

3.5 Initial positioning (other elements than subject)

In this section, we will be considering the place of adverbials (or modifiers) within a sentence. Adverbials or modifiers add extra information and are not part of the core (or argument) of the sentence. They should be distinguished from complements since these cannot be freely added or removed from the core sentence. The term adverbial can be misleading as the head of the adverbial phrase is not necessarily an adverb.

In French, temporal, spatial and logical adverbials tend to be placed in sentence initial position:

> Fatiguée, elle s'est arrêtée.

The adverbial phrase can be made up of an adjective, a past participle a noun, a conjunction or a preposition:

> Heureux d'avoir remporté le match, le joueur a affirmé que c'était sa plus belle victoire.

>Fondée en 1253 par Robert de Sorbon, la Sorbonne était à l'origine un
>collège pour étudiants en théologie.
>Dès qu'il l'a vu, le bébé a souri.
>Face à une telle situation, le sociologue est bien souvent démuni.

They do not go to the left of the main clause (*anteposition*) systematically; they can also appear to the right (*postposition*) or even be embedded within the main clause (*imbrication*).

Adverbials in initial position have a discourse-structuring function, ensuring clear transitions and coherent organisation of information. They often have a scene-setting function:

>Affaibli par sa maladie, Montaigne s'éteindra dans son château le 13
>septembre 1592.

They provide background information that frames the information presented in the main clause. They form the backdrop to the event presented in the main clause while retaining the focus on the event presented in the main clause.

There is a clear tendency in French to favour anteposition where English prefers postposition (Guillemin-Flescher, 1981: 127):

>Par terre, dans les angles, étaient rangés, debout, des sacs de blé.
>*Sacs of wheat stood in the corners of the room.*

Time adverbials in particular are often in anteposition in French and in postposition in English:

>Dimanche soir, une avalanche a fait deux morts.
>*Two people died in an avalanche on Sunday.*

>A 200 ans de distance, Goya et l'iranienne Farideh Lahsai ont tous deux
>chroniqué des périodes de conflit avec compassion et humour.
>*Francisco Goya and Iranian artist Farideh Lahsai chronicled periods of*
>*intense conflict 200 years apart, with humanity and humour.*

There are many cases of French sentences where the adverbial phrase which is placed in initial position cannot be placed in the same position in English. Guillemin-Flescher (1981: 128) gives the following sentences:

>A Deauville, faites des affaires immobilières!
>*Dans une jatte, faites tremper le pain spécial grillé émietté avec le vin blanc*
>*et le jus de crabe.*

Imbrication is also very common in French but is the least preferred option in English (Guillemin-Flescher, 1981: 125):

> Ils se livrent alors, <u>sous des dehors irrésistibles de drôlerie</u>, à une lutte sournoise et passionnée.
> *And, <u>from behind a cover of irresistibly funny wit</u>, they open fire in an artful and passionate battle.*

3.6 Absolute constructions, participial constructions, apposition, ellipsis and fronting

A number of constructions can occur in initial positions in both French and English.

The first is *absolute constructions* (i.e. a phrase that is syntactically independent from the main clause but semantically linked to it). The subject of absolute phrases is always different from the subject of the main clause:

> Sheila being late, the meeting was cancelled.
> *Sheila étant en retard, la réunion a été annulée.*

> The meeting being over, the team members went home.
> *La réunion (étant) terminée, les membres de l'équipe sont rentrés chez eux.*

In this construction: NP + being + X (a construction sometimes described as a *nominative absolute*), the participle (-ing/ant is a replacive for tense when the verb of the VP is *be/être*). It is important to note that French absolute constructions tend to be more elliptical than their English counterpart, as the present participle (*étant*) can be deleted easily.

It can be useful to distinguish *absolute constructions* from *participial constructions* (present or past participle). In participial constructions, the subject is not mentioned and is always the same as the subject in the main clauses:

> Singing at the top of his voice, the child entered the room.
> Being cunning, he will win the game easily.
> Exhausted from work, she went to bed early.
> Having driven for hours, she decided to stop at the motel.
> Disappointed with his results, he decided to appeal.

While these types of constructions can occur both in French and English, note that the French adverbial phrase is generally more elliptical than the English one, as the following example taken from Hervey and Higgins (1992: 227) shows:

> Etudiante, vous voyagerez à l'étranger.
> *While you're a student, you'll be travelling abroad.*

As Hervey and Higgins (1992: 230) point out, there is a generic quality to the verbless French construction.

According to Armstrong (2005: 123) and Hervey and Higgins (1992: 228), absolute constructions are commoner in French than English. While they are stylistically neutral in French and can appear in a number of contexts, in English they give the sentence an archaic flavour:

> Lui savant, on s'étonne de trouver une telle bévue
> *He a scholar, it is surprising to find such a blunder*
> (example from Armstrong, 2005: 123)

The fact that there is a tendency to place adverbial constructions in an initial position in French sentences seems to correlate with their elliptical nature. Constructions such as the ones below abound in French:

> Past participles:
> Inaugurée en 1995, la bibliothèque nationale est un chef d'œuvre architectural.

> Absolute construction (i.e. NP introduced by a definite article):
> L'air satisfait, Dominique est entré dans la salle.

> NPs with or without determiner:
> Fruit d'un projet ambitieux, le centre Pompidou demeure un chef d'œuvre architectural.

> Adjectival phrase:
> Novatrice par son recours aux nouvelles technologies, la bibliothèque nationale a immédiatement rencontré un grand succès auprès du public.

With the focus on the main clause, a principle of economy and expeditiousness seems to operate. The idea is to give background information in a way that does not distract attention from the focus. These constructions have a streamlining effect, correlated to their elliptical nature. These constructions always require some form of expansion when translating into English.

APPOSITION

The placing of these adverbials in initial position is reminiscent of apposition (i.e. placing two NPs that refer to the same logical subject side-by-side, which often appears at the beginning of a sentence:

> Jean-Paul Sartre, philosophe français du XXème siècle, a écrit de nombreux ouvrages.
> Jeanne d'Arc, personnage historique de grande envergure, est encore aujourd'hui une icône très largement évoquée.

Note the absence of an article in French in the apposed phrase. As Armstrong (2005: 122) points out, apposition is often better avoided when translating into English, especially when the first phrase in apposition is long.

Adjectives are often also apposed in French. As in the following example taken from an advert for a property which appeared in a bilingual magazine (Metropolitan, March 2017, p. 77):

> Intimiste, élégante et intemporelle, la résidence Neuilly-La-Grande-Jatte arbore fièrement une architecture du style Art Déco.

translated as:

> *With its Art Deco architecture, this dressed stone residence is of timeless elegance.*

Here the apposition was not kept in the English translation. This seems entirely justified since having three adjectives juxtaposed in such a way would be very awkward.

4 Passivisation and topicalisation – Voice

This section will focus on voice and pursue the discussion on topicalisation analysed in the previous section. Passives are particularly interesting to compare in French and English sentences. Firstly, they are more frequent in English than they are in French; secondly, there are several passive structures for which there is no equivalent in French.

4.1 Voice

Voice is linked to the direction of the activity or action presented in the sentence. It is useful to distinguish between *active* and *passive* voice and consider constructions that might show features of either or both (*middle* voice, *causative* forms). In the active voice, the activity or action is presented from the perspective of the *logical subject* (i.e. the entity that performs the action, often called the *agent* in grammar books), and there is a perfect fit between the *grammatical subject* and the *logical subject*:

> Paul mange la pomme.

In the passive voice, the activity or action is seen from the perspective of the logical direct object, which becomes the grammatical subject (*la pomme*):

> La pomme est mangée par Paul.

This means that the passive is a way of topicalising the direct object by placing it in the subject position (note that contrary to English, only direct objects can be passivised in French). This is obviously the case when the clause is about the logical direct object rather than logical subject:

Une journaliste irakienne a été enlevée lundi soir chez elle à Bagdad.

The passive allows to forgo mention of the logical subject. The agent (*par des hommes armés* for the sentence given earlier) could be mentioned, but it does not have to be mentioned if it is already known or seems irrelevant.

It is useful to remember that, in French, there is a strong preference for definite and animate NPs in the subject position, which means that an utterance such as:

Roland Barthes a été renversé par un camion.

will be preferred over:

Un camion a renversé Roland Barthes.

Guillemin-Flescher (1981: 207) points to a correlation between a more frequent use of the passive and a preference for animate subjects in English. She uses the translation of a sentence from *La Peste* by Albert Camus to exemplify this point, where the inanimate subject (*l'affiche*) is replaced by the animate *the townspeople*:

Elle (l'affiche) recommandait aux habitants la plus extrême propreté
    et invitait les porteurs de puces à se présenter dans les dispensaires
    municipaux.
The townspeople were advised to practise extreme cleanliness, and any who found
    fleas on their persons were directed to call at the municipal dispensaries.

Guillemin-Flescher also gives the following example (1981: 208) based on the translation of *Vendredi* by Michel Tournier:

Aussitot la vieille angoisse bien connue et si redoutée lui mordit le foie.
    Elle ne relâcha son étreinte qu'à moitié, lorsqu'il eut découvert dans une
    anfranctuosité de rocher un petit poulpe gris. . .
At once he was assailed by that familiar and dreaded sense of alienation,
    which was only partly relieved when he discovered, in a cavity in the
    rocks, a small grey squid. . .

The passive voice correlates with the use of an animate subject in English, where French tends to use the active voice and an inanimate subject, as in the following example (Demanuelli and Demanuelli, 1990: 25):

Son départ l'avait blessé.
He had been hurt when she left.

Middle voice is used to describe activities or actions for which the grammatical subject both performs and undergoes the action or activity in question, and it is typically associated with pronominal verbs used reflexively:

> Elle se lave. Il se rase. Elles s'habillent, etc.
> *She is washing and being washed. He is shaving and being shaved,* etc.

The *reflexive passive* can also be used to describe a general rule in sentences such as:

> Le participe passé employé avec le verbe avoir <u>ne s'accorde pas</u> avec son
>   C.O.D. lorsque ce C.O.D. est placé après le verbe.
> Le e final <u>ne se prononce pas</u> en français.
> Le vin blanc <u>se boit frais</u>.

Surprisingly, this type of construction, which suggests that the subject has some form of involvement in the action being performed, is typically used if the logical direct object is *inanimate*. Yet it is clear that the subject cannot play a part in carrying out the action.

Let us also mention the *causative voice*, labelled as such as the grammatical subject does not perform the action or activity in question but causes another entity to perform it:

> Elle lui fait passer l'aspirateur dans toute la maison.
> *She makes him vacuum the entire house.*

> Elle fait construire sa maison par un architecte renommé.
> *She is having her house built by a well-known architect.*

As mentioned previously, syntactical constraints on passivisation are more restrictive in French than in English, and only verbs that take a direct object can be made passive:

> (1) She was listened to.
>   *Elle a été écoutée.*

> (2) She was spoken to.
>   *Elle a été parlée.**

If we consider the infinitive, it is clear that with *écouter quelqu'un* we are dealing with a direct object in (1) and with an indirect object in (2): *parler à quelqu'un*. An alternative to the canonical passive is therefore needed in (2): *On lui a parlé.*

In the case of verbs that take both a direct and indirect object in the active voice (*donner/refuser quelque chose à quelqu'un*), a construction (*se faire/se voir* + *infinitive*) known as the *reflexive causative* is the only way of making the indirect object the subject of the passive:

> (1) Je me suis fait renverser par une voiture.
> *I was knocked over by a car.*

> (2) Un an plus tard, en prison, elle s'est vu décerner le prix Nobel de la paix.
> *A year later, while in prison, she was awarded the Nobel Peace Prize.*

This type of passive is similar to *get* passives in English (got run over): I got knocked over by a car. This construction cannot be used to translate every causative construction.

Here, again, the use of a pronominal verb is puzzling. Are we really dealing with a reflexive action? It certainly cannot be the case in (1) unless the logical subject actively tried to get run over by the car. In (2), her being awarded the Nobel Peace Prize is clearly associated with her actions, but she did not award the prize herself! Although not reflexive, the construction seems to imply that the subject contributed to the event happening. It emphasises the fact that the event in question is exceptional – something unusual (either good or bad) was done to the subject.

With main verbs that take a dative object in the active voice (*refuser qq à qq1*), the reflexive causative is the only means of promoting a logical dative object to grammatical subject position in a clause with passive meaning.

From a translation point of view, it is interesting to note that there is no way in English to translate the nuance that the use of this construction brings. Whether we are dealing with:

(1) Un an plus tard, en prison, elle s'est vu décerner le prix Nobel de la paix.
Or
(2) Un an plus tard, en prison, on lui a décerné le prix Nobel de la paix.

The translation in English will be the same:

> *A year later, while in prison, she was awarded the Nobel Peace Prize.*

4.2 Conclusion to the passive voice

When translating into French, it is useful to know the canonical ways of avoiding the passive in French: use of *on*, middle voice (*construction pronominale*), and nominalisation, which will be used in subsequent exercises. It is also useful to remember that some of the topicalising effects of the passive can be achieved via other means, via a cleft for instance:

A solution was found by the mayor.
C'est le maire qui a trouvé une solution.
Instead of:
Une solution a été trouvée par le maire.

Or left-dislocation if the logical subject is not mentioned:

La solution, on l'a trouvée.

5 Coordination and subordination

From the perspective of contrastive stylistics, analysing syntax is essential if we want to have a clear understanding of the linguistic constraints and preferences that each language show, as well as the the choices made by authors and speakers. A lot of observers (Chuquet-Paillard, Guillemin-Flescher, Demanuelli and Demanuelli, Delisle) have shown that there is a clear tendency in English to juxtapose independent clauses and to simply coordinate them using *and*. French, on the other hand, tends to use more complex sentences and subordination takes precedence over coordination. Coordination through the use of *et* is not therefore systematically used to translate the relation introduced by *and*:

Delisle (2003: 516):
Pleasant jobs find many applicants, <u>and</u> remuneration is bid down.
Les emplois agréables sont très recherchés, <u>ce qui fait</u> baisser la rémunération.

Read the text <u>and</u> translate it.
Lire le texte <u>avant de</u> le traduire.

Buy <u>and</u> save.
Achetez <u>tout en faisant</u> des économies.

Write <u>and</u> get our brochure.
Ecrivez <u>pour obtenir</u> notre brochure.

Demanuelli and Demanuelli (1990: 24) equate the preference for juxtaposition and coordination in English with a preference for *parataxis*, as opposed to a preference for *hypotaxis* in French. Parataxis is derived from a Greek word which means to place *side-by-side*. Parataxis can be used to describe the syntax of a text in which phrases and clauses are placed one after another independently, without coordinating or subordinating them using conjunctions. Hypotaxis is the opposite of parataxis. In hypotaxis, the sentences, clauses and phrases are subordinated and linked. Looking at a translation of *l'Etranger* by Camus (for which they use the Laredo translation), they give the following example:

> Il relatait un fait divers <u>dont</u> le début manquait, mais qui avait dû se passer.
> *It was a small news story. The beginning was missing, but it must have taken place.*

Where Camus uses a complex sentence (note the use of *dont* in the French original), the translator has opted for the juxtaposition of two independent clauses. Demanuelli and Demanuelli (1990) see the French predilection for hypotaxis as linked to a French preference for *abstract* forms where English favours more *concrete* ones – following Vinay and Darbelnet's analysis based on lexis (e.g. The picture hangs on the wall: *Le tableau est au mur*, where a verb of action is used in English, and the stative *être* in French; similarly, dress rehearsal in English, *répétition générale* in French). In their view, it is clear that what can be observed at the lexical level can be extended to syntax. They maintain that syntactical differences signal a predilection for *impressionism* in English where French favours *expressionism*. In English, coordination and juxtaposition are part of a linear process in which events are presented in chronological order and in a more organic way than in French. This process is also linked to a greater need in English to actualise events, which is exemplified (*ibid.* p. 24) by the translation of the following sentence (from *l'Etranger*):

> [. . .] une porte derrière laquelle on entendait <u>des voix, des appels, des bruits de chaises</u>.
> *[. . .] a door through which we could hear <u>people talking and shouting, chairs scraping</u>.*

Here, stative nominal forms (*voix, appels, bruits*) are replaced by a dynamic progressive form (*talking, shouting, scraping*).
It is the same need to actualise events that operates with apposition:

> J'avais trouvé un vieux morceau de journal presque collé à l'étoffe, <u>jauni et transparent</u>.
> *I'd found an old scrap of newspaper which had gone all yellow and transparent and was almost stuck to the material.*

Contrary to the French sentence, the English sentence is not elliptical and shows a complex sentence structure (use of the relative *which*). According to Demanuelli and Demanuelli, this is also due to the need to actualise the event. They also stress that English prefers an animate subject, which they see as being linked to a more concrete way of presenting events. They then discuss the translation of the following sentence taken from a novel by Nathalie Sarraute (Demanuelli and Demanuelli, 1990: 25):

Son départ l'avait blessé et il se souvenait encore. . .
He had been hurt when she left and he could still remember . . .

The inanimate subject (*son départ*) in French becomes animate in English (*he had been hurt*) – the object of the French clause (the third person personal pronoun *le*) becomes the subject of the English clause: *he* . . .).

Although Demanuelli and Demanuelli warn against overusing the principles they have identified, their description of the different ways the two languages express the same thing remains compelling. They successfully demonstrate that each language has its own set of syntactical constraints and preferences, with each language following its very own *démarche de langue*.

Conclusion

This chapter has shown that similarly to what was observed with lexis in Chapter 1, there is not always a direct equivalence between French and English syntactical structures. Interrogative forms are far more subject to variation in French than in English. Besides, there is a much wider repertoire of forms in French. Inversion in interrogative forms is strongly associated with a high register in French, which is not the case in English. Information management also greatly impacts how sentences are constructed in the two languages, as does topicalisation. Adverbial phrases tend to appear in anteposition in French (time adverbials in particular). Passivisation, which is grammatically not possible with an indirect object in French, is very frequent with animate subjects in English. There is also a predilection for coordination in English where French shows a preference for subordination.

The complexity of the relationship between French and English syntactical forms and the entanglement of structural, grammatical and stylistic constraints make syntax an area where the translator has to be particularly careful.

6 Activités de mise en pratique

I Identification des procédés de traduction

Observer les extraits de texte ci-dessous et essayer d'identifier les modifications survenues sur le plan syntaxique lors du passage de l'anglais au français. Ces extraits sont tirés du magazine bilingue Metropolitan disponibles dans les trains Eurostar entre Paris, Bruxelles et Londres.

Extrait 1:

Marseille

MAISON MOUTTE

Where could be more perfect for an emporium dedicated to 20th century design than Le Corbusier's Cité Radieuse? You'll find Gine Bel Moutte on the fourth floor, selling unique vintage pieces alongside contemporary design/*Rien de plus approprié que la Cité radieuse du Corbusier pour héberger un emporium dédié au design du XXe siècle. C'est au quatrième étage que Ginie Bel Moutte vend des pièces vintage uniques et du design contemporain.*

(Metropolitan, mai 2017, p. 27)

Qu'observez-vous au niveau de la première phrase? A quelle construction correspond "you'll find Ginie Bel Moutte" dans le texte français?

Extrait 2:

ARLES

ALICE NEEL: PAINTER OF MODERN LIFE

The American artist's portraits are curiously compelling: tender, scrappy and full of psychological insight. The cast of people she painted comprised friends and lovers, as well as New York art-world luminaries./*Tendres, décousus, révélateurs, les portraits de cette Américain exercent une fascination étrange. Elle a peint ses amis, ses amants et de grandes figures du monde de l'art new-yorkais.*

(Metropolitan, mai 2017, p. 49)

Qu'observez-vous au niveau de la syntaxe de la première phrase?

Extrait 3:

EN. Newly returned from Manhattan, where he's just opened a restaurant, Daniel Rose is happily perched at Cher la Vieille's zinc counter. First comes a succession of well-wishers: staff, friends, old customers, even a critic from *Le Monde.* There's a flurry of kisses, teasing, jokes and solicitous enquiries: "But Daniel, are they treating you right over there?"

FR. *Revenu de Manhattan où il vient d'ouvrir un restaurant, Daniel Rose a retrouvé avec bonheur le zinc de Chez La Vieille. Serveurs, amis, clients fidèles et même un critique du* Monde *viennent lui faire la bise, le taquiner et lui demander avec sollicitude: "Mais, ils te traitent bien là-bas?"*

(Metropolitan, février 2017, p. 37)

Qu'observez-vous au niveau de la syntaxe de la deuxième phrase du texte français?

Extrait 4:

It's said General de Gaulle, a Lille native, had a particular fondness for the light-as-air *gaufres* filled with Madagascan vanilla served at 18th-century tea room./*Natif de Lille, le Général de Gaulle aimait les douceurs, en particulier les gaufres légères à la vanille de Madagascar servies dans ce joli salon de thé/pâtisserie datant du XVIIIe siècle.*

(Metropolitan, avril 2017, p. 12)

Qu'observez-vous en ce qui concerne la place de l'adjectif "natif" dans la phrase du texte français?

Extrait 5: interview with film director François Ozon

The fear of others, of foreigners, is an important theme in Frantz, which opens in postwar Germany. Were you influenced by the current climate?

My primary interest was the point of view of those on the losing side, and of the young girl.

Dans Frantz, vous abordez notamment la peur de l'autre, de l'étranger. Avez-vous été inspire par le contexte actuel?

Ce qui m'intéressait d'abord, c'était le point de vue des perdants et de la jeune fille.

(Metropolitan, avril 2017, p. 15)

A quoi correspond "my primary interest was" dans le texte français?

Extrait 6:

HELLO CAULI

EN. My British friends constantly rave about their beloved cauliflower cheese, made with a rich, creamy cheddar sauce. It's great as an accompaniment to the majestic Sunday roast, or as a very pleasant – and pretty substantial – dish on its own.

LA SOUPE AU CHOU
FR. *Mes amis britanniques sont intarissables sur leur gratin de chou-fleur adoré et sa sauce crémeuse au cheddar, merveilleux accompagnement du rôti du dimanche. Seul, il est délicieux et roboratif.*

(Metropolitan, avril 2017, p. 42)

Commentez la syntaxe de la phrase: "Seul, il est délicieux et roboratif".

Extrait 7:

ON THE COVER

British artist Joe Cruz couldn't wait to crack out his panel sticks to make his mark on some of the most iconic works of Auguste Rodin; the results can be enjoyed alongside our feature (page 56) on this year's massive celebrations marking 100 years since the great French sculptor's death, which include must-see shows at the Grand Palais and the Rodin Museum. And, no we don't think Auguste would be offended by Joe's fluorescent doodlings – after all he was one of the art world's original enfant terribles, whose *Kiss* and *The Thinker* critics decried as risqué abominations. That was before their international renown elevated them to ambassadors of for French culture, of course./*L'artiste britannique Joe Cruz était impatient de sortir ses craies grasses pour apposer sa marque sur les œuvres emblématiques d'Auguste Rodin; admirez le résultat dans notre article (page 56) sur les célébrations majeures du centième anniversaire de la mort du grand sculpteur, notamment les expos immanquables du Grand Palais et du musée Rodin. Nous sommes persuadés qu'Auguste ne se serait pas offusqué des dessins fluo de Joe – après tout, lui aussi était un enfant terrible de l'art, et Le Baiser et Le Penseur furent dénigrés comme des abominations osées par certains critiques, avant d'être élevés au rang d'ambassadeurs de la culture française.*

(Metropolitan, avril 2017, p 57)

Identifier les passifs dans le texte anglais et dans le texte français: quels types de correspondance observe-t-on?

II Comparaison de traduction du Code civil

Identifier les différences qui apparaissent au niveau de la syntaxe et de la démarche de langue en comparant des extraits du Code civil[4] et leur traduction (détachement, inversion verbe-sujet, construction impersonnelle, etc.).

De la publication, des effets et de l'application des lois en général
The Publication, Effects, and Application of Legislation in General

Article 1:

Les lois et, lorsqu'ils sont publiés au Journal officiel de la République française, les actes administratifs entrent en vigueur à la date qu'ils fixent ou, à défaut, le lendemain de leur publication. Toutefois, l'entrée en vigueur de celles de leurs dispositions dont l'exécution nécessite des mesures d'application est reportée à la date d'entrée en vigueur de ces mesures.

En cas d'urgence, entrent en vigueur dès leur publication les lois dont le décret de promulgation le prescrit et les actes administratifs pour lesquels le Gouvernement l'ordonne par une disposition spéciale.

Les dispositions du présent article ne sont pas applicables aux actes individuels.

Statutes and administrative acts, when the latter are published in the Journal officiel de la République française, take effect on the date they specify or, if none is specified, on the day following the date of their publication. Nevertheless, if the enforcement of some provisions of such acts requires an additional enactment, the effective date of the enforcement of these provisions is deferred to the effective date of the additional enactment.

In case of an emergency, statutes whose decree of promulgation so declares and administrative acts for which the Government so orders by special provision, shall enter into force immediately upon their publication.

Article 3:

Les lois de police et de sûreté obligent tous ceux qui habitent le territoire.

Les immeubles, même ceux possédés par des étrangers, sont régis par la loi française.

Les lois concernant l'état et la capacité des personnes régissent les Français, même résidant en pays étranger.

Statutes concerning public policy and safety are binding on all those living on the territory.

French law governs immovables, even those possessed by aliens.

Statutes concerning the status and capacity of persons govern French citizens even those residing in a foreign country.

Article 4

Le juge qui refusera de juger, sous prétexte du silence, de l'obscurité ou de l'insuffisance de la loi, pourra être poursuivi comme coupable de déni de justice.

A judge who refuses to give judgment on the pretext of legislation being silent, obscure or insufficient may be prosecuted for being guilty of a denial of justice.

Article 5

Il est défendu aux juges de prononcer par voie de disposition générale et réglementaire sur les causes qui leur sont soumises.

In the cases that are referred to them, judges are forbidden to pronounce judgment by way of general and regulatory dispositions.

Des droits civils
Civil Rights

Article 7
L'exercice des droits civils est indépendant de l'exercice des droits politiques, lesquels s'acquièrent et se conservent conformément aux lois constitutionnelles et électorales.

The exercise of civil rights is independent of the exercise of political rights, which are acquired and preserved in accordance with constitutional and electoral statutes.

Article 8
Tout Français jouira des droits civils.

Every French person enjoys civil rights.

Article 9
Chacun a droit au respect de sa vie privée.
Les juges peuvent, sans préjudice de la réparation du dommage subi, prescrire toutes mesures, telles que séquestre, saisie et autres, propres à empêcher ou faire cesser une atteinte à l'intimité de la vie privée: ces mesures peuvent, s'il y a urgence, être ordonnées en référé.

Everyone has the right to respect for his private life.
Without prejudice to the right to recover indemnification for injury suffered, judges may prescribe any measures, such as sequestration, seizure and others, suited to the prevention or the ending of an infringement of the intimate character of private life; in case of emergency those measures may be provided for by summary proceedings.

Article 9.1.
Chacun a droit au respect de la présomption d'innocence.
Lorsqu'une personne est, avant toute condamnation, présentée publiquement comme étant coupable de faits faisant l'objet d'une enquête ou d'une instruction judiciaire, le juge peut, même en référé, sans préjudice de la réparation du dommage subi, prescrire toutes mesures, telles que l'insertion d'une rectification ou la diffusion d'un communiqué, aux fins de faire cesser l'atteinte à la présomption d'innocence, et ce aux frais de la personne, physique ou morale, responsable de cette atteinte.

Everyone is entitled to the presumption of innocence.
When, before any sentence is pronounced, a person is publicly portrayed to be guilty of acts that are subject to an inquest or preliminary judicial investigation,

the judge, even by summary proceedings and without prejudice to the right to recover indemnification for injury suffered, may prescribe any measures, such as the insertion of a correction or the circulation of a communiqué, in order to put an end to the infringement of the presumption of innocence, at the expense of the natural or juridical person responsible for that infringement.

III Coordination et subordination

Traduire les phrases ci-dessous en évitant de traduire "and" par "et".

1   The children were expected to be obedient and to watch <u>and</u> learn.
   Les enfants devaient . . .

2   Read the text <u>and</u> highlight the personal pronouns and verbs.
   Lire le texte . . .

3   I did <u>and</u> they said that they could not come <u>and</u> that they could not help.
   J'ai obtempéré . . .

4   Come <u>and</u> get me!
   Viens . . .

5   Our company employs 91 people <u>and</u> realised a turnover of 70 million euros from the processing of 100 million litres of milk in 2003.
   Notre entreprise emploie aujourd'hui 91 salariés . . .

IV Voix passive

La voix passive est beaucoup moins employée en français qu'en anglais. Le français a tendance à utiliser d'autres formes pour l'éviter. Traduire les phrases ci-dessous en évitant la voix passive et en utilisant les formes suggérées.

A ON. C'est la plus courante et la mieux connue:

1   French is spoken here.

2   Access to the Embassy has not been made easy to us.

B FORME PRONOMINALE DU VERBE.

Cette forme est employée surtout si l'on tient à garder le même ordre et la même emphase dans la phrase (sujet + verbe).

3   Ham is sold at the delicatessen.

4   Trainers can be bought in sports shops.

5   That is just not done.

6   Revenge is a dish best served cold.

C FORME IMPERSONNELLE DU VERBE. *Cette structure est assez courante, surtout lorsque le sujet est un participe présent en anglais.*

7   Smoking is prohibited.

8   No parking is allowed.

9   The use of street shoes is prohibited on the court.

D SE VOIR + INFINITIF

10   She was denied the chance to represent herself in court.

11   The European Union has been given greater administrative flexibility.

12   She was awarded a five-year research scholarship.

E FORME NOMINALE

13   Shortly after he was made redundant, his ex-employer contacted him.

14   Several modifications made to the vessel after she was built had not been reported.

15   The authorisation will lead to a torrent of requests for the rules to be relaxed.

Objet direct et objet indirect:

Attention à ne pas traduire la voix passive anglais par une voix passive en français quand le sujet de l'anglais devient l'objet indirect en français:

16   We were given a reward.

Traduire les phrases suivantes en utilisant la voix passive si cela est possible:

17   I have a lot of music on my phone that has never been listened to.

18   She was annoyed that she had been spoken to like that.

19   She has not been contacted.

V Le Participe présent

On l'utilise fréquemment pour renvoyer au sujet du verbe de la proposition principale:

> J'ai acheté ce dictionnaire ne sachant pas qu'il était mauvais.
> *I bought this dictionary not knowing it was a poor one.*

> (Etant) satisfaites de notre réponse, elles sont parties.
> *As they were satisfied with our reply, they left.*

Le participe présent appartient ici au groupe circonstanciel.

Attention, si en anglais on utilise le pp pour renvoyer à un nom (ou un pronom) le précédant on tend alors à utiliser en français une autre structure (notez que l'agent de l'action décrite par le pp est alors distinct du sujet de la principale). Traduire les phrases ci-dessous:

1   I could hear <u>dogs</u> **barking** all night.

2   I can see <u>him</u> **trying** to open the door.

En français, le pp tend à être utilisé pour renvoyer au sujet du verbe de la principale.

Attention également à certaines locutions prépositionnelles très utilisées dans les subordonnées circonstancielles:

3   **Depending on** your decision, I will stay or go.

4   **When speaking of the** euro, I would point out two things.

5   **Taking into account** inflation in the U.S., no significant fall can be expected.

En anglais, le pp peut exprimer le but ou la finalité:

6   They joined us in **expressing** deepest sympathies and support.

mais également la conséquence:

7   He has amassed an impressive array of awards and accolades, **making** him one of the greatest coaches in the history of French swimming.

et donner l'impression de simultanéité:

8   **Jumping** on his horse, he galloped away.

VI *Texte à traduire:* William and Mary, *Roald Dahl*

Traduire ce texte tiré d'une nouvelle de Roald Dahl, William and Mary. Eviter de traduire", <u>and</u> his will . . . "par", et son testament). *Est-il possible de déplacer le complément circonstanciel "when he died" dans la première phrase? Comment traduire la voix passive dans le dialogue du troisième paragraphe ("I have been instructed")? Faire attention également à la traduction proposée dans les trois dernières phrases du texte qui sont très elliptiques.*

William Pearl did not leave a great deal of money when he died, and his will was a simple one. With the exception of a few small bequests to relatives, he left all his property to his wife.

The solicitor and Mrs Pearl went over it together in the solicitor's office, and when the business was completed, the widow got up to leave. At that point, the solicitor took a sealed envelope from the folder on his desk and held it out to his client.

"I have been instructed to give you this", he said. "Your husband sent it to us shortly before he passed away." The solicitor was pale and prim, and out of respect for a widow he kept his head on one side as he spoke, looking downward. "It appears that it might be something personal, Mrs Pearl. No doubt you'd like to take it home with you and read it in privacy".

Mrs Pearl accepted the envelope and went out into the street. She paused on the pavement, feeling the thing with her fingers. A letter of farewell from William? Probably, yes. A formal letter. It was bound to be formal – stiff and formal.

(Roald Dahl, 2012)

TRADUCTION PROPOSÉE

A sa mort, William Pearl ne laissa que peu d'argent, aussi son testament ne posait-il aucune difficulté. A l'exception de quelques petits legs destinés à des parents, tous ses biens allaient à son épouse.

Dans l'étude notariale, le notaire et madame Pearl passèrent en revue le testament. Quand ils en eurent terminé, la veuve se leva pour partir. Le notaire tira alors une enveloppe cachetée du dossier qui se trouvait sur son bureau et la tendit à sa cliente.

"J'ai été chargé de vous remettre ceci, dit-il. Votre mari nous l'a fait parvenir peu de temps avant son décès". Le notaire paraissait blême et navré, par respect pour la veuve il gardait les yeux baissés, évitant de croiser son regard. "Cela doit être personnel Madame. Sans doute préfèrerez-vous la lire lorsque vous serez seule chez vous".

Madame Pearl prit l'enveloppe et sortit dans la rue. Elle s'arrêta un instant pour la palper du bout des doigts. Une lettre d'adieu de William? Probablement, oui. Une lettre pleine de formalité. Comment pourrait-il en être autrement? Pleine de formalité et de raideur.

COMMENTAIRE DE LA TRADUCTION PROPOSÉE

Première phrase: noter le déplacement de "when he died" ainsi que la nominalisa-tion de cette forme verbale (à sa mort), noter également la modulation par le con-traire (did not leave a great deal → ne laissa que peu de). En ce qui concerne ", and his will . . ." le rapport entre les deux propositions et rendu explicite par l'utilisation de "aussi" qui entraine une inversion du verbe et du sujet (inversion complexe).

Deuxième paragraphe: noter l'utilisation du passé antérieur (quand ils en eurent terminé) ainsi que l'étoffement de la préposition (from the folder on his desk → du dossier qui se trouvait sur son bureau).

Troisième paragraphe: éviter l'utilisation du passé simple dans le dialogue. La voix passive (I have been instructed) est ici traduite par une forme passive (j'ai été chargé), on aurait pu aussi envisager "on m'a demandé". Noter la nominalisation de "before he passed away" → "avant son décès".

Quatrième paragraphe: noter que le participe présent "feeling the thing" est traduit par "pour + infinitif", ce qui rend le but de cette action plus explicite. Noter que l'assertion "it was bound to be formal" est traduite sous forme de question "comment pourrait-il en être autrement?".

Notes

1 Note, however, that phrases are sometimes labelled in relation to their function.
2 "*Moi président de la République*, je ne serai pas le chef de la majorité, je ne recevrai pas les parlementaires de la majorité à l'Élysée. *Moi président de la République*, je ne traiterai pas mon Premier ministre de collaborateur. *Moi président de la République*, je ne participerai pas à des collectes de fonds pour mon propre parti, dans un hôtel paris-ien; etc."
3 Well-known song by Bénabar: Il y a une fille qu'habite chez moi/*there's a girl who lives in my house.*
4 Available at www.legifrance.gouv.fr (Accessed 10 February 2020).

References

Armstrong, N. (2005). *Translation, Linguistics, Culture: A French-English Handbook.* Buffalo, Toronto: Multilingual Matters.

Ayres-Bennett, W., Carruthers, J. and Temple, R.A.M. (2001). *Problems and Perspectives: Studies in the Modern French Language.* New York: Longman.

Ball, R. (2000). *Colloquial French Grammar: A Practical Guide.* 1st ed. Oxford and Mal-den, MA: Wiley-Blackwell.

Blanche-Benveniste, C. (1997). *Approches de la langue parlée en français.* Paris: Editions OPHRYS.

Coveney, A. (2002). *Variability in Spoken French: A Sociolinguistic Study of Interrogation and Negation.* Bristol: Intellect Books.

De Cat, C. 2007. *French Dislocation: Interpretation, Syntax, Acquisition.* Oxford: Oxford University Press.

Delisle, J. (2003). *La Traduction raisonnée: Manuel d'initiation à la traduction profes-sionnelle, anglais, français : Méthode par objectifs d'apprentissage.* Ottawa: Presses de l'Université d'Ottawa.

Demanuelli, C. and Demanuelli, J. (1990). *Lire et traduire: Anglais-français*. Paris: Masson.

Gadet, Françoise. 1997. *Le Français ordinaire*. 2nd edn. Paris: Armand Colin.

Gardelle, L. (2010). *Dislocations à gauche et antépositions de compléments en anglais : Formes, fonctionnalités et insertion en discours*. Discours – Revue de linguistique, psycholinguistique et informatique. ENS Lyon: Laboratoire LATTICE, pp.1–24.

Guillemin-Flescher, J. (1981). *Syntaxe comparée du français et de l'anglais: Problèmes de traduction*. Paris: Editions OPHRYS.

Hansen, M.-B.M. (2016). *The Structure of Modern Standard French: A Student Grammar*. Oxford and New York: Oxford University Press.

Hervey, S.G.J. and Higgins, I. (1992). *Thinking French Translation: A Course in Translation Method: French to English*. London: Psychology Press.

Jones, M.A. (1996). *Foundations of French Syntax, Cambridge Textbooks in Linguistics*. Cambridge: Cambridge University Press.

Leonarduzzi, L. and Herry, N. (2005). Les Dislocations: Textes et contextes. In: *Congrès de La Société Des Anglicistes de l'Enseignement Supérieur*. Toulouse, France: Publications de l'Université de Saint-Etienne, pp.127–148.

Meisel, J.M., Elsig, M. and Bonnesen, M. (2011). Delayed grammatical acquisition in first language development: Subject-Verb inversion and subject clitics in French interrogatives. Linguistic Approaches to Bilingualism 1. Amsterdam: John Benjamins Publishing Company, pp.347–390.

Planchenault, G. (2017). *Voices in the Media: Performing French Linguistic Otherness*. London and New York: Bloomsbury Publishing.

Chapter 4

A Tense affair

Summary

This chapter will specifically look at the tenses used in French to recount past events (*passé simple, passé composé, imparfait*, as well as the *présent*, which can also be used to relate past events). Firstly, we will consider canonical (i.e. unmarked) uses of each tense. We will look at what the *passé simple* implies, when it is expected, what context it should be used in, and what it implies in contrast to the *imparfait*. We will then examine when the *passé composé* is used to present past events and see whether it can ever replace the *passé simple*. We will then move on to less expected uses of the *passé simple* and *imparfait*, focusing on texts in which past events are primarily presented in the *passé composé* but in which the *passé simple* also crops up at times (in newspaper articles, for instance). We will also consider literary texts in which the *passé composé* is the tense mostly used to present past events, contrary to what some might have expected (*i.e. systematic use of the passé simple in literary narratives*). Finally, we will look at instances where the *imparfait* is used where the *passé composé* or *passé simple* might be expected. The chapter will examine the specificities of each tense and will look at ways of handling these when translating into French. We will reflect upon why certain text types make a greater use of the *passé simple* or *passé composé* than others and focus, in particular, on the relationship between the narrator and his/her text.

Introduction

As with lexis and syntax, there is no one-to-one fit between English and French verb forms and tenses. Hervey and Higgins (1992: 100) point to (at least) 13 different ways of translating a simple English utterance such as *he was injured* into French (*il était blessé, il a été blessé, il fut blessé, il avait été blessé, il se blessait, il se faisait blesser, il s'est blessé, il s'est fait blesser, il s'était blessé*, etc.). Learners of French will be aware that the *passé composé* (*je suis allé au magasin*) can be translated as the English simple past (*I went to the shop*) or as a present perfect (*I have been to the shop*). Similarly, an English simple past (*she saw the film*) might translate as a *passé composé* (*elle a vu le film*), as a *passé simple* (*elle vit le film*) or as an *imparfait* (*elle voyait le film*). It is essential when approaching the use of tenses to distinguish *tense* from *aspect*.

1 Time, tense and aspect

While *tense* is broadly the grammaticalised expression of time (past/present/future), *aspect* is a "grammatical category that indicates some temporal property of an action or state such as whether it is completed, ongoing, habitual, etc." (Fasold and Connor-Linton, 2006). Aspect is the notion we call upon to distinguish between *she was painting the kitchen* and *she painted the kitchen* in English for instance (and *elle peignait la cuisine* and *elle peignit la cuisine* in French). It is clear that the difference between these forms is not one of *tense* – we are with each one of those utterances dealing with a past tense – but one of *aspect*. Aspect is often described as the speaker/writer's perspective on events – the speaker might choose to present an event/action by highlighting a particular aspect over another. With *she was painting the kitchen* and *elle peignait la cuisine*, the stress is placed on the imperfective[1] aspect – the action is presented as ongoing and unbounded – whereas with *she painted the kitchen* and *elle peignit la cuisine*, the action is presented as completed and temporally bounded (perfective aspect).

2 Imperfective aspect

The imperfective aspect tends to be used to present supportive or background information, such as a description or a commentary. There is, generally, a static and permanent notion associated with it. The perfective aspect (*passé simple* or *passé composé*), on the other hand, is associated with actions and dynamism. It is used to present the main events within a sequence of past events and it provides the "plot line". Consecutive verbs in the *passé simple* (or *passé composé*) allow actions within a chronological sequence to proceed at a rapid pace. Let us imagine a simple story in order to illustrate the aspectual difference between *passé simple/passé composé* on the one hand and *imparfait* on the other. The story involves a character called P and is made up of three consecutive events: P buys a car, P has and accident, P sells the car.

The chronological development of the story is represented on the horizontal axis which represents time: event a) precedes event b) which precedes event c). The three main events, or anchor points, are placed on the horizontal axis, while extra information is given for each individual point on a vertical axis. The three main events are in the *passé simple*, while the extra information provided for each individual event is presented in the *imparfait*. Let us note that depending on the type of context in which this narrative is being told, the *passé simple* could be substituted for the *passé composé* (*P a acheté une voiture, P a eu un accident, P a revendu sa voiture*). Of course, the story could be made more complex (and perhaps rather more exciting) by adding new events (in the *passé simple*) on the

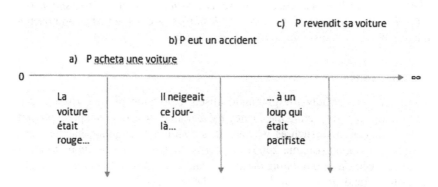

Figure. 4.1 Illustration of passé simple/imparfait opposition in a narrative.

horizontal line and extra information on the vertical axis: *P acheta une voiture. La voiture était rouge. P était très content(e) d'avoir une nouvelle voiture, elle était d'ailleurs très belle . . .* and so on.

   The aspect associated with situations in the *passé simple* (henceforth PS) or *passé composé* (henceforth PC) is the *punctual* aspect. The duration of events is brushed aside as not necessarily relevant. What matters is the fact that the action in question did, in fact, occur – the PS and PC place the focus on the terminal boundary of the process in question (note, however, that both PS and PC can present a duration: *la guerre a duré/dura cent ans*). The *imparfait*, on the other hand, views situations "from the inside", highlighting the internal development of the process and leaves the endpoint open. The endpoint is excluded from view. This has the effect of placing the emphasis on the process itself, not on its result, which explains why the *imparfait* is often said to be *durative* (or *progressive*). Of course, verbs and actions vary in that respect. There is a natural endpoint to *reconnaître quelqu'un* or *trouver quelque chose* or *naître* (these predicates are said to be *telic*). Other verbs such as *savoir quelque chose* and *être amoureux de quelqu'un* clearly refer to states and are *atelic*. Verbs that refer to activities, such as *chanter*, *courir* and *marcher* have inherent duration, while verbs that present achievements such as *remporter un prix* and *arriver à la gare* do not. While the former are likely to appear in the *passé simple* or *passé composé*, the latter are more likely to appear in the *imparfait*. *Lexical aspect* should therefore be taken into account when considering the selection of *passé simple/passé composé* over *imparfait*. The imperfective aspect underpins the different canonical uses of the *imparfait* to provide background information. This information provides the setting and framework for foregrounded events, as previously mentioned:

   Le jour où P eut un accident, il **neigeait** *beaucoup. Le ciel* **était** *sombre et la route* **était** *entièrement recouverte de neige. C'était la vieille de Noël.*

It is used to present ongoing and habitual actions that occurred in the past (often translated by "would" in English):

Chaque année, P se déguisait en Père Noël.
*Every year P **would** dress up as Father Christmas.*

It can also be used to describe an unchanging state in the past, as in the following paragraph taken from a newspaper article which was published in late May 1968 and describes the situation in France before the series of cataclysmic events that shook France:

Longtemps la France **se couchait** de bonne heure,[2] **c'était** un pays où officiellement on ne **posait** pas de questions. Du moins si on en **posait**, la réponse **était** connue d'avance.

(Claude Roy, Le Monde, 25/5/1968)

The use of the *imparfait* implies that the situation pre-May 1968 belongs to a bygone era. Here it is important for the author to stress that the events that shook France have transformed it irreversibly. The events are presented as a turning point: there is a before and an after May 1968 in France. This is *aspect révolu*, which is often translated by *used to* in English (*France used to go to bed early, etc.*).

Following the philosopher Hans Reichenbach (1947), it is useful to consider the type of time reference tenses imply in order to capture their intrinsic value. In his seminal study, Reichenbach distinguishes the *point of speech*, the *point of reference*, and the *point of the event*. If we consider an utterance such as:

Peter était parti

it should be noted that the *point of the event* is the time when Peter actually left. The *point of speech* is the moment when the sentence was uttered. The point of reference is usually given by context or cotext (*when I walked into the office*, for instance). Here, the *point of reference* is situated after the event and before the point of speech (Peter had already gone when I said Peter had gone; the event had already happened). Let us note that an event can take place before or after the point of speech or be simultaneous to it.

In the case of the *passé simple* or *passé composé*:

(1) Elle a vu Eve il y a deux jours.
(2) Elle vit Eve la veille de son départ.

The *point of event* coincides with the *point of reference*. The point of reference is explicit in the examples here: *il y a deux jours* for (1) and *la veille de son départ* for (2). The essential difference between the PS and PC, in contrast with the *imparfait*, is that the duration of the event is extended and left open-ended. As with the PS and PC, the point of event also coincides with the point of reference, so there is, from that point of view, no difference with the PS and PC.

3 Passé simple *as* temps du récit

The past tense, known as *passé simple* (*simple* needs to be understood in morphological terms, i.e. in opposition to *composé*), sometimes labelled *past historic* in English, is, for English speakers, a difficult tense to master since there is no direct equivalent in English. The *passé simple* is often said to be the *temps du récit par excellence*. Today, it is almost exclusively a narrative tense, typically used in written narratives such as novels, short stories, historical works, fairy tales, legends, biographies and obituaries. It tends, however, to be absent from other types of narratives such as letters, diaries and memoirs, especially when events are narrated in the first person. Unless the speaker is narrating a story, the PS is very unlikely to occur in speech (see Labeau, 2005). It typically involves a narrator who presents a text that does not require a verbal response, and it is, in that sense, intrinsically monological (Waugh and Monville-Burston, 1986).[3] It might be used in speech but by a speaker who does not expect his/her audience to interrupt the flow of the narrative and who presents a text prepared in advance. However, it tends not to be used in a narrative that requires audience participation. A person telling or reading a child a bedtime story is likely to use it, but not somebody telling their friends what they did the night before. In his theory of enunciation, the French linguist Emile Benveniste (1976) distinguished between two main types of texts: *discours* and *récit*. *Discours* involves a real speaker and a real addressee, and is characterised by subjective involvement of the speaker. *Récit*, on the other hand, implies detachment on the part of the speaker/writer – events are not presented in relation to the speaker but for their own sake. To put it simply, *discours* therefore deals with everyday matters and is linked to the subjectivity of the speaker/writer; *récit* on the other hand is used for events that are cut off from the speaker/writer's present. The events are presented objectively, without subjective involvement on the narrator's part.

The function of the *passé simple* was very eloquently delineated by the great literary theorist, linguist and semiotician, Roland Barthes:

> Le passé simple n'est plus chargé d'exprimer un temps. Son rôle est de ramener la réalité à un point, et d'abstraire de la multiplicité des temps vécus un acte verbal pur . . . Derrière le passé simple se cache toujours un démiurge, dieu ou récitant . . . le passé simple est précisément ce signe opératoire par lequel le narrateur ramène l'éclatement de la réalité à un verbe mince et pur, sans densité, sans volume, sans déploiement, dont la seule fonction est d'unir le plus rapidement possible une cause et une fin. . . . ces actions émergent

d'un <u>autrefois sans épaisseur</u> . . . le passé simple signifie une création: c'est-à-dire qu'il la signale et qu'il l'impose.

(Roland Barthes, *Le Degré zéro de l'écriture* 1953)

Its function is no longer that of a tense. The part it plays is to reduce reality to a point of time, and to abstract, from the depth of multiplicity of experiences, a pure verbal act. . . . Behind the preterite there always lurks a demiurge, a God, or a reciter . . . the preterite is precisely this operative sign whereby the narrator reduces the exploded reality to a slim and pure logos, without density, without volume, without spread, and whose sole function is to unite as rapidly as possible a cause to an end . . . such actions emerge from a past without substance . . . the preterite signifies a creation: that is, it proclaims and imposes it.[4]

Although the PS can be said to be a "once-upon-a-time tense" (cf. *temps du récit par excellence*), the fact that it is primarily associated with storytelling does not necessarily mean that it is systematically used in literary fiction. The narrative in Camus' *L'Etranger* is probably the most well-known illustration for this. If we look at the incipit of the novel:

Aujourd'hui, maman est morte. Ou peut-être hier, je ne sais pas. J'ai reçu un télégramme de l'asile: "Mère décédée. Enterrement demain. Sentiments distingués". Cela ne veut rien dire. C'était peut-être hier. L'asile de vieillards est à Marengo, à quatre-vingts kilomètres d'Alger. Je prendrai l'autobus à deux heures et j'arriverai dans l'après-midi. Ainsi, je pourrai veiller et je rentrerai demain soir. J'ai demandé deux jours de congé à mon patron et il ne pouvait pas me les refuser avec une excuse pareille. Mais il n'avait pas l'air content. Je lui ai même dit: "Ce n'est pas de ma faute". Il n'a pas répondu. J'ai pensé alors que je n'aurais pas dû lui dire cela. En somme, je n'avais pas à m'excuser.

We can note that (1) the *passé composé* is used for the past events presented in the text (*maman est morte, j'ai reçu, j'ai demandé*, etc.); (2) we are dealing with a first-person narrative (the narrator is the main protagonist in the story that is being told); and (3) the narrator presents past events which have only just happened to him: *Aujourd'hui, maman est morte* – the time elapsed between the moment when the events took place and the narration of these events is short. If we apply the time reference approach developed by Reichenbach, we can see that the distance between the *point of event* and the *point of speech* is short and that the *point of reference* is determined in relation to the present of the character (which coincides with the *point of speech*). This would not be the case with the *passé simple*; using the latter would for that reason be incongruous in this context. From a narratological point of view, Camus' text is very distinct from Zola's novel *Germinal*, the opening of which is presented below:

> Dans la plaine rase, sous la nuit sans étoiles, d'une obscurité et d'une épaisseur d'encre, un homme suivait seul la grande route de Marchiennes à Montsou, dix kilomètres de pavé coupant tout droit, à travers les champs de betteraves. Devant lui, il ne voyait même pas le sol noir, et il n'avait la sensation de l'immense horizon plat que par les souffles du vent de mars, des rafales larges comme sur une mer, glacées d'avoir balayé des lieues de marais et de terres nues . . .
>
> L'homme était parti de Marchiennes vers deux heures. Il marchait d'un pas allongé, grelottant sous le coton aminci de sa veste et de son pantalon de velours . . . Une seule idée occupait sa tête vide d'ouvrier sans travail et sans gîte, l'espoir que le froid serait moins vif après le lever du jour. Depuis une heure, il avançait ainsi, lorsque sur la gauche à deux kilomètres de Montsou, il aperçut des feux rouges, trois brasiers brûlant au plein air, et comme suspendus. D'abord, il hésita, pris de crainte; puis, il ne put résister au besoin douloureux de se chauffer un instant les mains.

Here, we are dealing with a third-person narrative, with an omnipresent and omniscient narrator. The events are presented in a more distant and less subjective way than in the Camus text. The narrator might borrow the perspective and language of the protagonist, and the reader might be able to momentarily inhabit his mindset, but the viewpoint adopted by the narrator is wider than in the previous text. The fact that the PC lends itself to the expression of subjectivity explains why it is more frequently used in autobiographical narratives than the PS. As Fleischman puts it, the PC is linked to a particular type of discourse: "the discourse of a speaker-observer whose psychological centre permeates the discourse" (Fleischman, 1990: 31). In Camus' text, the story is held together not by external events or by the narrator's actions, but by the strength and dynamism of the narrative style. We are not dealing with a narrative where past events are presented as the result of a long and reflexive process, but as they are happening. The narrative presents what the protagonist is experiencing as events take place in the "here-and-now" of the character. To put it in Reichenbachian terms, the *point of reference* is the present of the character, not his past. This obviously prevents the use of the PS, which implies distance (*aujourd'hui maman mourut* would be impossible, the PS clashing with the adverbial *aujourd'hui*).

According to Waugh and Monville-Burston (1986: 851), two fundamental notions define the PS: *detachment* and *dimensionalisation*. *Detachment* is understood as a "separation within a universe, of a dimensionalised entity (a delimited unit) which is highlighted in some way" and *dimensionalisation* as "the delimitation of a figure with clear-cut contours or dimensions". As the function of the PS is primarily to delimit and detach the past events it presents from the everyday (i.e. chronological and emotional detachment), it is not surprising that it should be expected in fairy tales:

> Pendant qu'Ivan dormait, la princesse quitta sa peau de grenouille et se transforma aussitôt en une belle jeune fille. Elle ouvrit la fenêtre et vit une araignée qui tissait sa toile dans l'embrasure.
>
> (La Princesse Grenouille, Russian fairytale)

Of course, the PC would be grammatically possible. However, it would not frame these events as belonging to the particular realm of fairy tales, as the PS does. Its use is not compulsory but it is part of the convention of storytelling. In fact, the use of the PS is akin to using a set formula such as "Once upon a time" at the beginning of a fairy tale. With this particular genre, the reader has usually no interest for the present of the narrator, who tends to be an abstract entity and not a character in the story. Instead, the focus is on the events themselves.

The PS is similarly expected in historical narratives such as dictionary or encyclopaedia entries:

> Augustin, saint (354–430), théologien, prédicateur, père et docteur de l'Église, auteur des Confessions et de la Cité de Dieu.
>
> Augustin **naquit** le 13 novembre 354, à Thagaste (aujourd'hui Souk-Ahras en Algérie). Son père Patricius était païen. Sa mère Monique était en revanche une ardente chrétienne qui **œuvra** inlassablement pour la conversion de son fils et qui sera canonisée par l'Église catholique. Augustin **fit** des études de rhétorique dans les villes de Thagaste, Madaure et Carthage, en Afrique du Nord.

Here, the subjectivity of the entity presenting the events cannot be called upon, since we are dealing with an abstract entity. This detachment has the effect of presenting the events in an objective manner (*this is how things really happened*), which grants them a certain permanence and solemnity (*these are important historical facts*). This also has the effect of presenting these events as detached from the present of the reader (*the events are detached from the here-and-now*). The *passé composé* would imply an unwelcome closeness to the events, *il est né* could imply that Saint Augustin is still alive and would not convey the same sense of deference towards his birth.

4 Passé simple *and* passé composé

In the previous section, we examined what motivates the selection of the *passé simple* over the *passé composé* and focused on texts in which all the past events that are foregrounded were either in the *passé simple* or in the *passé composé*. In this section, we will focus on texts in which the tense primarily used is the *passé composé*, but in which the *passé simple* also appears. This can occur in both narrative and non-narrative texts. This phenomenon is most frequent in newspaper articles but can also appear in first-person narratives such as in autobiographies and novels. When the PS appears in a context where the PC is mostly used, its function is usually to draw attention to a particular event. Its function is then to present the elements in question as important or special and, in any case, worthy of the reader's attention. The PS/PC contrast might then be used in order to distinguish between different time sequences, as is the case below:

> L'ordinateur familial: la micro-informatique **fut** initialement conçue pour un public de passionnés. Afin d'arriver à élargir un public alors restreint, les constructeurs de micro-ordinateurs **introduisirent** le concept de l'ordinateur familial, machine prévue pour toute la famille. Avec l'ordinateur familial, monsieur ferait son travail, madame stockerait ses recettes de cuisine et les enfants joueraient et s'instruiraient. En fait, le micro-ordinateur **a élu** domicile dans la chambre du fiston (= fils, familier) et **n'a** principalement **été utilisé** que pour les jeux.

The contrast between the two tense forms has the effect of highlighting the distinction between two time sequences:

- a first sequence that describes the spirit in which personal computers were created
- a second sequence that describes the actual use that people made of personal computers.

By using the PS in the first one and the PC in the second one, the text highlights the clash between the initial expectations people had in relation to computers and the actual use of computers. The PS/PC contrast is used similarly in the following extract (taken from a novel by Jules Verne):

> On sait généralement et l'on **répète** volontiers que la poudre **fut inventée** au XIVe siècle par le moine Schwartz, qui **paya** de sa vie sa grande découverte. Mais il **est** à peu près **prouvé** maintenant que la poudre **n'a été inventée** par personne; elle **dérive** directement des feux grégeois, composés comme elle de soufre et de salpêtre. Seulement, depuis cette époque, ces mélanges, qui n'étaient que des mélanges fusants, **se sont transformés** en mélanges détonants.

> (Jules Verne, De la terre à la lune)

The contrast is between two sequences of a different nature: one belonging to the realm of myth and preconceptions (i.e. the alleged origin of gunpowder) and the other being an objective and true depiction of reality (what effectively happened). As Waugh and Monville-Burston (1986) signal, the PS is often used at the beginning of a text, especially when presenting the beginning of a process, or presenting the origin of something that is presented in the text where it usually occupies a predominant place. In this promotional text taken from the bilingual magazine *Métropolitain*, which presents a hotel spa in the South-West of France, the PS is used only once. It is used in the first sentence to point out that the hotel is the first one of its kind across France:

LES SOURCES DE CAUDALIE

Tucked away in pony-tilled vineyards, this spa hotel was France's first. We'd happily wager it's still the best: everything here – from the fleet of powder-blue bikes to the sweet goats in the tiny farm – coaxes guests into casting their urban worries away. A recent spruce-up saw the addition of a church-like indoor pool, a grocery-cum-tapas bar and a scattering of sprawling, contemporary suites. Don't miss the chef's garden-fresh creations in the two-star greenhouse restaurant: his surprising "angry egg" is superb with a glug of something special from the Château across the road.

Niché au milieu des vignes labourées au cheval, cet hôtel-spa fut le premier en son genre en France. On parierait que c'est encore le meilleur. Des bicyclettes bleu ciel aux adorables biquettes de la petite ferme, tout invite les clients à se défaire de leurs soucis citadins. Une récente rénovation a vu l'ajout d'une piscine couverte aux allures d'église, d'un bar à tapas-épicerie et de vastes suites modernes. Ne ratez pas les créations tout droit sorties du potager du restaurant-serre deux fois étoilé. Le surprenant "œuf de ferme en colère" est exquis avec un bon verre du château d'à côté.

(Métropolitan, juillet 2017 p. 32)

The use of the PS highlights the uniqueness of the hotel. Syntactically, it is interesting to note the use of the presentative construction "ce + être" since the *passé simple* is often used with this type of construction (precisely to highlight something in a particular situation). The PS is also often used to place emphasis (*mise en relief*) on an event, as in this bilingual advert for a primary school in Brussels:

While the PC is used in the first sentence ("nous avons choisi la BSB"), which is expected since it is important to frame that event in relation to the present of the speaker, the PS is used in the second sentence ("ce fut une expérience enrichissante"). Interestingly, the event in the PC precedes the event in the PS – chronologically, the event in the PC took place first. The use of the PS reinforces the idea that the experience in question was exceptional (this use of the *passé simple* is often compared to a camera "zooming in" on an event). The PC could obviously have been used in the second sentence ("cela a été une expérience

Figure. 4.2 Metropolitan, March 2017 p. 78.

enrichissante"), but the sentence would lose some of its impact and would appear more factual. In terms of the forms used, it is interesting to note that, as in the previous example, the PS appears in a presentative construction and in the third-person singular of *être* (i.e. a form that is easily recognisable and familiar).

5 Imparfait de narration

We discussed the imperfective aspect in Section 2 and stressed the role of the *imparfait* in providing background information. The *imparfait* denotes an event that is incomplete and open-ended and assumes an internal viewpoint that lends itself to introspection (rather than retrospection, which is normally associated with the *passé simple*). We also noted that there is normally no temporal progression with the *imparfait*. Let us compare (examples taken from Saussure and Sthioul, 1999: 10):

(1) Paul entra. Marie téléphonait.
(2) Paul entra. Marie téléphona.

It is obvious that in (2) the point of event for *téléphona* is posterior to the point of event of *entra*, while in (1) the point of event for *téléphonait* is concomitant to the point of event for *entra*. Both events are happening at the same time; one receives the "narrative" focus (what Paul did: *Paul entra*); the other is contextual information that pertains to this particular focalised event (i.e. what was happening when Paul entered the room: *Marie téléphonait*).

There are cases, however, where the *imparfait* is clearly associated with a completed event that takes the narrative line forward (as in the example here from Jubb and Rouxeville, 2008):

Albert Camus mourait accidentellement en 1960.

Here, it is clear that the event described is not open-ended; of all processes death obviously signals the end of something. Therefore, there is something contradictory, on the surface at least, in referring to an event that is clearly the end of a process, on the one hand, and using the *imparfait* on the other. This use of the *imparfait*, which is generally described as *imparfait de narration*,[5] seems to contradict the intrinsic value of the *imparfait*. Some linguists, however, have shown that this contradiction is precisely what triggers the meaning associated with the *imparfait de narration* (Labeau and Larrivée, 2005). Since the normal interpretation fails, the reader has to make an inference (Saussure and Sthioul, 1999). The internal viewpoint associated with the *imparfait* is retained and this is used interpretatively rather than literally. It provides the viewpoint of the narrator. In the present case, it gives the impression that the narrator was there when the event took place and this adds extra poignancy and drama to Camus' untimely death. To draw an analogy, the use of the *imparfait de narration* is reminiscent of the film technique known as subjective camera, which replicates the point of view or mindset of a character in a film. It also gives the impression of slowing down the action, which results in presenting the action in a more dramatic way than the PS or PC. This interpretative detour should not be discarded. As Saussure and Sthioul (1999: 6) demonstrate, the *imparfait de narration* and the *passé simple* are not interchangeable, and the *imparfait de narration* cannot be considered to convey the same meaning as the *passé simple*.

(1) Le train quitta Genève. Quelques heures plus tard, il entrait déjà en Gare de Lyon.
(2) Le train quitta Genève. Quelques heures plus tard, il entra déjà en Gare de Lyon.

While sentence (1) is perfectly acceptable, the adverb *déjà* clashes with the use of the *passé simple* (*entra*) in sentence (2), as it signals an internal viewpoint which is incompatible with the *passé simple*. The subjective and personal viewpoint explains why the *imparfait de narration* is often used in sports reports, as in the following sentence taken from an article that narrates a basketball game:

A partir de là, les deux équipes se rendaient coup pour coup (19–19, 14éme), et c'est finalement dos à dos que chacun regagnait son vestiaire à la pause (24–24, 20éme).[6]

By using the *imparfait*, the journalist signals that he or she was there when the events took place. From a translation point of view (French-English), the shade of meaning introduced by the *imparfait de narration* is usually lost in English since the only possibility that exists in English (for a verbal form such as *regagnait* here, for instance) is the simple past. The simple past, however, does not convey the internal viewpoint, so the "viewpoint effect" is lost. If no other means can be found to convey that nuance, the translation results in a translation loss, as in the following example taken from *Le Monde Diplomatique* (and borrowed from Chuquet in Granger, 2003).

Le 19 janvier dernier, le gouvernement <u>annonçait</u> que 300 000 immigrés seraient expulsés dans les six mois.

Le Monde Diplomatique, avril 1998

In the translation, taken from the English edition, the nuance introduced by the *imparfait* is entirely lost:

On 19 January last, the Thai government <u>announced</u> that 300,000 immigrants would be expelled within six months.

6 Présent de narration

The present tense can also be used to present past events a narrative. The *présent* can also be used as the main *temps du récit* in a narrative and/or in alternance with the *passé composé*. It is often used in sports reports and in oral narratives that sportspeople might give when being interviewed after a sporting event (*présent de reportage*):

Que s'est-il passé au troisième set?

Dans le deuxième jeu du troisième, quand <u>je me fais breaker</u>, j'ai un peu trop regardé l'adversaire. Je me disais que ça allait tenir, que physiquement ça irait mais il a remis de l'intensité et changé son plan de jeu en jouant plus souvent décroisé sur mon coup droit. . . .
    Avez-vous été surpris qu'il joue aussi bien dans le troisième set?
Non. <u>Tu subis</u>, <u>tu ne peux pas suivre</u>. Il <u>faut reconnaître</u> quand le mec <u>est</u> plus fort. 6–0, <u>c'est</u> dur mais il <u>est</u> au-dessus. Il <u>lâche</u> ses coups, je le vois en total contrôle, il <u>est bien</u>, il <u>tape</u> très fort. Il avait sa proie.[7]

It can also appear in literary and historical texts, in combination with the *passé simple*, as in the following text (*présent historique*):

Je ne trouvai point Mme de Warens; on me dit qu'elle venait de sortir pour aller à l'église. C'était le jour des Rameaux de l'année 1728. Je **cours** pour la suivre: je la **vois**, je l'**atteins**, je lui **parle** . . .

J.-J. Rousseau, *Les Confessions*

The present tense adds vivacity and dynamism to the text. The events appear to be more actual and immediate, while combining the internal viewpoint normally associated with the *imparfait*. As with the *imparfait*, the events are presented as ongoing and non-accomplished. The *present* is usually associated with speech and *discours* so adding it in a context where the *passé simple* is normally used gives the narrative a conversational and oral element. Although the present tense is used in the second paragraph as a *présent de vérité générale* to describe permanent situations and facts that are always true (*Il faut reconnaître quand le mec est plus fort. 6–0, c'est dur mais il est au-dessus*), it is clearly used as a *présent de narration* in the rest of the text (*je me fais breaker, Il lâche ses coups, je le vois en total contrôle, il est bien, il tape très fort*). In English, when events are clearly in the past, and temporal indications are provided (such as *C'était le jour des Rameaux de l'année 1728* in the Rousseau passage), the preterite tends to be used. However, it is also possible for the present tense to be used even if the preterite is the usual choice. Sports broadcasters and other live reporters tend to use the present simple to commentate on events in real time. They do not, however, use the present tense so readily when narrating events that clearly happened in the past.

Conclusion

This chapter examined the difference between tense and aspect in order to make a distinction between the *passé simple* and the *imparfait*. Unsurprisingly, the imperfective aspect is crucial to all the uses of the imparfait including the *imparfait de narration*. The opposition between the *passé simple* as *temps du récit* and the *passé composé* as *temps du discours* was also discussed. By so doing, we were able to account for uses of the *passé composé* in literary fiction and for uses of the *passé simple* in nonliterary texts. The chapter showed that contrasting tenses is a way of creating effects which cannot often be rendered through the same process in English. This means that a translator must pay particular attention to past tenses when translating from English into French. When translating verb forms from French into English, a process of neutralisation often occurs (i.e. a less expressive form is used in the TT than in the ST). It can happen the other way around. This can also be the case when translating from English into French, especially when dealing with forms such as *would*, *used to*, and *be+-ing*, in the context of the description of past events. We have seen that these can then be translated with one single form in French, namely, the *imparfait*.

7 Activités de mise en pratique

I Analyse des temps dans un article de journal

Lire le texte puis commenter l'emploi des temps. Comment expliquer l'emploi du passé simple dans le premier paragraphe? Aurait-on pu utiliser le passé composé à la place? Aurait-on pu utiliser le passé simple dans le deuxième et troisième paragraphes? Comment expliquer l'utilisation du présent dans le premier paragraphe, dans le troisième paragraphe?

Le tourisme de l'espace

Il y a peu de temps encore, on pensait que le tourisme spatial allait exploser. Hélas, les explosions qui se <u>produisirent</u> n'étaient pas celle que l'on avait escomptée. En 2003, l'explosion de la navette américaine Columbia, qui <u>fit</u>

sept victimes, et celle de la navette de Vigrin Galactic qui <u>eut lieu</u> une dizaine d'années plus tard, <u>mirent</u> un terme à la poursuite de ce rêve.

Face aux difficultés techniques et aux coûts astronomiques d'une telle entreprise, les entrepreneurs de l'espace <u>ont décidé</u> de miser sur la stratosphère. Il n'est point nécessaire en effet de sortir de l'atmosphère pour faire l'expérience de l'espace.

"A une trentaine de kilomètres d'altitude le spectacle est saisissant: le ciel se fait d'un noir profond et les étoiles semblent à portée de main", <u>affirme</u> un spécialiste des voyages dans la stratosphère. Reste que des voyages de ce type ne sont destinés qu'à un nombre très réduit de privilégies. En effet, le coût de plus de centaines milliers de dollars en est prohibitif, ce qui n'est peut-être pas plus mal quand on <u>connait</u> l'empreinte carbone de ce type de vols.

II Analyse des temps dans un prospectus touristique

Cet extrait est tiré d'un dépliant touristique destiné aux visiteurs de l'église du village de Pradelles en Haute-Loire (France), église dans laquelle on peut voir une statue de la Sainte Vierge. 1). Expliquer l'emploi des temps dans cet extrait: quels sont les temps utilisés? Pour quelles raisons? 2). Comparer l'emploi des temps dans le texte français et dans le texte anglais? Quelles correspondances observe-t-on entre les temps utilisés en français et en anglais?

La découverte de la statue

Le culte de Notre-Dame apparait en 1512, date à laquelle un hospitalier, voulant relever une muraille au coin du pré joignant l'hôpital, découvre dans le sol un coffre contenant une statue en bois. Cette statue, à l'origine en bois de cèdre (mesurant une soixante de cm), fut restaurée avec des pièces de pin pour réparer les dégâts de l'incendie sous la "Terreur" de juin 1973.

Elle fut cachée pendant plusieurs décennies avant de réintégrer la chapelle en 1802 où elle trône "en majesté" sur le maitre-autel. Trois restaurations successives ont été effectués au cours des deux derniers siècles.

The discovery of the statue

The Cult of our Lady appears in 1512, when a hospital worker, wishing to rebuild a wall at the corner of a field adjacent to the hospital, discovers in the earth a chest containing a wooden statue. This statue, originally made of cedar wood (measuring about 60 cm, less than 2 ft.), was restored with pieces of pine to repair the damage due to a fire during the "Terror" of June 1973.

It was hidden for several decades before returning to the chapel in 1802 where Our Lady sits enthroned "in majesty" on the high altar. Three successive restorations have been carried out during the last two centuries.

III Traduction des temps dans un article de journal

Observer les deux textes ci-dessous (le text source est en anglais, le texte cible en français) puis commenter la traduction des temps:

In March 2016 the Drug Controller General of India (DCGI) <u>issued</u> a notice stating that it had received a proposal for switching gelatin capsules with hydroxypropyl methylcellulose (HPMC) or cellulose capsule shells. The notice <u>has caused</u> panic in the Indian pharmaceutical industry because if implemented, it <u>will raise</u> the cost of production <u>and increase</u> the price of medicines significantly.[8]

En mars 2016, le Drug Controller General of India (DCGI) [. . .] <u>annonçait</u> dans une note qu'il <u>avait reçu</u> une proposition ayant pour but de remplacer les gélules en gélatine par des gélules en cellulose ou en hypromellose. Cette nouvelle <u>a semé</u> la panique dans le secteur pharmaceutique indien: si la proposition est acceptée, le coût de production et le prix des médicaments <u>augmenteront</u> significativement.[9]

IV Traduction des temps dans un article de journal

Le paragraphe ci-dessous est écrit dans le style d'un article de journal. Cet article présente les témoignages de personnes qui vivent dans une province qui font part des changements qu'a connus leur région.

1   *Lire le paragraphe ci-dessous et répondre aux questions suivantes: quelles sont les formes verbales utilisées? Comment vont-elles être traduites en français? La situation décrite est-elle encore valable au moment de l'énonciation?*

   "When I was a child we lived in a tiny house built by my father, at the bottom of a mountain", he says. "My mother used to take me to school by bicycle every day, and after school I would often go to look at the books in the nearby shop. Although they were not expensive, I could not afford them".

   Quel(s) temps va-t-on utiliser pour les verbes laissés à l'infinitif dans la traduction ci-dessous?

   "Enfant, dit-elle, nous _____ (vivre) dans une maison que mon père avait construite au pied de la montagne. Ma mère m'_____ (emmener) tous les jours à l'école en bicyclette et après l'école j'_____ (aller) souvent faire un tour dans la librarie à côté Même, si ces livres n'étaient pas chers, je ne _____ (pouvoir) pas me permettre de les acheter"

2   *Dans l'entretien ci-dessous, un célèbre chef cuisinier explique ses débuts en cuisine:*

   Quel(s) temps va-t-on utiliser pour les verbes laissés à l'infinitif dans le texte français? Les événements décrits se sont-ils produits une seule ou plusieurs fois?

   When did you realise you were a bit of a dab hand at cooking? From the age of eight, I was always in the kitchen; my dad was a chef, and it was the only time I'd get to see him. I'd sit on the side, doing silly jobs, like cleaning mussels, before graduating to making sauces. I would experiment with ingredients, and create these bizarre flavour combinations that I thought were revolutionary – things like olive oil peppered toast and burnt caramel – and test them out on my poor mum![10]

Quand avez-vous compris que vous ___ (être) bon cuisinier? Dès 8 ans, j'___ (être) toujours fourré en cuisine. Mon père ___ (être) chef c'___ (être) la seule façon de passer du temps avec lui. Je ___ (rester) dans les parages à faire de menues tâches, comme nettoyer les moules, avant d'être promu aux sauces. J'_____ (expérimenter) avec des ingrédients pour créer des combinaisons bizarres de saveurs que je ____ (trouver) révolutionnaires – comme du toast à l'huile d'olive et au caramel brulé – et je les ____ (tester) sur ma pauvre maman!

V Traduction des temps dans un récit

Simon Waller was sitting at the bar in the only pub in the village, drinking a pint and wondering what to do that afternoon when a woman tapped him on the shoulder. She looked vaguely familiar but he could not quite place her and, in the dimly lit bar, he attempted a half-smile and blinked at her, remaining confused and at a loss for words.

Quel temps va-t-on utiliser pour présenter les actions qui font progresser le récit (a woman tapped him on the shoulder; he blinked at her): passé simple ou passé composé? Quel temps va-t-on principalement utiliser dans le reste du texte? Pour quelles raisons?

VI Traduction d'une entrée biographique dans une encyclopédie

Marie Curie, née Maria Salomea Skłodowska (born November 7, 1867, Warsaw, Congress Kingdom of Poland, Russian Empire – <u>died</u> July 4, 1934, near Sallanches, France), Polish-born French physicist, famous for her work on radioactivity and twice a winner of the Nobel Prize. With Henri Becquerel and her husband, Pierre Curie, she <u>was awarded</u> the 1903 Nobel Prize for Physics. She <u>was</u> the sole winner of the 1911 Nobel Prize for Chemistry. She <u>was</u> the first woman to win a Nobel Prize, and she is the only woman to win the award in two different fields.

Encyclopaedia Britannica[11]

Quel temps utiliser dans la première phrase pour traduire l'événement principal (died July 4)? Passé simple ou passé composé? Qu'en est-il pour le reste du texte?

VII Texte à traduire: passé simple ou passé composé, alternance de ces deux temps?

Cet extrait est tiré d'un ouvrage de psychologie intitulé Emotion, écrit par Dylan Jones, il s'agit d'une introduction à la "science des sentiments".[12] Dans ce passage, l'auteur utilise une anecdote personnelle pour présenter une émotion pour laquelle il n'y a pas de mot en anglais.

When I was 15, some friends of mine invited me to join their punk rock band. The previous singer, while very good in rehearsals, suffered from stage fright and could not perform in public. I was just the opposite: my voice was terrible, but I had no qualms about making a fool of myself. Just the right ingredients for a punk rock singer!

After the first rehearsal, we sat around planning our careers in the music business. It was then that Tim told me how happy he was that I had joined the band. I can still remember vividly the intense reaction that comment produced in me. The warm wave spread outwards and upwards from my stomach, rapidly enveloping the whole of my upper chest. It was a kind of joy, but unlike any moment of joy I had felt before. It was a feeling of acceptance, of belonging, of being valued by a group of people whom I was proud to call my friends. I was momentarily lost for words, shocked by the novelty of the sensation. In the years since then the feeling has never repeated itself exactly, and I have never forgotten it. I am certainly not the only person to have experienced this particular emotion.

1   Quelle est la fonction du récit présenté ici par rapport au reste de l'ouvrage?

2   Quelle est la structure temporelle de ce passage?

3   Serait-il possible et souhaitable d'utiliser le passé simple dans une partie du texte?

4   Pourrait-on utiliser le passé simple dans la dernière phrase du texte?

1   Ce récit a une valeur illustrative. Sa fonction est de venir appuyer l'idée que certaines émotions ne peuvent facilement être exprimées. Il n'y a pas de terme en anglais, ni d'ailleurs en français, pour décrire l'émotion ressentie par l'auteur lorsqu'on lui a demandé de rejoindre le groupe de musique (contrairement au japonais: *amae*). Ce récit a donc une valeur anecdotique et ne s'inscrit pas dans une séquence d'évènements qui représenteraient l'essentiel du texte.

2   Le premier paragraphe fournit le contexte dans lequel s'est produit l'événement central (le fait de ressentir une émotion particulière). Le deuxième paragraphe présente cet événement de façon détaillée. On notera que les observations de l'auteur quant à cette émotion sont repérées par rapport au moment de l'énonciation (*in the years since then*). On notera aussi l'utilisation du présent dans la dernière phrase.

3   Bien qu'il ne soit pas obligatoire, le passé simple peut être judic-
ieusement utilisé pour décrire le moment où l'auteur a ressenti la
sensation nouvelle (*The warm wave spread outwards and upwards
from my stomach, rapidly enveloping the whole of my upper chest*).
Cela permet de mettre l'emphase sur la particularité de la sensation
ressentie par l'auteur, événement qui constitue l'élément principal du
texte.

4   Le passé simple serait impossible pour traduire la dernière phrase du
texte, puisque cet événement est repéré par rapport au moment de
l'énonciation (*I am certainly not the only person to have experienced
this particular emotion*).

Traduction du texte de Dylan Evans

A l'âge de 15 ans, des amis m'ont proposé de faire partie de leur groupe de
punk rock. Le chanteur précédent, excellent en répétition, avait le trac et était
incapable de se produire sur scène. Pour moi c'était tout le contraire, j'avais
une voix terrible mais n'avais pas le moindre scrupule à me ridiculiser. Tout
ce qu'il fallait donc pour un être un bon chanteur de punk rock!

Après la première répétition, on devisa de notre avenir dans le monde du
show-business. C'est alors que Tim me dit combien il était heureux que j'aie
rejoint le groupe. Je me rappelle encore très bien la sensation que ce commentaire produisit en moi. Une sensation de chaleur qui partit de mon abdo-
men et se répandit dans tout le haut de mon torse: une sorte de joie comme je
n'en avais jamais ressenti auparavant. Le sentiment d'appartenir à un groupe,
d'avoir la reconnaissance d'un groupe de personnes que j'étais fier d'avoir
pour amis. Je restai interloqué, étonné par la nouveauté de cette sensation.
Je n'ai jamais ressenti depuis ce sentiment dans la même mesure, je ne l'ai
pourtant pas oublié. Je ne suis certainement pas le seul à avoir éprouvé cette
émotion si particulière.

VIII *Texte littéraire – Talking it over, Julian Barnes*

*Dans ce texte tiré d'un roman, le narrateur s'adresse à son ami Stuart qui est
lui-même un personnage de l'histoire. Comment traduire le prétérit anglais dans
ce texte?*

Stuart, shall I tell you something I always slightly resented? This is probably
going to sound incredibly petty, but it's true.

At the weekends she used to have a lie-in. I'd be the first to get up. We
always had a grapefruit, or at least, one of the mornings we did, either Saturday or Sunday.

I'd be the one to decide. If I went down and felt like a grapefruit on Saturday, I'd take it out of the fridge, cut it in half and put each in a bowl.

Otherwise we'd have it on the Sunday. Now, when I'd eaten my half, I'd look at Gillian's sitting in its bowl. I'd think, that's hers, she's going to eat that when she wakes up. And I'd carefully take out all the pips from her half, so she wouldn't have to do it herself.

Do you know, in all the time we were together, she never noticed this. Or if she did notice, she never mentioned it. I used to think, perhaps she believes some new strain of seedless grapefruit has been invented. How does she think grapefruit reproduce?

Maybe she's discovered the existence of pips by now.

1   Quel temps utiliser pour traduire le prétérit dans la première phrase du paragraphe "shall I tell you something I always slightly resented"?

2   Quel temps va-t-on utiliser pour la majorité des verbes du deuxième paragraphe?

TRADUCTION PROPOSÉE

Stuart, tu veux que je te raconte quelque chose qui m'a toujours un peu gêné? Ça va certainement te paraître mesquin, mais c'est pourtant vrai.

Le week-end, elle avait l'habitude de faire la grasse matinée. C'était toujours moi qui me levais le premier. On mangeait toujours un pamplemousse, au moins un matin sur les deux, soit le samedi, soit le dimanche, c'était moi qui décidais. Si je me levais et si j'avais envie d'un pamplemousse, j'en prenais un dans le frigidaire, je le coupais en deux puis mettais chaque moitié dans une assiette . . . ou alors, on le mangeait le dimanche. Et puis, une fois que j'avais mangé ma moitié, je regardais celle de Gillian dans l'assiette, je pensais alors, c'est sa part, elle la mangera quand elle se réveillera, et, minutieusement, je retirais tous les pépins un à un; tout ça, pour lui éviter d'avoir à le faire elle-même.

Sais-tu que pendant tout le temps que nous avons passé ensemble, elle ne s'en est jamais rendu compte . . . ou si elle s'en est rendu compte elle n'en a jamais rien dit. A l'époque je me disais, peut-être qu'elle croit qu'on a inventé une nouvelle variété de pamplemousse sans pépins. Ils se reproduisent comment les pamplemousses, à son avis?

Peut-être a-t-elle aujourd'hui découvert l'existence des pépins.

COMMENTAIRE DE LA TRADUCTION PROPOSÉE

Temps verbaux: une des particularités de ce texte se situe dans la façon dont cette histoire est narrée puisque le narrateur, qui est un personnage de l'histoire, s'adresse directement dans un monologue à l'un de ses amis (Stuart), c'est donc sur le ton de la confidence que l'histoire est présentée. Le texte comporte des éléments d'oralité et porte sur des événements douloureusement liés au présent du personnage, le passé composé s'impose donc comme temps de la narration.

L'imparfait est évidemment utilisé pour décrire les événements habituels qui se produisaient à l'époque maintenant révolue (cf. *used to, would* dans le TS) où le narrateur vivait avec sa compagne. Pour *when she wakes up*, noter que le présent de la subordonnée du TS correspond en français au futur *quand elle se réveillera* (9, when I'm sixty four→quand j'aurai soixante-quatre ans).

Syntaxe: la syntaxe comporte des éléments d'oralité: on notera l'absence d'inversion dans la question de la première phrase: *tu veux que . . .* de même que l'utilisation de *peut-être qu'elle croit* plutôt que *peut-être croit-elle*. L'inversion apparaît en revanche dans la dernière phrase, dans laquelle *peut-être* est en antéposition, et confère à l'énoncé un caractère emphatique qui correspond à l'agacement du personnage.

Noter également l'utilisation de *vouloir* (1, *tu veux que je te raconte*) qui traduit *shall I tell you* – *shall* a ici une valeur modale et on ne saurait en aucun cas le traduire par un futur, c'est l'utilisation de *vouloir* qui permet de retrouver la valeur de consultation de *shall*.

IX Texte littéraire – The Kite Runner, *Khaled Hosseini*

Dans ce roman écrit à la première personne, le narrateur se remémore des événements qui ont marqué son enfance. C'est le coup de téléphone de son ami Rahim khan qui l'amène à se replonger dans des événements qui ont eu lieu une vingtaine d'années auparavant:

Excerpt 1

December 2001

I became what I am today at the age of twelve, on a frigid overcast day in the winter of 1975. I remember the precise moment, crouching behind a crumbling mud wall, peeking into the alley near the frozen creek. That was a long time ago, but it's wrong what they say about the past, I've learned, about how you can bury it because the past claws its way out. Looking back now, I realise I have been peeking into that deserted alley for the last twenty-six years.

One day last summer, my friend Rahim Khan called from Pakistan. He asked me to come see him. Standing in the kitchen with the receiver to my ear, I knew it wasn't just Rahim Khan on the line. It was my past of una-toned sins. After I hung up, I went for a walk along Spreckels Lake on the northern edge of Golden Gate Park. The early-afternoon sun sparkled on the water where dozens of miniature boats sailed, propelled by a crisp breeze. Then I glanced up and saw a pair of kites, red with long blue tails, soaring in the sky. They danced high above the trees on the west end of the park, over the windmills, floating side by side like a pair of eyes looking down on San Francisco, the city I now call home. And suddenly Hassan's voice whispered in my head: *For you, a thousand times over.* Hassan the harelipped runner.

Si les événements narrés ci-dessus sont temporellement proches du moment de l'énonciation, le roman comporte également de longues séquences dans lesquelles sont présentés les événements qui ont marqué son enfance – le roman se caractérise par un va-et-vient incessant entre les deux plans temporels:

Excerpt 2

One day, we were walking from my father's house to Cinema Zainab for a new Iranian movie, taking the shortcut through the military barracks near Istiqlal Middle School – Baba had forbidden us to take that shortcut, but he was in Pakistan with Rahim Khan. We hopped the fence that surrounded the barracks, skipped over a little creek, and broke into the open dirt field where old, abandoned tanks collected dust. A group of soldiers huddled in the shade of one of those tanks, smoking cigarettes and playing cards. One of them saw us, elbowed the guy next to him, and called Hassan.

"Hey, you!" he said. "I know you".

We had never seen him before. He was a squatty man with a shaved head and black stubble on his face. The way he grinned at us, leered, scared me. "Just keep walking," I muttered to Hassan.

1   Réfléchir à la façon de traduire les événements passés présentés dans les deux textes ci-dessus: souligner les formes verbales et proposer une forme verbale française pour chacune d'elle. Quel(s) temps utiliser?
2   Lire les deux extraits ci-dessous tirés de la traduction de Valérie Bourgeois (Editions Belfond, 2007) et souligner les formes verbales: quels sont les temps utilisés?

Extrait 1

Décembre 2001

Je suis devenu ce que je suis aujourd'hui à l'âge de douze ans, par un jour glacial et nuageux de l'hiver 1975. Je revois encore cet instant précis où, tapi derrière le mur de terre à demi éboulé, j'ai jeté un regard furtif dans l'impasse située près du ruisseau gelé. La scène date d'il y a longtemps mais, je le sais maintenant, c'est une erreur d'affirmer que l'on peut enterrer le passé: il s'accroche tant et si bien qu'il remonte toujours à la surface. Quand je regarde en arrière, je me rends compte que je n'ai cessé de fixer cette ruelle déserte depuis vingt-six ans.

L'été dernier, mon ami Rahim Khan m'a téléphoné du Pakistan pour me demander de venir le voir. Le combiné à l'oreille, dans la cuisine, j'ai compris que je n'avais pas affaire seulement à lui. Mes fautes inexpiées se rappelaient à moi, elles aussi. Après avoir raccroché, je suis allé au bord du lac Spreckels, à la limite nord du Golden Gate Park. Le soleil du début d'après-midi faisait miroiter des reflets dans l'eau où voguaient des douzaines de bateaux miniatures poussés par un petit vent vif. Levant la tête, j'ai aperçu deux cerfs-volants rouges dotés d'une longue queue qui volaient haut dans le ciel. Bien au-dessus des arbres et des moulins à vent, à l'extrémité ouest du parc, ils dansaient et flottaient côte à côte, semblables à deux yeux rivés sur San Francisco, la ville où je me sens maintenant chez moi. Soudain, la voix d'Hassan a résonné en moi: Pour vous, un millier de fois, me chuchotait-elle. Hassan, l'enfant aux cerfs-volants affligé d'un bec de lièvre.

Extrait 2

Un jour que nous nous rendions à pied au cinéma Zainab, où passait un nouveau film iranien, nous avons coupé par les baraquements militaires situés près du collège Istiqlal. Baba nous avait interdit d'emprunter ce raccourci, mais il était alors au Pakistan avec Rahim khan. Nous avons sauté par-dessus la barrière ceignant les casernes, franchi un petit ruisseau et débouché sur le terrain vague où de vieux tanks abandonnés prenaient la poussière. Quelques soldats s'étaient serrés à l'ombre de l'une de ces carcasses pour fumer et jouer aux cartes. L'un d'eux nous aperçut, décocha un coup de coude à son voisin et interpella Hassan.

– Hé, toi là-bas! Je te connais!

Nous n'avions jamais vu cet homme trapu au crâne rasé qui affichait une barbe noire de quelques jours. Son sourire goguenard m'effraya.

– Ne t'arrête pas, murmurai-je à Hasan.

Notes

1 Hence the term "imparfait" to describe the French past tense.
2 Readers might have noticed the reference to the opening sentence of Proust's *A la Recherche du temps perdu*: "Longtemps je me suis couché de bonne heure". While the imperfect is used in the newspaper article, Proust opted for the *passé composé* which is in line with the inchoative aspect of the verb. Rather than stressing that the event *used to* happen, Proust stresses that the event *did* happen.
3 Here is how the presenter of the France Inter programme *Remèdes à la mélancolie* introduced the actor Virginie Efira on 14/05/2017. Although we are dealing with spoken language, the text is clearly monological as it does not call for a response from the audience: "*Notre apothicaire de l'âme est une actrice qui a d'abord imprégné de son charme ébouriffant les planches du conservatoire de Bruxelles et les canaux de la télévision belge. Sur le petit écran français, dans une émission populaire qu'elle présentait, sa drôlerie était telle qu'on lui demanda de se réfréner un peu. Par la suite, heureusement, on la sollicita justement pour ce qu'on lui avait demandé de modérer.*"
4 The translation is from the Barthes Reader edited by Susan Sontag (Barthes, 1993).
5 The term *imparfait de rupture* is also often used for utterances of this kind.
6 Available at: http://usmb-tigers2016.clubeo.com/actualite/2017/10/08/superbe-succes-des-seniors-filles-a-herin-46-40.html (Accessed 10 February 2020).

7 Available at: www.lequipe.fr/Tennis/Actualites/Gael-monfils-il-avait-sa-proie/653412 (Accessed 10 February 2020).
8 Available at www.outlookindia.com/magazine/story/the-pure-veg-prescription/299301 (Accessed 10 February 2020).
9 Available at www.courrierinternational.com/article/medicaments-la-prescription-veg ane-du-gouvernement-indien (Accessed 10 February 2020).
10 *Metropolitan* July 2017, p. 16.
11 Available at www.britannica.com/biography/Marie-Curie (accessed 10 February 2020).
12 Dylan. 2001. *Emotion: The science of sentiment.* Oxford and New York: Oxford University Press.

References

Barthes, R. (1953). *Le Degré zéro de l'écriture.* Paris: Éditions du Seuil.

Barthes, R. and Sontag, S., eds. (1993). *A Barthes Reader.* London: Vintage Books.

Benveniste, Emile. 1976. *Problèmes de linguistique générale, tome 1.* Paris: Gallimard.

Chuquet, H. (2003). Loss and Gain in English Translations of the French Imparfait. In: S. Granger, J. Lerot and S. Petch-Tyson, eds., *Corpus-based approaches to contrastive linguistics and translation studies.* Amsterdam and New York: Rodopi.

Fasold, R.W. and Connor-Linton, J. (2006). *An Introduction to Language and Linguistics.* Cambridge: Cambridge University Press.

Fleischman, S. (1990). *Tense and Narrativity: From Medieval Performance to Modern Fiction.* Austin: University of Texas Press.

Hervey, S.G.J. and Higgins, I. (1992). *Thinking French Translation: A Course in Translation Method: French to English.* London: Routledge.

Jubb, M. and Rouxeville, A. (2008). *French Grammar in Context.* 3rd ed. London: Routledge.

Julian Barnes (2009). *Talking it Over.* London : Vintage, pp.244–5.

Labeau, E. (2005). *Beyond the Aspect Hypothesis: Tense-aspect Development in Advanced L2 French.* Bern and Oxford: Peter Lang.

Labeau, E. and Larrivée, P. (2005). *Nouveaux développements de l'imparfait.* Cahiers Chronos. Amsterdam: Rodopi.

Reichenbach, H. (1947). *Elements of Symbolic Logic.* New York: Macmillan Co.

Saussure, L. de and Sthioul, B. (1999). L'imparfait narratif : Point de vue (et images du monde). *Cahiers de praxématique*, 32, 167–188.

Waugh, L.R. and Monville-Burston, M. (1986). Aspect and discourse function: The French simple past in newspaper usage. *Language*, 62, 846–877.

Chapter 5

Traduttore, traditore!

Summary

With its memorable parallel structure, the well-known Italian adage suggests that every translation is a betrayal (*translator, traitor*). This is a reminder of one of the most pressing questions in translation studies, namely, how far should the translator transform the text? How far is this new work a true reflection of the original? This chapter will analyse issues which might lead translators to make choices that might indeed be perceived as a betrayal or result in translation distortion or loss of the ST. The chapter will shed light on questions such as: when do the decisions a translator has to make become truly problematic and put the translation process at risk? What do we mean when we talk about *translatability*? What are the features of a text that might make the translation process particularly difficult?

In order to illustrate a clear case of malpractice, one section will deal with the early translation of Beauvoir's *Second Sex* by H.M. Parshley. Another section will consider the translation of the opening paragraph of *l'Etranger*. The relationship between translation and sounds will also be discussed in relation to political slogans and proper nouns.

Introduction

As we discussed in Chapter 1, translating lexical items is often linked to the fact that linguistic systems organise the world into different conceptual categories and, often, there is no direct or full equivalence between a lexical item in language A and in language B (recall Vinay and Darbelnet's mantra: "full synonymy is the exception not the rule" (1958)). Indeed, translators' notes abound with examples of words that cannot be rendered in the TL without exposing the arbitrariness of the translator's decision. For instance, as Graham Burchell, the translator who translated Foucault's lectures *On the Government of the Living*, notes in his preface to the translated text, the French word *pénitence*, which is central to the text, can be translated as *penitence*, but could also be translated as *penance* or *repentance*:

> [the] reader should bear in mind that "repentance" perhaps falls short of the early Church sense of paenitentia/metonia, and that in these lectures

"penance" does not usually mean penalty or punishment, and, unless explicitly indicated, does not refer to the sacrament of penance.

Similarly, in the note that prefaces the 2007 edition of Robespierre's speeches *Virtue and Terror* published by Verso, the translator discusses the translation of the French word *patrie*, which recurs throughout the French text. Although the nearest equivalent is *fatherland*, the translator opted for the term *homeland*: "For people of my age, though, the word 'fatherland' has a tainted ring, and 'motherland' seems a gratuitous inversion. I have chosen to translate it as 'homeland'". Examples of this type abound, especially when dealing with philosophical texts; however, as long as the translator makes the reader aware of the translatability issue they pose, they do not constitute acts of betrayal, as such.

1 Translatability and text types

Clearly, translatability depends on the type of text a translator has to translate and is, to a large extent, linked to its function and purpose. The way a translator approaches the translation of a given text is largely linked to the communicative purpose of the text in question. If we consider two text types of a very different nature, a notice for a prescription drug and a poem, for instance, we can anticipate that the translation process will be approached very differently. Translating the notice for a prescription drug, or the operating instructions for any manufactured product, does not pose the same kind of difficulty as translating a poem, since both texts have very different functions. There might be more room for a translator to betray the writer's intention in the case of a poem; however, the risk of getting the translation wrong might have graver consequences in the case of a pharmaceutical drug notice. With the latter, the success of the translation can be assessed in objective terms and independently of the ST (*Is the text clear enough? Will the user know exactly what they have to do?*). With a poem, assessing the reliability and success of a translation will always rely more largely on comparing the TT with the ST and more heavily on the translator's subjectivity – how a reader appreciates and interprets a poem calls on a reader's subjectivity more so than understanding instructions on how to use a tool. Procedural language can therefore be translated in a more mechanical and predictable way.

When assessing machine translation, poetry is often invoked as the text type that will always resist automation – digital companies might have managed to create very efficient translation tools and programmes (e.g. *Trados, DeepL Translator* or *Google Translate*), which can produce accurate and competent translations for some texts, or at least assist the translator in the translation process. It is hard to imagine how machine learning, which is mostly based on using probability, could be applied to poetry in a systematic way (see the next chapter on the discussion of Douglas Hofstadter's inclusions of translations via machines in his book showcasing different versions of the same poem).

2 Translatability and the heterogeneity of meaning

Translatability is obviously also largely linked to the heterogeneity of meaning. Leech (1974) distinguishes seven types of meaning which can be roughly split into two subcategories: *conceptual meaning* vs. *associative meaning*. In broad terms, conceptual meaning is synonymous with propositional meaning or denotative meaning. From that point of view, the meaning of a sentence is the sum of its linguistic components, while associative meaning, which encompasses connotative, social and affective meaning, is peripheral and somehow incidental. Conceptual meaning can be reduced to a finite number of traits, whereas associative meaning is by nature open-ended. Connotative meaning refers to the qualitative associations we make when a noun and adjective or a verb is used: two words with the same denotative meaning might trigger different associations (cf. Chapter 1) – *père* vs. *papa*, mom vs. *mother*. Associative meaning is also linked with "social" meaning. We recognise some words or pronunciations as being dialectal, as belonging to a particular geographical, social variety of the language or to a particular historical period. In the first translation of *The Old Man and the Sea* by Hemingway, which was produced by Jean Dutourd and published in 1952, the old man's use of the French language is colloquial and clearly socially marked, which is not at all the case in the original English. For instance, when the old man asks in the original: "who can we borrow that from", it is translated by Dutourd as: "à qui c'est-y qu'on va les emprunter"? which is a nonstandard and low prestige form. This shift in register has the effect of associating the old man's speech with a particular social group and with a whole range of stereotypes. That does not alter the story, which obviously remains the same, but it gives the French text a distinct flavour the original does not possess.

Leech (1974: 23) also mentions *affective meaning* – "what is communicated of the feelings and attitudes of the speaker/writer" – as well as *reflected* and *collocative meaning* – "what is communicated through association with another sense of the same expression". Associative meaning is also linked to intertextuality, that is, *the shaping of a text's meaning by another text*. The meaning of a text does not solely arise from the compositional meaning of the words on the page but in relation to other texts embedded within a whole cultural context.[1]

3 The Translator as traitor – H.M. Parshley's translation of The Second Sex

If translation can lead to minor and isolated cases of betrayal on the translator's part, there are also clear cases of outright betrayal. Because the translator acts as an intermediary between two texts, or *passeur* in French, he or she can, from this vantage point, smuggle in elements which should never have appeared in the TT. The translator, therefore, has the power to alter the text in a way which will remain totally hidden from the foreign language reader. The translation of Simone de Beauvoir's 1949 book *Le Deuxième Sexe* is a case in point. In the first English-language translation by H.M. Parshley, which was released in 1954, and which is still widely available in British bookshops, large segments of the original text are missing as they were simply axed by Parshley (Simons, 1983). Indeed, the literary theorist Toril Moi described the cuts and omissions to the French text as a "sorry mess" (Moi, 2004). An equivalent of 145 pages from the original 972-page French text were edited out. However, not only were large sections of the text edited out but the cuts are not signaled in the text, nor is the reader warned in any way that the text has been "abridged". As commentators have shown (Simons, 1983; Moi, 2004; Grosholz, 2017), this drastic process is obviously not innocent and forms a clear case of censorship. Shockingly for a book that deals with the unfair treatment women have received throughout history, the names of 78 women were eliminated from the original: medieval chatelaines, noblewomen who lived around the time of Charlemagne and the knights of the Round Table, and women of the Italian Renaissance. All were pushed into oblivion; quotations were deleted, and the love poems by the lesbian poet Renée Vivien were removed. The translation process was clearly not simply a case of altering the text for the sake of brevity and readability.

The translation also shows severe misunderstandings. Parshley, who was not a philosopher, often mistranslates terms that are specific to the vocabulary of existentialism. One of the most fundamental distinctions in Sartrean existentialism and phenomenology, the philosophical school Beauvoir belonged to, is the distinction between *être-en-soi* and *être-pour-soi, being-for-itself* and *being-in-itself. Being-in-itself* refers to objects in the external world – a mode of existence that simply is and does not involve awareness of being. It is not conscious of its own existence, so it is neither active nor passive and harbours no potentiality for transcendence. On the other hand, *being-for-itself* is consciousness of being.

However, consciousness poses a major difficulty since it is always linked not to what we are but to what we are not. As they are constantly striving to attain *being-in-itself*, which is impossible, human beings are trapped into experiencing nothingness – and therefore experience the existential disease, *mauvaise foi.*

Beauvoir uses this distinction to show that, for women, the confusion between the two modes of being is particularly difficult. As society tries to impose an essence onto them, *être-pour-soi* is, for women, simply not possible.

As Simons and Moi have pointed out, these terms which are central to existentialist thought are badly translated by Parshley. The translation below shows his lack of understanding of French existentialism:

> *Beauvoir:* "La femme se connait et se choisit non en tant qu'elle existe pour soi mais telle que l'homme la définit".
> *Literal translation:* "Woman knows and chooses herself not as she exists for herself, but as man defines her". (as translated by Moi)
> *Parshley:* "Woman sees herself and makes her choices not in accordance with her true nature in itself but as man defines her".

Indeed, the issue is not whether woman can be true *to her true nature* but whether it is possible for her to establish a true nature for herself.

This other example taken from Moi (2004: 1022) also contains a gross distortion of the original:

> *Beauvoir:* "En refusant des attributs féminins, on n'acquiert pas des attributs virils; même la travestie ne réussit pas à faire d'elle-même un homme: c'est une travestie".

> *Literal translation*: "One does not acquire virile attributes by rejecting female [feminine] attributes; even a transvestite doesn't manage to turn herself into a man – <u>she remains a transvestite</u>".
>
> *Parshley*: "One does not acquire virile attributes by rejecting feminine attributes; even the transvestite fails to make a man of herself – <u>she is a travesty</u>".

In English, a travesty is never a person, unlike in French. Instead of simply stating that the female transvestite remains a transvestite in the eyes of others, Parshley makes a pronouncement – *attempting to pass for a man is wrong and cannot be achieved* – virtually making Beauvoir say the opposite of what she intended to say and completely distorting her argument in the process.

There are also gross *contresens* based on basic language errors, which show poor knowledge of basic French (Moi, 2004: 2024–2025):

> *Beauvoir:* "Il y a une fonction féminine qu'il est <u>actuellement</u> presque impossible d'assumer en toute liberté, c'est la maternité".
>
> *Literal translation:* "There is one female function which it is almost impossible to undertake in complete freedom <u>today</u>, namely motherhood".
>
> *Parshley*: "There is one feminine function that it is <u>actually</u> almost impossible to perform in complete liberty. It is maternity".

Parshley has made an elementary French mistake: *actuellement* in French does not mean *actually, as a matter of fact* or *really*; it means *now, today* or *nowadays*.

Similarly, in the following example:

> *Beauvoir:* "Il faut ajouter que <u>faute de</u> crèches, de jardins d'enfants convenablement organisés, il suffit d'un enfant pour paralyser entièrement l'activité de la femme".
>
> *Literal translation:* "I should add that <u>given the lack of</u> appropriately organised day nurseries and kindergartens, having a child is enough to paralyze a woman's activity entirely".
>
> *Parshley:* "It must be said in addition that <u>in spite of</u> convenient day nurseries and kindergartens, having a child is enough to paralyze a woman's activity entirely".

Contrary to what Parshley writes, according to Beauvoir, more nurseries and kindergartens are needed – their existence is a precondition to a woman's freedom, not the other way around.

To translate *actuellement* as *actually* and *faute de* as *in spite of* (and *convenable* as *convenient*) in the same text is quite a feat. Parshley's attempt at demeaning Beauvoir's argument is perhaps at its most glaring when he translates *réalité humaine* (i.e. human reality/human existence) as *the real nature of man*. Making a feminist writer use the term *man* to refer to a *woman* is the height of dishonesty. Despite these fundamental changes, Parshley's translation is still widely available in British bookshops.

4 Translatability and connotative meaning in Camus', L'Étranger

We previously discussed the opening paragraph of *L'Étranger* (Chapter 4), an extract which has received considerable scholarly attention. The opening line ("Aujourd'hui, maman est morte") has been hailed as one of the most powerful opening lines in modern fiction. In a blog article, the *Guardian* journalist Guy Dammann compared the opening line to the first bars of Beethoven's Fifth Symphony, its resonance filling the entire novel. From a translation point of view, the opening paragraph is fascinating since it poses a great number of difficulties. Interestingly, there are no fewer than five different translations of Camus' 1942 novel in English – the first translation appeared shortly after the release of the novel in French, three other versions were released in the 1980s, and one by the multi-award-winning translator Sandra Smith was published by Penguin in 2013. Let us look back at the original Camus paragraph and consider the first sentence:

> Aujourd'hui, maman est morte. Ou peut-être hier, je ne sais pas. J'ai reçu un télégramme de l'asile: "Mère décédée. Enterrement demain. Sentiments distingués." Cela ne veut rien dire. C'était peut-être hier.

Here, the narrator introduces the death of his mother. This is an event which is both tragic and sad, yet there seems to be a certain casualness to the way this particular event is introduced. The contrast between the tragic reality of the mother's death, and the seemingly casual words the narrator uses, immediately arouses the reader suspicion's regarding his reaction to his mother's death (*What sort of a man is he? What sort of relationship did he have with his mother?*). The rest of the paragraph sustains the readers' curiosity and suspicion (*What does the narrator's uncertainty regarding whether his mother died today or yesterday mean? Does this mean he cared for her or not?*).

The nature of the relationship among Meursault, the narrator, and his mother is obviously key to the novel. How we ultimately view Meursault relies to a large extent on how we assess his relationship to his mother. The judgement the court will pass later on in the novel, when Meursault is tried for the murder he commits, will largely depend on the assessment the jury makes of that relationship. The prosecutor will repeatedly come back to Meursault's attitude at his mother's funeral and in the days following her death. This will memorably lead the defence lawyer to exclaim: "Est-il accusé d'avoir enterré sa mère ou d'avoir tué un homme?" (*Is the defendant on trial for having buried his mother of for having killed a man?*), to which the prosecutor will reply: "J'accuse cet homme d'avoir enterré une mère avec un cœur de criminel" (*I accuse this man of having buried his mother with the heart of a criminal*).

Translating the deceptively simple opening line and paragraph in a way that does not betray the original is therefore key in order to give the English reader the impression it conveys in French. However, this is no easy feat.

If we look at the five translations available and consider how *maman* was trans-lated, we can see that three translators opted for "<u>mother</u> died today", one for "<u>maman</u> died today", and one for "<u>my mother</u> died today":

> Mother died today. Or, maybe, yesterday; I can't be sure. The telegram from the Home says: YOUR MOTHER PASSED AWAY. FUNERAL TOMOR-ROW. DEEP SYMPATHY. Which leaves the matter doubtful; it could have been yesterday.
> (Tr. Stuart Gilbert, *The Stranger*, New York, Vintage, 1954 (1946))

> Mother died today. Or maybe yesterday, I don't know. I had a telegram from the home: 'Mother passed away. Funeral tomorrow. Yours sincerely' That doesn't mean anything. It may have been yesterday.
> (Tr. Joseph Laredo, *The Outsider*, London, Penguin, 1983 (1982))

> Mother died today. Or maybe it was yesterday, I don't know. I received a tele-gram from the rest home: MOTHER DECEASED. BURIAL TOMORROW. VERY TRULY YOURS. It doesn't say anything. Maybe it was yesterday.
> (Tr. Kate Griffith, *The Stranger*, Washington, D.C.,
> University Press of America, 1982)

> Maman died today. Or yesterday maybe, I don't know. I got a telegram from the home: "Mother deceased. Funeral tomorrow. Faithfully yours." That doesn't mean anything. Maybe it was yesterday.
> (Tr. Matthew Ward, *The Stranger*, New York, Vintage, 1989 (1988))

> My mother died today. Or maybe yesterday, I don't know. I received a tele-gram from the old people's home: "Mother deceased. Funeral tomorrow. Very sincerely yours." That doesn't mean anything. It might have been yesterday.
> (Tr. Sandra Smith, *The Outsider*, Penguin, 2013)

As Ryan Bloom pointed out in his excellent article *Lost in Translation: What the First Line of The Stranger Should Be* that appeared in the New Yorker, 11 May 2012, the detached formality of *mother died today* does not get across the close relationship that *maman* implies. Similarly to *mère*, *mother* is more for-mal than *maman* and is very rarely used as a term of address or when referring to one's mother in the third person. It conveys social and emotional distance and presents Meursault as more distant from his mother than *maman* does. One could perhaps envisage other possibilities: *mommy* or *mummy*, *mom* or *mum*. However, all of these terms would also present an inaccurate view of the nar-rator's relationship to his mother, presenting him as an affectionate and loving son. The difficulty is that *maman*, in terms of the level of affection it connotes, seems to occupy a space between "mother" at one extreme end of the spectrum and "mum/mom" at the other. We should then, perhaps, as Matthew Ward did, decide to keep the French word in the English translation. After all, the French word is transparent enough for an English-language reader to understand what it means. However, "it will carry no baggage, it will plant no unintended seeds in our head. The word will neither sway us to see Meursault as overly cold and heartless nor as overly warm and loving" (Ryan Bloom in *The New Yorker*). Ward's solution to the dilemma, which from the point of view of translation studies would be labelled as a *foreignising* strategy, is therefore a non-choice as it does not tell the reader anything about the nature of the relationship between the son and his mother.

Sandra Smith opted for "my mother died today" with the possessive "my" before "mother". This has the advantage of presenting Meursault as less distant and more emotionally affected by the death of his mother. In numerous interviews and in discussions we have had with her, Sandra Smith has explained that it was important for her not to alienate the reader from Meursault and present him as cold-hearted and aloof. She also felt that Meursault addresses the reader directly:

> I chose "My mother" because I thought about how someone would tell another person that his mother had died. Meursault is speaking to the reader directly. "My mother died today" seemed to me the way it would work, and also implied the closeness of "maman" you get in the French. Afterwards, I used "mama", partly because it sounds like "maman" and partly because I was aware that a British audience would probably prefer "Mum" and an American reader "Mom" so I needed something that worked on both sides of the Atlantic.
>
> (Sandra, Smith *On translating Camus – The Guardian*, Thursday 28 Nov.)

In the 2016 translation of the graphic novel by Jacques Ferrandez that came out in 2013, which was also translated by Sandra Smith, "mama" was used.

Apart from the use of "mama", the syntax is also noticeable as closer to the original. Rather than having the adverbial at the end of the sentence, "mama died today", which, as we saw in Chapter 3, seems more natural in English, Smith here decided to place "today" at the beginning of the sentence. The fact we are dealing with a graphic novel probably means that the orality of Meursault's words can be made more salient. Do we then have an utterance that is closer to the original from the point of view of what it tells us about the protagonist's psychological and philosophical makeup? As will become apparent in the rest of the novel, what is odd about Meursault is that he lives his life almost unconsciously, sleepwalking through it, the past and the future not seeming to matter to him. For instance, he realises during the procession at his mother's funeral that he did not know how old she was. Throughout the course of the novel, he remains detached, letting life pass him by. This attitude will be fatal. His detachment will lead to his downfall.

Meursault's inability to reflect upon his life and his lack of self-consciousness are what make him an iconic absurdist figure. Retaining the syntax of the French sentence is, therefore, absolutely crucial.

Figure 5.1

5 Translatability and sounds

We saw previously that translatability depends largely on the function of a text and the text type it belongs to. Poetry was used as an example of as a text type that poses great difficulty and resists mechanisation.

In a famous article published in 1959, Roman Jakobson argued that the translation of poetic texts is simply not possible as poetry calls on all the "constitutents of the verbal code" (Jakobson, 1959). The only possibility that is left is "creative transposition" or adaptation; in the same way a play might be adapted into a film or a novel into a play, the poetic object will be turned into another type of poetic object. The text in question will have a similar effect in the original language as in the translation (as cognitive experience is universal); however, as a textual object, it will be significantly different.

One of the things that Jakobson insisted on in his seminal essay on translation is that poetic texts are different from other texts as the language of poetry is not arbitrary. In Saussurean linguistics, words are said to be arbitrary insofar as there is no direct link between the form (*signifiant*) and the meaning (*signifié*) of a word, or to put it differently, there is no direct connection between the form of a word and what it refers to in the real world (a word acquires its meaning within a linguistic system and in relation to other words). The word *cat* does not acquire its meaning because it bears any resemblance with a real cat, but because it is distinct from lion, dog, table and so on. Poetic language, however, is *motivated*, as poetry does not simply rely on the meaning of words but also on their sounds. It also relies on rhythm, contrasts, repetition, alliterations, assonances and so on. We discuss these in more detail in the following chapter.

Although for the purpose of his argument, Jakobson draws a clear line between poetic and non-poetic text types, we could argue that the kind of the textual features that Jakobson associates with poetry can be found to a varying degree in a great variety of text types. The features Jakobson points outs are naturally present in poetry, but these features are not the preserve of poetry and can appear in other text types.

If we consider the headlines of newspaper articles, the slogans of political campaigns, or even academic articles, it is immediately clear that they also involve using sounds and prosody, wordplay, repetition and so on. In a 1952 lecture, Jakobson famously commented on the three-word slogan that was used in Dwight Einsehower's 1952 campaign, "I like Ike" – the repetition of |ai| which appears in every word of the slogan (i.e. three times) and the repetition of |aik| in *like* and *Ike* create a very powerful effect. The repetition of beginning consonants (alliteration) can be found in a lot of slogans: "Go Green"; "Fair Is Worth Fighting For" (UK Green Party's 2010 election campaign); or "For Your Future"; "Britain Can Be Better"; "Stronger for Scotland"; "Working for Wales", and so forth. Parallelism and the repetition of syllables, words or morphemes is also common: "Equality Not Austerity"; "Prosperity Not Austerity"; "Stronger Safer, and Better Off In" (EU referendum); "Taking Our Seats Taking a Stand", and so on.

French political slogans use the same devices (i.e. alliterations, parallelism, repetition, etc.): "Tonton, c'est tentant" (1988 presidential campaign); "La France forte"; "Une force pour la France", as well as aphorisms and formulaic statements: "Le cœur battra toujours à gauche", "le socialisme, une idée qui fait son chemin".

Similarly, if we consider the following book titles taken from children's books, which all involve play on sounds, it is clear that the author has selected them carefully in order to give them maximum impact:

The Very Greedy Bee
Gruff the Grump
David's Dream Team

Translating these titles adequately forces us to avoid a literal translation, which would lose the playfulness of the original titles and requires modulation.

In the French edition of the book, *The Very Greedy Bee* was translated as *L'abeille qui aimait le miel*, which allows for the repetition of almost identical sounds (cf. *abeille* and *miel*); similarly, *Gruff the Grump* became *Ce grognon de Gédéon* (note that the name of the protagonist has changed). *David's Dream Team* was translated as *Les Caïds de David*.

As these examples show, the features involved in giving those titles particular strength and energy can be replicated in French, and similar effects to the effects produced in the ST can be produced in the TT. However, the translation process requires modulation and necessitates creativity. Translatability therefore does not depend entirely on the text type we are considering. In a lot of cases, translatability will depend on the features of the text we are considering, regardless of the text type to which it belongs. The translation of a large section of a text might be fairly mechanical, but that might not be the case for all of it. A wide range of texts might contain elements which are akin to what might be encountered in a poem.

6 Translatability and onomastics

In fiction, made-up names can also display the playfulness encountered in headlines and slogans and interweave sounds and content. The school house names in *Harry Potter* are a good example of this: *Gryffindor, Hufflepuff, Ravenclaw, Slytherin*. These proper names were obviously created by the author of the novel to give the four houses a strong identity, in line with the theme of sorcery which is central to the books.

These very expressive and evocative terms are all made up of three syllables. Apart from *Hufflepuff*, they all refer to an animal or a mythical creature and arouse a strong image in the reader's mind. It is both the combination of the meaning of these items and their sounds that contribute to making them particularly effective. So, when translating them both, their form and meaning must be taken into account. The French translator opted for *Gryffondor* for *Gryffindor*. In French, a griffin is *un griffon*, and the suffix *-dor* has the same connotation as in English. *Ravenclaw* could have been translated literally as *serre de corbeau* but the translator obviously felt it did not sound very good and opted for *Serdaigle* instead (i.e. eagle claw, as it happens, the eagle is the one of the house's symbols). For *Hufflepuff*, which is a play on words based on what the big bad wolf tells the three little pigs in the eponymous tale (*I'll huff and I'll puff and I'll blow your house down*), the translator came up with *Poufsouffle*. This sounds similar to *Hufflepuff* and recalls the action the wolf threatens. *Slytherin* was translated as *Serpentard*. Both evoke a snake and the same action, the suffix *-ard* in French also adds a negative connotation in keeping with the original.[2]

Contrary to what we might have expected, the translation of proper names also often raises translation issues. The use of proper names is only licensed by an assumption that the reader/hearer can identify the noun in question. Let's consider the examples below:

She looks a bit like Beyoncé.
I have never been to London.
You are starting to sound like Theresa May.

The reader/hearer does not need to know the referent in person in order to understand what their interlocutor is trying to communicate to them. They do not need to know Beyoncé or Theresa May personally or to have been to London to understand what their interlocutor is saying. Their ability to understand what their interlocutor means when using these items calls on background and nonlinguistic knowledge about the world. The speaker/writer and hearer/reader have to share knowledge about the referent in order for the reader/hearer to be able to retrieve the speaker's intention – what he/she meant by using that item. The difficulty with items of this kind is that they are largely embedded in a particular cultural context – unless one lives in the UK and/or follows British politics closely, it might be hard to know what Theresa May might "sound like". When translating, should the translator opt for foreignisation and keep the original term or opt for domestication and adaptation?[3]

If we look at how items of this kind were translated in the English-language subtitles of the 1995 French film directed by Mathieu Kassovitz, *La Haine*, often described as a *banlieue* film, these terms have been transposed to culturally fit an American frame of reference. There is a lot of banter between the main characters. In one scene, one of the three protagonists tells one of the other two, as a way of a mock insult:

– Ta mère, elle boit de la Kro.

Translated as:

– Your mother drinks Bud.

Here the translator substituted the French beer brand (*Kronenbourg*) for an American one (*Budweiser*).

When looking for the person nicknamed *Astérix,* the subtitles instead use the American cartoon *Snoopy*.
Similarly, one of the characters in the film is comically called *Darty*, which is the name of a well-known French chain of electrical shops – the humour comes from the use of that well-known brand name to refer to a petty criminal who deals in stolen goods:

– Qui est Darty?
– Le receleur de la tour B?

Translated as:

– Who's WalMart?
– That fence in Tower B?

In the following intervention, in which one of the protagonists tries to justify his carrying a gun, he says:

– Je m'appelle pas Malik Oussekine!

Malik Oussekine was a French-born student of North African origin who died of a heart attack during the 1988 student protests after he was chased and beaten by police.

This intervention is translated as:

– My name's not Rodney King!

Rodney King was an African-American taxi driver who became known internationally as the victim of Los Angeles Police Department brutality after a videotape was released of several police officers beating him during his arrest on 3 March 1991. In the examples here, the overall strategy of the translator consisted in transforming French references into American ones. This process of domestication, while it might make the understanding of the TT more straightforward, obviously negates the sociocultural context the films are supposed to represent. One could argue, however, that this is inevitable if we want the effect on the target-language audience to be immediate and powerful. However, it remains contradictory, given that we are dealing with a film that specifically exemplifies a form of suburban social realism and presents a very French reality.

Conclusion

This chapter has considered the issue of translatability from different angles: from the sheer difficulty, and sometimes impossibility of selecting the right term in the TL as none is available, to the issues that arise because of the heterogeneity of meaning (connotative and affective meaning, associative meaning and intertextuality). It has also looked at the interplay between form and content, sounds and meaning. This has led us to consider the types of strategies that are deployed by translators (foreignisation and domestication). These strategies are dependent on the type of text and context in which the difficulties arise. While the chapter has not sought to advocate particular strategies, it has highlighted the importance of taking into account the richness and complexity of meaning. As translation theorists have pointed out (Malmkjær and Windle, 2011), translations tend to display recurring features (some observers such as Chesterman, 2004 talk about *translation universals*; others such as Gideon Toury (1995) talk about *translation norms* and *laws*). These observers have noted that translations tend for instance to be more explicit than their original. They also tend to *standardise* the ST (cf. Toury's *law of growing standardisation*) – any element that stands out in the ST will tend to be smoothened out in the TT. Translations will also tend to use more standard language and err towards conservatism. Translations also tend to be longer than their STs and tend to display more usual collocations than their STs. They tend to be more explicit. Translated texts exhibit a larger quantity of patterns that are untypical of the language than nontranslated. Translated texts are less varied lexically than nontranslated texts, are less lexically dense, and use more high-frequency terms. In sum, translations tend towards standardisation, sanitisation and normalisation. While it is important to consider the role of translation and to bear in mind those limitations, it is equally important not to view the translation process as a lost cause. The perennial question of "faithfulness" to the ST, central to the issue of translatability, or in other words, the conflict between fidelity and freedom in translation, needs to be put in terms that allow us to reconcile the two. From this point of view, Walter Benjamin's seminal essay, *The Translator's Task*, provides interesting clues (Rendall, 1997). In his article, Benjamin disputes the traditional theory of translation which views the translation process as the reproduction of meaning. In his view, a poem does not "say" or "communicate" anything; it has no message. Focusing on conveying a message when dealing with a literary text results in bad translation, that is, "the inexact transmission of an inessential content" (ibid. p. 152). The essential content is not tangible; it cannot be broken down into an equation or a set of well-defined traits. The translation's language must therefore free itself from "bondage to meaning" (ibid. 161): "True translation is transparent, it does not obscure the original, does not stand in its light, but rather allows pure language, as if strengthened by its own medium, to shine even more fully on the original" (ibid. 162). For Benjamin, translation is closely seen as a gain rather than a loss. The translated text is not simply a copy of the original, bound to be imperfect and flawed. Benjamin introduces a distinction between *what is meant* and *the manner of meaning it*. What is unique to languages is not what is meant but the manner of meaning it. In a way that recalls Chomsky's universal grammar, albeit in a more metaphysical and transcendental form, Benjamin invokes the notion of *pure language*. Languages are no stranger to one another; they are interrelated in what they can express. Pure language is an aggregate of all the languages in the world, of all the potentialities languages offer, a space where the mutually exclusive differences among languages can coexist. Translation is about the relationship between languages rather than texts, and the translator's work should "ultimately serve the purpose of expressing the innermost relationship of languages to one another". Seen from this perspective, the translation process involves a triangulation among the original language, the TL, and *pure language*:

> in translation the original grows into a linguistic sphere that is both higher and purer. It cannot, however, go on living indefinitely in this sphere, since it is far from attaining it in all parts of its form; but it nevertheless points, with wonderful penetration, toward the predetermined, inaccessible domain where languages are reconciled and fulfilled.
>
> (ibid. 157–158)

7 Activités de mise en pratique

I Traduire les slogans politiques

1   No taxation without representation – slogan of American revolutionaries

2   A chicken in every pot – Herbert Hoover, 1928 U.S. presidential campaign

3   Happy Days Are Here Again – Franklin Delano Roosevelt, 1932

4   Labour isn't working – Margaret Thatcher, Tories 1979

5   Things can only get better – Tony Blair, Labour 1997

6   Yes, we can – Barack Obama, 2008

7   Change We Can Believe In – Barack Obama, 2008

8   It's the Economy, Stupid – Bill Clinton, 1992

9   Don't Be a Loser, Be a Chooser

10   Enough is enough

11   Good times ahead

12   It's time to make a change

13   Putting people first

14   Think Global, Act Local

II   Comparer la traduction d'une chanson et son original. Ne me quitte pas de Jacques Brel

Classique du répertoire de la chanson française, ce titre de Jacques Brel a été repris en français par de nombreux artistes, mais aussi dans d'autres langues, notamment en anglais. Une des plus célèbres adaptations en anglais, et la version de Rod McKuen: If you go away, qui sera reprise par Frank Sinatra.

Ecoutez et comparez les deux versions (disponibles sur Internet):

1   Est-ce que l'une vous semble plus sombre que l'autre?

2   A quoi correspond "On a vu souvent rejaillir le feu d'un ancien volcan qu'on croyait trop vieux" dans la version anglaise?

3   Comment "Laisse-moi devenir l'ombre de ton ombre . . ." a-t-il été traduit? Que pensez-vous de cette modification?

4   Ressentez-vous la même impression, le même sentiment, à l'écoute des deux chansons?

III   Traduction d'éléments lexicaux culturellement marqués

Cette activité porte sur l'analyse d'exemples tirés du roman Intimacy écrit par Hanif Kureishi (Faber and Faber, 1998) et traduit par Brice Mathieussent

(Editions 10/18). Les phrases sélectionnées comportent des éléments culturelle-ment chargés difficiles à traduire.

Traduisez les phrases suivantes puis reportez-vous à la traduction proposée à la fin du livre et comparez-la à la vôtre:

1   Being lower-middle class and from the suburbs, where poverty and preten-sion go together, I can see how good the middle class have it, and what a separate, sealed world they inhabit.

2   The desks – which my parents bought me when I was taking my A-levels – I have lugged around form squat to squat, via shared houses and council flats, until it ended up here, the first property I have owned.

3   But my first weeks at university shocked me into attention. I had to get home to read *Teach Yourself* books and *The Children's Guide to . . .*

4   Perhaps I should remind myself that I am absconding, not appearing on *Desert Island Discs.*

5   I have started to visit hospitals. I know where they all are now, without the *A-to-Z.*

IV Analyse d'un texte non-standard et de sa traduction: Kiffe Kiffe demain, Faiza Guène

Lire cet extrait du roman de Faiza Guène, Kiffe Kiffe demain dans lequel la nar-ratrice, une jeune fille qui vit dans un quartier de banlieue, livre un témoign-age de son quotidien à la fois tendre et amer. Sur le plan linguistique, on trouve dans le texte de nombreux marqueurs d'oralité ainsi que des éléments asso-ciés au "parler des banlieues". Identifier les marqueurs linguistiques (lexicaux, morphologiques, syntaxiques: dislocation) qui n'appartiennent pas à la langue "standard" (ils sont répertoriés dans le chapitre de réponses "Key answers" à la fin de l'ouvrage).

Depuis que le vieux s'est cassé, on a eu droit à un défilé d'assitantes sociales à la maison. La nouvelle, je sais plus son nom. C'est un truc du genre Dubois, Dupont, ou Dupré, bref un nom pour qu'on sache que tu viens de quelque part. Je la trouve conne et en plus, elle sourit tout le temps pour rien. Même
5   quand c'est pas le moment. Cette meuf, on dirait qu'elle a besoin d'être heu-reuse à la place des autres. Une fois, elle m'a demandé si je voulais qu'on devienne amies. Moi, comme une crapule, je lui ai répondu qu'il y avait pas

moyen. Mais je crois que j'ai gaffé parce que j'ai senti le regard de ma mère me transpercer. Elle devait avoir peur que la mairie ne nous aide plus si je
10 devenais pas copine avec leur conne d'assistante.

Avant Mme Dumachin, c'était un homme . . . Ouais, son prédécesseur, c'était un monsieur, un assistant de la mairie. Il ressemblait à Laurent Cabrol, celui qui présentait "La Nuit des héros" sur TF1 le vendredi soir. C'est dommage que ce soit fini. Maintenant, Laurent Cabrol, il est en bas à droite de la
15 page 30 du TV Mag en tout petit, habillé en polo à rayures jaunes et noires, en train de faire une pub pour les chauffages thermiques. Donc, l'assistant social c'était son sosie. Tout le contraire de Mme Dutruc. Il plaisantait jamais, il souriait et il s'habillait comme le professeur Tournesol dans *Les Aventures de Tintin*. Une fois, il a dit à ma mère qu'en dix ans de métier, c'était la premi-
20 ère fois qu'il voyait "des gens comme nous avec un enfant seulement par famille". Il ne l'a pas dit mais il devait penser "Arabes". Quand il venait à la maison, ça lui faisait exotique. Il regardait bizarre les bibelots qui sont posés sur le meuble, ceux que ma mère a rapportés du Maroc après son mariage. Et puis comme on marche en babouches à la maison, quand il entrait dans
25 l'appartement, il enlevait ses chaussures pour faire bien. Sauf que lui, il avait des pieds bioniques, son deuxième doigt était au moins dix fois plus long que le gros orteil. On dirait qu'il faisait des doigts d'honneur à l'intérieur de ses chaussettes. Et puis il y avait l'odeur. Il jouait le type compatissant mais c'était un mytho. Rien du tout. Il en avait rien à foutre de nous. D'ailleurs, il
30 a arrêté le travail d'assistant social. Il s'est installé à la campagne à ce qu'il paraît. Si ça se trouve, il s'est reconverti en maître fromager. Il passe avec sa camionnette bleu ciel dans les petits villages de la bonne vieille France, le dimanche après la messe, et vend du pain de seigle, du roquefort tradition et du saucisson sec.
35 [. . .]

Quel destin de merde. Le destin, c'est la misère parce que t'y peux rien. Ça veut dire que quoi que tu fasses, tu te feras toujours couiller. Ma mère, elle dit que si mon père nous a abandonnées, c'est parce que c'était écrit.

TRADUCTION PROPOSÉE

Traduction de l'extrait tirée de la traduction du roman réalisée par Sarah Adams et publiée aux éditions Harvest Books. Lire l'extrait et répondre aux questions:

Since the old man split we've had a whole parade of social workers coming to the apartment. Can't remember the new one's name, but it's something like Dubois or Dupont or Dupré, a name that tells you she's from somewhere, from a real family line or something. I think she's stupid, and she smiles all
5 the time for no good reason. Even when it's clearly not the right time. It's like the crazy woman feels the need to be happy for other people because they aren't happy for themselves. Once, she asked if I wanted us to be friends.

Like a little brat I told her I didn't see that happening. But I guess I messed up, because the look my mother gave me cut me in half. . . . She was probably
10 scared social services would cut off our benefits if I didn't make nice with their stupid social worker.

Before Mme Du-Thingamajig, it was a man. . . . Yeah, she took over from this guy who looked like Laurent Cabrol, the one who hosted "Heroes' Night" on TF1 on Friday nights. Shame it's not on anymore. Now Laurent
15 Cabrol's in the bottom right-hand corner of *TV Mag*, page 30, wearing a yellow and black striped rugby shirt, advertising central heating. Anyway, this social worker was his spitting image. Total opposite of Mme DuWhatsit. He never cracked a joke, he never smiled, and he dressed like Professor Calculus in *The Adventures of Tintin*. Once, he told my mom that in
20 ten years on this job, this was the first time he'd seen "people like you but with only one child." family. He was thinking "Arabs", but he didn't say so. Coming to our place was like an exotic experience for him. He kept giving weird looks to all the knick-knacks around the house, the ones my mom brought over from Morocco after she got married. And since we
25 wear *babouches* at home, he'd take off his shoes when he walked in, trying to do the right thing. Except he had alien feet. His second toe was at least ten times longer than his big toe. It looked like he was giving us the finger through his socks. And then there was the stench. The whole time he played the sweet, compassionate type, but it was all a front. He didn't
30 give a shit about us. Besides, he quit. Seems he moved to the countryside. Remade himself into a cheese-maker, for all I know. He drives around the little villages of dear old la belle France in his sky blue van on Sunday mornings after Mass, selling rye bread, old-fashioned Roquefort cheese and *saucisson sec*.
35   [. . .]

What a shitty destiny. Fate is all trial and misery because and you can't do anything about it. Basically no matter what you do you'll always get screwed over. My mom says my dad walked out on us because it was written that way.

Guène, 2006

Comment les éléments d'oralité et les marqueurs non-standard ont-ils été traduits? Quelle stratégie a été adoptée par la traductrice pour traduire les éléments de la langue source qui n'ont pas d'équivalents directs? Le caractère spécial de l'original est-il maintenu dans la traduction?

V Traduire un sociolecte – extrait de Trainspotting (1996) de l'auteur écossais Irvine Welsh

Réflexion sur la valeur du sociolecte dans le roman. Analyse d'une scène. Analyse de trois traductions différentes de ce même extrait. Cette activité s'appuie sur un excellent article du traducteur Alex Gauthier (Gauthier, 2017) dans lequel il plaide pour la traduisibilité de tout sociolecte.

CARACTÉRISTIQUES DU TS

- Caractère oral du texte
- Caractère subversif de la langue utilisée, la voix du narrateur: un psychopathe.
- Dialecte (spécificité géographique et sociale), vulgarité, langue non conventionnelle: graphie. Le dialecte comme affirmation identitaire.

QUE FAIRE DE CETTE LANGUE?

- Vulgarité: intensité du terme utilisé, idiomaticité, intensité affective et spontanéité de l'idiome.
- La fonction des variantes graphiques: véracité et fidélité (paroles qui correspondent à celles de ce groupe), aspect dialectal,

ANALYSE DE LA FONCTION DU SOCIOLECTE DANS LE ROMAN

Cet extrait est tiré du roman *Trainspotting* qui se caractérise par l'utilisation d'une langue non-conventionnelle et dialectale qui comporte des spécificités géographiques et sociales, ce que dénote la graphie non-standard utilisée dans tout le roman. Cette langue comporte un caractère subversif, vulgaire et provocateur, indéniable, en lien direct avec son oralité. Cette langue se veut volontairement difficile à déchiffrer et vient bousculer les habitudes de lecture de tout lecteur anglophone. Elle représente, en outre, l'insubordination des personnages à l'ordre établi, ou ici l'inadaptabilité du personnage à la société qui l'entoure. La langue est ici symptomatique du décalage que vit le personnage – le texte est en fait une féroce critique de l'ère thatchérienne – et l'incompréhension initiale du lecteur est à mettre en parallèle avec la difficulté que les personnages ont à se faire une place dans un pays en crise et en pleine mutation. Cette langue est, par ailleurs, un grand coup de pied dans la fourmilière des conventions littéraires.

La traduction de cette langue (ou sociolecte) est donc particulièrement cruciale et les risques de ne pas être fidèle au TS sont grands. La traduction de tout sociolecte soulève la question du type de variété linguistique à sélectionner dans la langue cible: peut-on substituer un sociolecte au sociolecte de la langue source un sociolecte de la langue cible et produire le même effet que celui produit par la langue utilisée dans le TS?

PRÉSENTATION DE LA SCÈNE À ANALYSER

Dans la scène proposée ci-dessous, Begbie, le narrateur, personnage violent, sadique et brutal, qui représente à lui seul cette Ecosse qui sombre, se livre à un échange verbal dans un train avec deux canadiennes en voyage qui ne comprennent pas un traitre mot de ce qu'il leur dit. Cette incompréhension, emblématique du rapport du personnage au monde (inadapté à son milieu, il est appelé à disparaître) est évidemment en lien avec la langue qu'il utilise. Paradoxalement, ce ne sont pas ici les deux Canadiennes qui apparaissent comme étrangères mais lui, l'autochtone – elle parle une langue qui, si elle porte la trace de leur origine géographique, reste néanmoins très standard, ce qui n'est pas le cas de Begbie:

> – No fuckin shy, they British Rail cunts, eh? ah sais, nudgin the burd next tae us.
> – Pardon? it sais tae us, sortay soundin likes, 'par – dawn' ken?
> – Whair's it yis come fae then?
> – Sorry, I can't really understand you. . . . These foreign cunts've goat trouble wi the Queen's fuckin English, ken. Ye huv tae speak louder, slower, n likesay mair posh, fir the cunts tae understand ye.
> – WHERE . . . DO . . . YOU . . . COME . . . FROM?
> That dis the fuckin trick. These nosey cunts in front ay us look roond. Ah stares back at the cunts. Some fucker's oan a burst mooth before the end ay this fuckin journey, ah kin see that now.
> – Ehm . . . we're from Toronto, Canada.
> – Tirawnto. That wis the Lone Ranger's mate, wis it no? ah sais. The burds jist look it us. Some punters dinnae fuckin understand the Scottish sense ay humour.

Voici une traduction réalisée par Eric Lindor Fall (Paris, L'Olivier, 1996):

> – Putain, ils manquent pas d'air, ces cons du British Rail, hein? je fais en coudoyant dans le flanc de la caille posée à côté de moi.
> – Je vous demande pardon? qu'elle me fait et ça sonne genre "démainde pairdon".
> – Attends, toi, tu viens d'où?
> – Je rgraitte, je ne vous comprin pas bien . . .
> Les cons qui viennent d'ailleurs ont de vrais problèmes avec notre putain d'anglais anglais. Pour que ces cons prennent, il faut leur parler fort, lentement et surtout façon je ne suce que des virgules épluchées avec des gants.
> – PUIS-JE . . . SAVOIR . . . D'OÙ . . . TU . . . VIENS . . .?
> C'est le seul moyen, putain. Et les connards de devant qui se retournent pour mater. Je leur douche le cul d'un seul regard. Y a un enculé qui va se faire éclater la bouche avant la fin de ce foutu voyage, je le vois d'ici.
> – Ehm . . . Nous sommes de Troïnto, Canédé.
> – Tonto. C'était le pote du Lone Ranger, non? je fais.
> La caille me regarde. Y a des gens qui n'ont vraiment pas le sens de l'humour écossais.

Voici une deuxième traduction réalisée par Jean-René Etienne (Au diable Vauvert, 2011):

> – Y se goinfrent bien, ces enculés de British Rail, hein? j'y dis, en donnant
>   un ptit coup de coude à la nana d'à côté.
> – Pardon? qu'elle me fait, mais ça sonne "par-dawn" ou quoi.
> – Mais ouais, mais d'où tu viens?
> – Désolée, je ne comprends pas très bien ce que vous dites. C'est quoi ces
>   connasses de métèques qu'ont du mal avec l'anglais de la Reine. Faut
>   leur parler plus fort, plus lentement, et comme qui dirait plus bourge pour
>   qu'elles te comprennent.
> – D'OÙ . . . VIENS . . . TU?
> C'est ça qu'il lui fallait. Et les fouille-merde de devant qui se retournent
>   pour mater, jles toise. Y a un enculé qui va se faire péter la gueule avant
>   la fin du voyage, jle sens.
> – Euh . . . On est du Canada, de Toronto.
> – Tirawnto. C'était le pote à Lone Ranger ça, non? j'y dis. La nana me
>   regarde, y en a qui pigent rien du tout à l'humour écossais.

1   Comment le parler du narrateur a-t-il été traduit dans les deux traductions
     ci-dessus?
2   Quel est le rapport entre la langue parlée par les Canadiennes et celle parlée
     par le narrateur?
3   Pensez-vous que l'effet produit par ces deux traductions soit le même que
     celui produit par le TS?

Voici une troisième version dans laquelle le traducteur (Alex Gauthier) propose un parler qui utilise le français québécois vernaculaire et "déforme" la langue standard:

> – Sont câlissement pâh geinés, les crosseurs d'la British Rail, ein? heuj'dzis
>   en donnant un coup d'coude à fille à côté.
> – Pardon? qu'a m'dzit, pis c't'à crouére qu'a dzit "par-dawn", t'sé?
> – D'oussé qu'tsu viens coudonc?
> – Désolée, je suis pas sûre de vous comprendre . . . Ah ben h'ai mon
>   vouéyage, lé tsites tourisses ont d'la misère a'ec l'angla' d'la réine
>   d'Angleterre, tabarnac. Faut leu' parler ben fort, ben lentement, pis ben
>   fancé, tsu comprends-tsi, pour qu'è comprennent.
> – D'OÙ . . . VIENS . . . TSU?
> C'tait çâh qu'y falla' pour qu'a l'allume. Y'âh dé z'osties d'fouines à marde
>   a n'avant d'nous z'aut' qui s'eurtournent. Y vont s'manher deux, trois
>   dents câssées avant 'a fin du vouéyage, h'eul'sens, estsie.
> – Euh . . . On vient de Toronto, au Canada.

– Tirawno . . . c'tait pâh l'partner dzu Lone Ranger, çâh? heuj'dzis. Les deux m'orgarent, ben scotchées là. Eh boy, y'en a qui catchent pas pentoute heul'sens de l'humour écossa'.

1   Que pensez-vous de cette troisième version en comparaison avec les deux précédentes?
2   Laquelle de ces trois traductions vous paraît le plus fidèle à l'original?
3   Pour une discussion plus approfondie de ces questions: consultez l'article susmentionné qui est disponible en ligne.[4]

VI Traduction d'un texte de fiction: The Hotel New Hampshire, John Irving

Ce texte met en scène des personnages germanophones s'exprimant en anglais avec un fort accent allemand, ce qui contribue à l'élaboration d'un ensemble de stéréotypes et de représentations négatives quant à leur identité. Avec cet accent allemand, c'est en fait l'amalgame entre langue allemande et antisémitisme qui s'opère, ce qui contribue évidemment à la tension dramatique de la scène dans laquelle apparaît Freud, l'un des personnages principaux du roman, juif de surcroît.

La difficulté principale que pose la traduction de ce texte tient donc dans la reconstitution d'un accent allemand crédible en français: comment créer un accent allemand permettant d'activer les stéréotypes précédemment évoqués?

Alphonse Allais, écrivain de la Belle Epoque, nous donne quelques indications quant à la manière d'aborder cette difficulté. Dans un de ses textes, il évoque une lettre envoyée par un ami qui explique que les Allemands confondent le p et le b, le t et le d, f et v, g et k, j et ch, etc (Allais 2016). Et l'ami d'ajouter qu'un Allemand commandant un verre de Bordeaux se voit souvent servir un verre de Porto.

Ce qu'identifie Allais est un phénomène que les phonologues connaissent bien puisqu'il s'agit d'une confusion entre consonnes voisées et non voisées (avec b d g v z, les cordes vocales vibrent; avec p t k f s, elles ne vibrent pas). En introduisant des "erreurs" à ce niveau, on pourra alors créer un accent allemand convaincant.

The Germans, now in the driveway outside the entrance, were grinding a large trunk across the gravel; someone would have to rake the stones in the morning. "Is der not enough help at dis hotel to help us?" one of the Germans yelled.

5   On the spotless counter, in the serving room between the main dining hall and the kitchen, the big German with the gashed cheek lay like a corpse, his pale head resting on his folded-up dinner jacket, which would never be white again; his propeller of a dark tie sagged limply at his throat, his cummerbund heaved.

"It'z a *goot* doctor?" he asked the desk manager. The young giantess in the
10 gown with the yellow ruching held the German's hand.

"An excellent doctor", the desk manager said.

"Especially at stitching", my father said. My mother held his hand.

"It'z not too civilized a hotel I tink" the German said.

"It'z in der *vilderness*", the tawny, athletic woman said, but she dismissed her-
15 self with a laugh. "But it'z *nicht* so bad a cut, I tink", she told Father and Mother,
and the desk manager. "We don't need too goot a doctor to fix it up, I tink".

"Just so it'z no Jew", the German said. He coughed. Freud was in the small
room, though none of them had seen him; he was having trouble threading
a needle."It'z no Jew, I'm sure". The tawny princess laughed. "They haf no
20 Jews in Maine!" When she saw Freud, she didn't look so sure.

The Hotel New Hampshire, John Irving (1986)

TRADUCTION PROPOSÉE

Les Allemands, regroupés dans l'allée, traînaient une grosse malle sur le gra-
vier; le lendemain matin, il faudrait enlever les pierres au râteau.

— Y a tonc pas assez te bersonnel tans cet hôtel bour nous aiter? hurla un
des Allemands.
5 Sur le comptoir immaculé, dans le petit office coincé entre la grande salle à
manger et la cuisine, le gros Allemand à la joue entaillée gisait blême comme
un cadavre, la tête posée sur sa veste de smoking soigneusement pliée, qui
jamais plus ne redeviendrait blanche; l'hélice de son nœud papillon noir pen-
dait mollement sur sa gorge, sa ceinture se soulevait.
10 — Est-ce que c'est un *pon* tocteur? demanda-t-il au chef-réceptionniste.
La jeune géante à la robe ornée d'un ruché jaune tenait la main de l'Allemand.
— Un excellent docteur, affirma le chef-réceptionniste.
— Un spécialiste des points de suture, renchérit mon père, sa main dans
celle de ma mère.
15 — Bas drès zifilisé cet hôtel, à mon avis, dit l'Allemand.
— On est en *blein tésert*, fit la femme athlétique et bronzée, en s'excusant
avec un éclat de rire. Mais cette plessure, c'est *nicht* trop grave, je crois. Pas
besoin d'avoir un trop pon tocteu pour arrancher ça, je crois.
— Bourvu qu'il zoit bas *juif*, dit l'Allemand.
20 Il toussota. Freud, que personne n'avait vu, avait fait son entrée dans la
petite pièce; non sans mal, il enfilait une aiguille.
— Imbossible qu'il zoit juif, j'en zuis zûre, s'esclaffa la princesse bronzée.
Y a bas de Juifs tans le Maine!
Quand elle vit Freud, elle n'en eut pas l'air aussi sûre.
25 — *Guten Abend, meine Dame und Herr*, dit Freud. *Was ist los?*

L'Hôtel New Hampshire, traduit par Maurice
Rambaud (Editions du Seuil, 1982)

COMMENTAIRE LINÉAIRE DE LA TRADUCTION PROPOSÉE

• *Les Allemand, regroupés (1)*: étoffement (absence de forme verbale dans le
TS: *the Germans now in the driveway*).

- *Traînaient une grosse malle (1)*: noter l'absence de référence au bruit produit par la malle glissant sur le sol, *ils faisaient grincer* pourrait impliquer que le but premier de l'action est de produire un grincement. En outre, ajouter *ce qui produisait un grincement*, serait stylistiquement très lourd.
- *Il faudrait enlever les pierres / someone would have to rake the stones*: construction impersonnelle en anglais.
- *Le lendemain matin* (2): noter le caractère elliptique du TS, *in the morning* signifie bien le lendemain matin, le matin ne serait pas suffisamment explicite en français.
- *Le gros Allemand à la joue entaillée* (7–8): noter que *with* (*with the gashed cheek*), comme c'est très souvent le cas dans les descriptions, est traduit par *à*.
- *gisait blême comme un cadavre (8)*: *gisait* correspond au verbe *gésir* à l'imparfait, en français moderne, ce verbe qui a un sens très spécifique ne s'utilise qu'à l'indicatif présent, à l'indicatif imparfait et au participe présent; noter que *blême* traduit l'adjectif *pale* du TS, qui portait sur le visage de l'homme (*pale head*).
- *la tête posée* (8): participe passé en français, participe présent en anglais; noter l'absence de possessif en français (sa tête posée*).
- *soigneusement* (9): noter l'absence de forme correspondant à cet adverbe dans le TS.
- *ceinture* (11): terme hyperonymique en français, terme hyponymique en anglais (*cummerbund*).
- *demanda-t-il* (12): noter l'inversion sujet-verbe quasi-systématique en français dans les dialogues.
- *tenait la main de l'Allemand (14–15)*: utilisation de l'imparfait: description d'un état.
- *affirma (16), renchérit (17), dit (19), s'esclaffa (28)*: noter que ces verbes très spécifiques correspondent à un seul et même verbe en anglais: *to say*.
- *On est en blein tésert* (20, *en plein désert*) noter l'utilisation de la collocation qui s'impose dans ce contexte – *on est dans le désert* serait trop faible.
- *Non sans mal, il enfilait une aiguille* (26–27): noter la construction de cette phrase: complément circonstanciel en antéposition dans le TC,
- *Bourvu qu'il zoit bas juif (24)*: utilisation du subjonctif avec *pourvu que*.
- *Le Maine (29)*: noter la présence de l'article défini devant le nom (les noms d'états ou de contés sont généralement précédés d'un article défini: *le Missouri, la Californie, l'Oxfordshire, le Dorset*, etc.)

Notes

1 For a discussion of intertextuality and translation in three recent French-language Holocaust novels, see Angela Kershaw's excellent article of May 2014, Intertextuality and translation in three recent French Holocaust novels. *Translation and Literature*, 23(2), 185–196.

2 See the following for an interview in which the translator Jean-François Ménard discusses how he approached the translation of these names: www.lepoint.fr/pop-culture/livres/legende-en-anglais-harry-potter-decrypte-par-son-traducteur-26-10-2017-2167477_2945.php (Accessed 10 February 2020).
3 See section on cultural adaptation in Chapter 2.
4 Available at www.erudit.org/en/journals/ttr/1900-v1-n1-ttr03236/1041657ar/ (Accessed 2 June 2020).

References

Allais, A. (2016). *Alphonse Allais: Oeuvres completes*. Arvensa Editions, p. 1463.
Chesterman, A. (2004). Beyond the particular. In: A. Mauranen and P. Kujamäki, eds., *Translation Universals: Do they Exist?* Amsterdam: Benjamins Publishing, pp.33–49.
Gauthier, A. (2017). These Foreign C*nts've Goat Trouble Wi the Queen's F*ckin English, Ken, ou ré-énoncer la voix scots de Trainspotting au moyen du Québec et de la (socio-) linguistique. *TTR Traduction, Terminologie, Rédaction*, 28(1–2), 207–237.
Grosholz, E.R. (2017). Two English Translations of Simone de Beauvoir's The Second Sex. In: L. Hengehold and N. Bauer, eds., *A Companion to Simone de Beauvoir*. Hoboken: Wiley Blackwell, pp.59–70.
Guène, F. (2006). *Kiffe Kiffe Tomorrow*, trans. S. Adams. London: Chatto and Windus, pp. 7–10.
Irving, J. (1986). *The Hotel New Hampshire*. London: Black Swan, p. 44.
Jakobson, R. (2000 [1959]). On Linguistic Aspects of Translation. In: L. Venuti, ed., *The Translation Studies Reader*. London: Routledge, pp.113–118.
Leech, G.N. (1974). *Semantics*. Harmondsworth: Penguin.
Malmkjær, K. and Windle, K., eds. (2011). *The Oxford Handbook of Translation Studies*. Oxford and New York: Oxford University Press.
Moi, T. (2004). While We Wait: Notes on the English Translation of The Second Sex. In: E.R. Grosholz, ed., *The Legacy of Simone de Beauvoir*. Oxford: Clarendon Press.
Rendall, S. (1997). The Translator's Task, Walter Benjamin (translation). *TTR: Traduction, Terminologie, Rédaction*, 10, 151.
Simons, M.A. (2017 [1983]). The Silencing of Simone de Beauvoir: Guess What's Missing from The Second Sex. In: B. Mann and M. Ferrari, eds., *On ne naît pas femme, on le devient: The Life of a Sentence*. New York: Oxford University Press.
Toury, G. (1995). *Descriptive Translation Studies and Beyond*. Amsterdam and Philadelphia: Benjamins Publishing.
Vinay, J.-P. and Darbelnet, J. (1958). *Stylistique comparée du francais et de l'anglais*. Paris: Didier.

Chapter 6

The Perils of poetry

Pour Un Art Poétique

Bon dieu de bon dieu que j'ai envie d'écrire un petit poème
Tiens en voilà justement un qui passe
    Petit petit petit
    viens ici que je t'enfile
sur le fil du collier de mes autres poèmes
    viens ici que je t'entube
dans le comprimé de mes œuvres complètes
    viens ici que je t'enpapouète
    et que je t'enrime
    et que je t'enrythme
    et que je t'enlyre
    et que je t'enpégase
    et que je t'enverse
    et que je t'enprose

la vache
il a foutu le camp

(*Bucoliques* Raymond Queneau, 1947)[1]

Summary

One of the principal aims of this chapter is to demonstrate the perils and the pleasures of the translation of poetic texts. Poetry is understood here as a genre of literary text (although all texts can contain what can be termed "poetic features" of language, as we discussed in the previous chapter, and songs can also fall into this category). This section explores translating poetry from a practical angle, although it will touch on theoretical approaches. These practical considerations are explored in order to demystify what is generally believed to be the most difficult form of translation. Furthermore, by providing an awareness of the process and encouraging experimentation, these exercises can underscore the playful and creative enterprise of translation. This chapter reminds the reader of the vital recognition of qualities of language beyond the semantic. Thinking about strategies to replicate these features within poetry allows us to have a greater understanding more generally of how translation operates both as a linguistic and cultural practice. Ultimately, this section acts as a reminder that working on poetry can also enhance our grasp of difference, not just between languages, but also between literary and historical traditions and their cultures.

"J'ai envie d'écrire/traduire un petit poème"

Raymond Queneau's playful poem, cited above, begins with the speaker having a creative itch. He feels the need to "write a little poem" and suddenly one appears. As if it were floating past him in the air or swimming around like a little fish, he seeks to catch and reel it in. He beckons it to "come here" in order to then add it to his existing collection. Once it is captured, he will, albeit very crudely, fool around with it (with the verbs *empapouète*, a distortion of the word *empapaouter* "to sodomise" and *enfile* and *entube*, which all sugest the poem is something with which he plans to toy). In the sequence of (mostly invented) verbs, we see how he fantasises about how he will treat his prospective poem while he mocks the ennobling poetic transformative craft, telling it "I'll enrhyme you, I'll enrhythm you, I'll enlyric you, I'll enpegassus you, I'll enverse you, I'll enprose you". A difficult poem in itself to translate, it has been selected here not simply for its creative use of language but because it draws attention to the range of features to which any student of poetry or translator of poetry must be alert. Namely, it explores the poetic process and poetic convention (which it exploits, even if to flout it with its colloquial register and *comptine*-like structure), and it humorously showcases an arrogant need to master and tame a poem into submission. Translators, try as they might to fully grasp a poem and then subject it to a series of transformations in the act of translation, might find their version far removed from the original. In what follows, we will thus discuss the spectrum of translations from the very literal to the extremely free. We will look at whether we can keep hold of a poem and not let it disappear like Queneau's slippery subject, and how we can attempt to bring forth the myriad features present in poetic writing.

1 What is poetry? Is it what is "lost in translation"?[2]

What makes poetry so different from prose? Why has the former been described as the "most complex of all linguistic structures" (Holmes, 1998: 9)? Owing to the historical tradition of oral performance, poetry exploits the sonic features of a language (i.e. the use of sound and rhythm). Regardless of whether there is any formal metre or rhyming pattern, poetry can also be seen to possess an inner rhythm or a "musical mode" (Raffel, 1991: 95). Crucially, the form (or the aesthetic devices which make up the form) and the content (or the semantic content or "message") are inseparably linked. A characteristic feature of poetry is also the way in which it uses language in a way that is compact and condensed. It may also deviate from prose norms of syntax or collocation. Poetic language is predominantly connotational rather than denotational. It is therefore unsurprising that interpreting poetry is challenging and translating it, even more so.

Identifying the semantic level where some "message" or statement is communicated is by no means a straightforward task since the implicit and connotative manner in which such messages can be expressed leads to a range of interpretations. Arguably then, since there is no single way of reading a poem, there can be no single translation of one poem. We saw, in the previous chapter, how Benjamin firmly rejected the idea that a poem communicates anything at all. Additionally, as Susan Bassnett neatly sums up (1980: 120):

> some have suggested that there is a "spirit" or "essence" of a poem that the translator must discover and seek in some way to recapture in the new version, others totally reject the idea of an indefinable essence that resists concrete analysis.

Furthermore, poetry does not only operate in terms of semantic content or aesthetic form. It also aims to produce an emotional effect. This pragmatic dimension is often the most difficult to identify. Readers react intellectually, imaginatively or emotively. This subjective response needs to be kept in mind while also attending to the objective observable facts of the poem (the patterns of sounds, words and meanings, etc.)

It may well be impossible to translate poetry, if by translating poetry we mean taking into account *all* the factors involved and conveying *all* the features of the original into another language and form that works within the TL's own culture and tradition. As Michael Ferber underlines, the translator must attempt to capture primary senses of words, but secondary connotations may be lost and different ones inserted. Among secondary meanings, there may be allusions to the Bible or the classics and they may depend on precise wording (2019: 251). Admitting such obstacles, we can nevertheless attempt to find ways to render as much as possible of the original poetry and make strategic choices as to how to represent what we have identified. Different theorists have conceptualised ways in which this process might be undertaken. Here we will focus on two different systematisations as a useful way for thinking about how one might rework material.

Of course, not all poetry represents the same level of difficulty for the translator. A descriptive or narrative poem in blank verse might pose less difficulty "than a sonnet with its rhyme constraints, or a surrealistic poem with its disruption of conventional syntax, thought patterns, words and image associations" (Jones, 2014: 226). In the activities at the end of this section, we will encourage work on a range of poems and songs which underscore different challenges in both French and English traditions.

2 Different strategies

How literal should a translator be? What aspects should be privileged? There has been considerable debate over this throughout history, with trenchant attitudes on the impossibility of the task and injunctions that poetry only ever be rendered literally. Those who favour a freerer interpretation, however, argue that the translator must also produce a text that will function as a poem in the TL. To do so requires a more creative approach and not a mechanical attempt at fidelity. We shall not rehearse this thorny debate here; suffice is it to say that fears of distorting the original poem have led to those on one side of the debate viewing the transformative process with intense scepticism. Such reluctance has meant that many writers have deemed only an absolute exact rendering to be acceptable. However, this idea of a totally literal translation is itself a myth since, as we know, no two languages are identical. Instead of attempting total replication, a task that will of course set one up for failure, it is more fruitful to think about various ways of reworking poetic texts with each method producing different kind of results. Holmes (1970: 94–99) sets out four different strategies to translate verse form: the first comprises the "mimetic form", where the translated poem attempts to retain the form of the original. The second is the "analogical form", where a culturally corresponding form is used. The third refers to the "organic form". Here the semantic material is allowed, rather loosely, to "take on its own unique shape as the translation develops". The fourth, termed "deviant or extraneous" is where the form used is in no way implicit in either the form or content of the original. A more comprehensive model is clearly laid out by André Lefevere (1975: 19–84), who lists seven possible strategies the translator can adopt. Holmes' categories can be seen to fit within this model.

1   Phonemic translation: reproducing the SL sound in the TL
2   Literal translation: word-for-word translation
3   Metrical translation: reproducing the SL metre
4   Verse to prose translation: distorting the sense, communicative values and syntax of ST
5   Rhymed translation: transferring the rhyme of the original poem into the TL
6   Blank/free verse translation
7   Interpretation: version and imitation

Point 7 draws attention to a more free approach. Interpretation or adaptation, as it is also known, has been met with criticism and a certain nervousness has surrounded it. This relates back to the issue of remaining faithful to the original text and potentially "betraying" the author. Such a pious approach can limit creative engagement and wider assess to a text. France was, in fact, responsible for the golden age of adaptation. This was the period of the *belles infidèles* (in the 17th and 18th centuries), where very free translations were undertaken and justified by arguing that foreign texts needed to be adapted to the tastes and habits of the target culture. Cultural transposition is not without its problems, but rewriting and taking inspiration from the ST can be a very illuminating activity. If not pure translation, the process still involves reading and closely analysing features of the ST in order to make strategic choices and present a new version. Adaptation should not be confused with cultural adaptation as a translation technique (as defined by Vinay and Darbelnet) which, we have seen, is a procedure used whenever the context referred to in the original text does not exist in the culture of the TT and thus necessitates some form of re-creation. Adaptation in this context need not be a reaction to encountering something in the text that cannot be replicated. Rather, it can be an inventive way to transform and play with the text, expand certain aspects of it, update it and use it to draw attention to certain features of the original. The activities in Section 3 engage with this. Douglas Hofstadter's book, *Le Ton de Marot: In Praise of the Music of Language* (1997) showcases bold experimentation, specifically in relation to the 16th-century poem by Clément Marot, *A une Damoyselle Malade*. The poem is rather elegant and simple. In the 28-line poem, Marot, adopting an avuncular role, encourages a little girl who has fallen ill to make a speedy recovery. It is composed in rhyming couplets with lines of only three syllables and with the last "Ma mignonne", identical with the first. Midway the poem changes from formal (*vous*) to informal (*tu*), and the poet inserts his own name directly into the poem. However, throughout the book, Hofstadter proposes over 60 versions of the poem (reproducing, in the majority of the versions, these key formal properties of the poem). Many of the poems are penned by Hofstadter himself, but he also sent copies and collated the attempts of friends, family members and colleagues. He also included poems generated by computer programmes for translations (which he admits produce absurd results). There are even translations of the poem into Italian, German, Russian and modern French which are then retranslated into English. It is fascinating to see the range produced. There are versions in Elizabethan English, the language of rap, and with 1920s American slang, for instance. Across the different versions, Marot's invocation to "Ma Mignonne" that starts and ends the poem is transformed into a range of terms of endearment: "Honey bun", "Sugar lump", "Turtle dove", "Chickadee" and "Pal petite", only to name a few. Throughout, Hofstadter cleverly points to the possibilities that emerge (in terms of transforming the verbs, images and the tone, for instance,) when one transposes a poem from one cultural context to another.

3 Versification

The following section is only a very brief overview into a very complex subject. However, when engaging with different kinds of poetry, the translator must have a basic understanding of the conventional patterns of French and English prosody. This does not necessarily require an in-depth knowledge of versification, the various forms and structures of poems, metres, rhymes, syllablism or stress (or accentuation), but the rudiments of such features will help in identifying and unpacking the particular organisation of a poem. Furthermore, understanding the two systems will help in making an informed choice about what English metre to use to replicate a French one if the translator attempts to produce a translation in verse.

As Mary Lewis Shaw underlines, "the French language, like every other, has an inherent rhythm (or beat) and this derives from the relative emphasis placed on certain sounds, that is its *accent*. This 'natural' rhythm plays an important role in the development of poetic metres" (2003: 8). The way in which an accent falls in a specific language can involve the duration given to a sound (as with long or short syllables) or be a matter of stress. In English, this stress is built into the pronunciation of words, but in French accent is determined by the order in which a sound comes within a given sequence of sounds (whether this sequence is a word or word group). Whereas English is heavily marked and varying, French stress is relatively light and evenly distributed. In French the stress always falls on the last accentuable syllable (i.e. the last tonic (or pronounced) vowel of any word or syntactic word group, with the silent *e* unpronounced).

Lewis Shaw further points out that the relative weakness of French accent and its association with endings can be seen as an explanation as to why French poetry, unlike English poetry, has no tradition of blank (or unrhymed) verse (9). Additionally, French words with their frequent word endings (with suffixes and grammatical inflections) are more easy to rhyme with each other than English words.

French metres comprise equal numbers of syllables (they are *isosyllabic*), whereas English metres are made up of rhythmic measures or *feet*. A foot is a preset rhythmic measure with at least one accented syllable and one or more unaccented syllable depending on whether it is *iambic, trochaic, anapestic* and so forth. Since English words, unlike French ones, carry variable built-in accents of intensity, they must be arranged in verse in a manner that will fit a given metre (the preset sequence of accented and unaccented syllables chosen for the poem).

Significantly, in French, metre is formulated differently. French words tend to lose their individual accents within the context of a word group. Additionally, the terminal accent is syntactically determined. This means that all syllables are equal in French verse (with the exception of those formed by the mute *e*). The syllables may or may not be accented depending on where they fall. On account of syllable linking (or *enchaînement*) which is created by the grammatical rules of *élision* (the eliding of a word's final *e* in front of a word beginning with a vowel) and *liaison* (the linking of final consonants with beginning vowels), boundaries between words tend to be inaudible in French.

The most common line lengths in French verse traditionally have an even number of syllables. These include the *alexandrine* (12 syllables), the *decasyllable* (ten) and the *octosyllable* (eight). The alexandrine was the most popular choice for poets and playwrights from the 16th to the 19th century. Until the mid-19th century, it had a pause or *caesura* after the sixth syllable after which the break was often placed more flexibly. Lines with an odd number of syllables are less common in traditional verse and are impossible to divide up into equal halves.

One needs to remember that in French verse there is no rigid pattern of feet (or *pied* as it is termed in French) superimposed onto the line. The pattern of stresses in the line almost always coincides with the "natural" stresses of the words in prose. Poets, of course, will use these stresses and the rhythmical effects created to emphasise certain words.

Rhyme within the framework of regular verse is a required structuring feature. One prescribed feature in French verse that was little contested until the end of the 19th-century, and is still widely used, is that of alternating rhyme (*l'alternance des rimes*). This means that a pair (or set) of masculine rhymes must be followed by a pair (or set) of feminine rhymes. A feminine rhyme is defined as a word whose last vowel is a mute *e* (e.g. *fouete, squelette*). A masculine rhyme is any word whose final vowel is not a mute *e* (e.g. *nuit, bruit*). The prominent patterns of French rhyme are *rimes plates* (aabb), *rimes croisées* (abab), and *rimes embrassées* (abba). There is a further distinction in that rhyme can be classified as *rime pauvre* (weak rhyme), which has only one identical element (the tonic vowel; e.g. *bleu/feu*); *rime suffisante* (sufficient rhyme), which has two identical elements, the tonic vowel and a supporting consonant (*cardinal/légal*); and *rime riche*, which has more than two elements in the tonic syllable (*santé/hanté*). A very rich rhyme involving two syllables is called a *rime léonine* (*cardinal/matinal*). Rich rhyme is often encountered in 19th-century poetry. *Rimes équivoques* (equivocal rhymes) should also be added to this list. This involves having homophonous elements which extend to entire words.

Valéry playfully draws attention to such poetic stipulations in the famous passage describing the predicament of a poet reaching the end of a line:

> Je cherche un mot (dit le poète) un mot qui soit:
>   féminin,
>   de deux syllabes,
>   contenant P ou F,
>   terminé par une muette,
>   et synonyme de brisure, désagrégation,
>   et pas savant, pas rare.
>   Six conditions-au moins!

The translator need not fixate on all the constituent parts that make up the form of the poem but needs to be aware of the mechanics of the patterning to see what is given prominence, follow the unfolding of the poem's central ideas, and see how the key connections are highlighted among certain words, lines and ideas. In the next section we will focus on phonic features, but we should not forget that rhyme also creates a particular pattern visually on the page. As such, the translator also needs to be alert to the words as graphic features positioned in a specific manner and must think about whether the translated text can mirror such a design. This would be particularly crucial for the "visual" poetry of Apollinaire's

Calligrammes, for example, in which typeface and arrangement of the specific words on the page add to the meaning of the poems.

4 Sounds

We have touched upon the way verse exploits the sounds of words in a systematic way – using rhythm and rhyme – but let us now look at other sound effects which can be employed to heighten and intensify expression. Many of the effects of verse derive from the control of the sound of the words in ways apart from their rhythms. This can be achieved by repeating (or echoing) word sounds or by using sounds in themselves to suggest something of the subject and feeling.

In relation to repetition, the poet can, for example, repeat:

- complete words through, for example, rhetorical devices such as *anaphora* which is the repetition of the same word or phrase at the beginning of a sequence of grammatically parallel constructions, at the beginning of a series of lines or stanzas, for example, *Rome, l'unique objet de mon ressentiment!/ Rome, à qui vient ton bras d'immoler mon amant* (Corneille, *Horace*)
- single consonants (usually at the beginning of words), called *alliteration* (e.g. *l'heure menteuse et molle aux membres sur la mousse* (Paul Valéry))
- the vowel sound only, called *assonance* (e.g. *Quand du stérile hiver a resplendi l'ennui* (Mallarmé)). We can see that Verlaine combines both alliteration and assonance in a very concentrated way in the following three lines:

  > *Les sanglots longs*
  > *Des violons*
  > *De l'automne (Chanson d'automne)*.

- the sounds from the last word of line (as we have discussed, through rhyme)

Two prominent rhetorical figures related to sound pattern are *homoioteleuton* and *paronomasia*. *Homoioteleuton* is the repetition of words with the same endings (e.g. *Ni vu ni connu* (Paul Valéry)). *Paronomasia* is a playful device that brings together words that sound very similar but are not quite the same (e.g. *Sans rien en lui qui pèse ou qui pose* (Verlaine)).

Apart from repetition, sounds in themselves can be used to suggest something of the subject and feeling. The device of *onomatopoeia* is used in a way that sound echoes the sense, as in words such as *crash*, *hiss* and *thud*. In French, examples include *plouf* (*splash*) *chut* (*shh*) and *toc toc* (*knock knock*). We hear the sound of the rain dropping in the following line, *Il tomb' de l'eau plic ploc plac* (Jule Laforgue). In Racine's famous line from *Andromaque*, we hear, through the repetition of the *s* sound, the hissing of the Furies' snakes hallucinated by Oreste: *Pour qui sont ces serpents qui sifflent sur vos têtes?*

One also needs to be sensitive to the individual sounds in words. These often assist the meaning of a word by reminding us of other words with similar meaning, or by the way in which the sound is formed. Consonants such as *p*, *b*, *t*, *d*, *k* and *g* in English are called *plosives*. When they occur in words and phrases with a hard and forceful meaning they emphasise this very quality. The sounds *bitter* and *batter* add to the harshness of their sense. Other consonants like *m*, *n*, *s*, *l* and *w* are much softer and can be used to produce a gentler mellow mood, such as with *slumber*, *sleep* or *wistful*. The particular quality of vowels is how they can be sustained like a held note in music. Some can be just be short like *hot* or *met*, or they can be drawn out in the sounds like *low* and *moon*. In French, similarly, we describe the sounds as *consonnes labiales* and *consonnes dentales* and can use vowel sounds as specific ways of accentuating a mood within individual words (these can be sustained throughout a line or throughout a whole poem). When a poem has such prevalent features so that the literal sense and the mood of the text are reinforced by the phonic qualities of the text (known as *sound symbolism*), then it is obviously important to try and replicate this as much as possible in the ST in order to avoid translation loss.

Conclusion

In this section, we have concentrated on looking at how poetry, when employing verse, makes sound and formal structure a component part of its means of expression. These interdependent features are by no means easy to render into another language and may require some radical reordering and verbal calisthenics so as to replicate the devices and effects of the original poem. Furthermore, As Ferber points out, if

> there are rhymes in the original, we want rhymes in the translation, but words of similar meaning seldom rhyme in both source and target languages, so if we insist on a complete rhyme scheme, we may well force the poem into a Procrustean bed and distort its pattern of meaning.
>
> (251).

One can make use of rhyming dictionaries (examples of online dictionaries include *www.rhymezone.com* or *www.rhymer.com*), but it may be worth seeing whether a translation can be made without using rhyme. Tortuous inversions to achieve a rhyme are quite painful, and couplets in English can end up sounding like greeting-card doggerel.

There are, as has been noted, suggested methods to approach the translation of a poem which privilege one particular feature over an other. However, the aim of this chapter has not been to engage with or advocate one specific approach. Rather, it has signalled recurrent devices that a reader of French and English poetry will encounter and about which the translator will have to make strategic decisions.

More than this, however, this section has also sought to show that poetry is a complex textual object that cannot be reduced simply to what the words it uses mean, or to the sounds it embraces, or uniquely to the general feeling it conveys. Rather, all of these elements have to be taken into account and this renders the translator's task particularly difficult. A certain kinship between translator and poet can be identified. Both poet and translator need to have an acute awareness of both form and content.

Furthermore, it should be noted that poetry, even before we have attempted to translate it, can be viewed as a product of translation. After all, scores of great poets have translated poems from other languages and have taken inspiration from earlier models and traditions reworking them into their own. Poetic forms (the sonnet, the ballad or the rondeau) have travelled across languages, and poetic styles (e.g. symbolist romantic, futurist) have permeated Europe. From this perspective, "the history of Western poetry *is* the history of poetry in translation". Since poets themselves have been "imitators, plagiarists, surreptitious importers and translators since the beginning of time" (Bellos, 152), translators of poetry therefore should be emboldened to work with the material they have before them and transform it into something new. They should do so in the knowledge that such a craft makes them akin to the poets they might struggle to imitate.

After this rallying cry to climb the poetic heights of Mount Helicon, the following advice might seem surprisingly prosaic. However, the aim of this book is to provide practical strategies and, as such, it is hoped that providing a sequence of steps can help the student begin the task of unravelling the complex layers of a poem for translation purposes.

A basic strategy for creating your own translation will involve:

1   Reading closely and decoding the original text (paying attention to meaning and form (including language, the architecture of the poem and its sound)
2   Deciding on whether to keep the particular form of the original poem (or swapping it for another)
3   Producing a draft version
4   Revising and polishing to ensure it reads well in the TL.

As Clare Sullivan underlines in *The Routledge Handbook of Literary Translation*, access to "quality monolingual and bilingual dictionaries" is also important, and it is essential to look "up every word in the original poem, to plumb for unknown meanings or connotations" (2019: 278). Additionally, it is worth remembering, as she stresses that:

•   academic editions of the source-text poems and historical source-languages dictionaries can be helpful.
•   corpora can help determine and help replicate the style of a text.
•   parallel texts and poetry written in the TL with similar language, style and tone can help provide some models.

5 Activités de mise en pratique

I Les jeux phoniques

Traduire les extraits des poèmes, des virelangues et des chansons ci-dessous en tenant compte des jeux phoniques (allitération, assonance et onomatopée) et en essayant de les reproduire.

1   Once upon a midnight dreary, while I pondered, weak and weary,
     Over many a quaint and curious volume of forgotten lore –
     While I nodded, nearly napping, suddenly there came a tapping,
     – *The Raven*, Edgar Allan Poe

2   Betty Botter bought some butter,
       "But," she said, "the butter's bitter;
     If I put it in my batter,
     It will make my batter bitter;
     But a bit of better butter,
     That would make my batter better
     – *Tongue twister*

3   yes i am sad
     says the majestic mackerel
     i am as sad
     as the song
     of a soudanese jackal
     who is wailing for the blood red
     moon he cannot reach and rip.
     – *Archy interviews a pharaoh*, Don Marquis

4   Les masques sont silencieux
     Et la musique est si lointaine
     Qu'elle semble venir des cieux
     Oui je veux vous aimer mais vous aimer à peine
     Et mon mal est délicieux
     – *Alcools*, Guillaume Apollinaire

5   L'opium agrandit ce qui n'a pas de bornes,
     Allonge l'illimité,
     Approfondit le temps, creuse la volupté,
     Et de plaisirs noirs et mornes
     Remplit l'âme au-delà de sa capacité.
     – *Le poison*, Charles Baudelaire

6   Ta Katie t'a quitté
     Ce soir au bar de la gare
     Igor hagard est noir
     Il n'arrête guère de boire
     Car sa Katia, sa jolie Katia
     Vient de le quitter
     Sa Katie l'a quitté
     – *Ta Katie t'a quitté*, Bobby la Pointe (Chanson)

7   Viens faire des bulles, viens faire des WIP!
     SHEBAM! POW! BLOP! WIZZ!
     – *Comic Strip*, Serge Gainsbourg (Chanson)

II Pour un art poétique

Lire encore une fois le poème de Queneau qui ouvre ce chapitre.

1   Comment traduiriez-vous le titre?

2   Comment traduiriez-vous le style familier du poème?

3   Quels sont les expressions argotiques qui sont particulièrement difficiles à traduire?

4   Comment traduiriez-vous les répétitions?

5   Que feriez-vous avec les néologismes?

6   Essayez de produire votre propre version.

III Variantes de traduction

Voici un poème de Charles Baudelaire, *L'albatros* (publié dans le célèbre recueil de poèmes *Les Fleurs du mal*).

Souvent, pour s'amuser, les hommes d'équipage
Prennent des albatros, vastes oiseaux des mers,
Qui suivent, indolents compagnons de voyage,
Le navire glissant sur les gouffres amers.

À peine les ont-ils déposés sur les planches,
Que ces rois de l'azur, maladroits et honteux,
Laissent piteusement leurs grandes ailes blanches
Comme des avirons traîner à côté d'eux.

Ce voyageur ailé, comme il est gauche et veule!
Lui, naguère si beau, qu'il est comique et laid!
L'un agace son bec avec un brûle-gueule,
L'autre mime, en boitant, l'infirme qui volait!

Le Poète est semblable au prince des nuées
Qui hante la tempête et se rit de l'archer;
Exilé sur le sol au milieu des huées,
Ses ailes de géant l'empêchent de marcher.

Maintenant, examinez la traduction rimée de James McGowan (2008):

Often, when bored, the sailors of the crew
Trap albatross, the great birds of the seas,
Mild travellers escorting in the blue
Ships gliding on the ocean's mysteries.

And when the sailors have them on the planks,
Hurt and distraught, these kings of all outdoors
Piteously let trail along their flanks
Their great white wings, dragging like useless oars.

This voyager, how comical and weak!
Once handsome, how unseemly and inept!
One sailor pokes a pipe into his beak,
Another mocks the flier's hobbled step.

The poet is a kinsman in the clouds
Who scoffs at archers, loves a stormy day;

But on the ground, among the hooring crowds,
He cannot walk, his wings are in the way.[3]

1   A votre avis, en retravaillant les vers pour les faire rimer, le traducteur en a-t-
il gardé le sens?

2   Qu'est ce qui manque dans la nouvelle version, qui était crucial dans la syntaxe de l'original, et qui souligne les mouvements de l'oiseau gaffeur?

3   Baudelaire fait une comparaison entre l'oiseau maladroit et la figure du poète. La
similarité des mots "tempête" et "empechênt" qui sont liés à ses deux personnages
renforcent ce lien. Les sons de ces mots sont-ils reproduits dans la traduction?

Voici une version plus ludique de ce poème de Kinsley Amis, intitulée, *The
Helbatrawss*[4]

THE HELBATRAWSS

aht of the froggie of Charlie Bowdylair

Qvite horfen, for a lark, coves on a ship
Ketches a uge sea-bird, a helbatrawss,
A hidle sod as mucks in on the trip
By follerin the wessel on its course.

Theyve ardly got im on the deck afore,
Cackanded, proper chocker- never mind
Es a igh-flier- cor, e makes em roar
Voddlin abaht, is vings trailin beind.

Up top, yus, e was smashin, but es grim
Like this: e aint alf hugly now es dahned:
Vun perisher blows Voodbine-smoke at im,
Auvver tikes im orff by oppin rahnd!

A long-aired bloke's the sime: ead in the clahds,
E laughs at harrers, soups is cupper tea;
But dahn to earf in these ere bleedin crahds,
Them uge great wings balls up is plates, yer see.

Cette version est intéressante car elle est à la fois assez précise (et proche de
l'original) tout en étant un pastiche amusant. La langue utilisée constitue une variété marquée de l'anglais (une forme stylisée du cockney archaïque). En outre,
cette version est une parodie du poème *The Rime of the Ancient Mariner*. Cette
version ludique vise à se moquer de la renaissance du dialecte contemporain
parmi les écrivains qui était à la mode quand Amis l'a écrit.

Pour un autre exemple d'un pastiche, voir le poème de Baudelaire Tu mettras tout l'univers dans ta ruelle *et comparez-le, par exemple, à la version de Jeremy Reed (*You'd Sleep with Anything*) Cette version exagère la vulgarité de l'original. Qu'est-ce que vous en pensez? Est-ce que vous pensez que les vulgarités et le ton argotique sont efficaces dans ce contexte? Les poèmes de Baudelaire étaient considérés comme scandaleux à l'époque, peut-être le traducteur essayait-il de choquer les lecteurs à travers ce langage. . .*

IV Variantes de traduction

Lisez le sonnet du Ronsard et la version de Yeats.

QUAND VOUS SEREZ BIEN VIEILLE

Quand vous serez bien vieille, au soir, à la chandelle,
Assise aupres du feu, devidant et filant,
Direz, chantant mes vers, en vous esmerveillant:
Ronsard me celebroit du temps que j'estois belle.

Lors vous n'aurez servante oyant telle nouvelle,
Desja sous le labeur à demy sommeillant,
Qui au bruit de mon nom ne s'aille resveillant,
Benissant vostre nom de louange immortelle.

Je seray sous la terre et fantosme sans os,
Par les ombres myrteux je prendray mon repos:
Vous serez au fouyer une vieille accroupie,
Regrettant mon amour et vostre fier desdain,

Vivez si m'en croyez, n'attendez à demain:
Cueillez dés aujourd'huy les roses de la vie.

(Pierre Ronsard)

When you are old and grey and full of sleep,
And nodding by the fire, take down this book,
And slowly read, and dream of the soft look
Your eyes had once, and of their shadows deep;

How many loved your moments of glad grace,
And loved your beauty with love false or true,
But one man loved the pilgrim soul in you,
And loved the sorrows of your changing face;

And bending down beside the glowing bars,
Murmur, a little sadly, how Love fled

And paced upon the mountains overhead
And hid his face amid a crowd of stars.

(W.B. Yeats)

1   Quels sont les principaux changements que Yeats a introduits? Quels sonts
les éléments manquants du poème de Ronsard? Le poète Ronsard a un rôle
important dans le déroulement du poème. Est-ce que Yeats a essayé de reproduire cette dimension?

2   *La volta* (ou *charnière*) d'un sonnet (qui signale un changement d'argument
et fournit une sorte de résolution) est dans la version de Ronsard, un plaidoyer
en faveur de la personne aimée. Il dit "carpe diem" (ou "cueillez les roses
de la vie") essayant ainsi de convaincre son amour de se soumettre. Yeats
propose-t-il une conclusion similaire?

V Variantes de traduction

*Lisez le poème ci-dessous et essayez de créer une version plus libre en anglais,
dans laquelle le texte sera modernisé (les deux interlocuteurs s'envoient des tex-
tos, par exemple). Toutefois, essayez de reproduire la distinction entre le premier
personnage qui essaie de parler avec l'autre à travers les mots romantiques et
hyperboliques, et l'autre personnage qui répond d'une manière sèche et mièvre.*

Colloque sentimental

Dans le vieux parc solitaire et glacé
Deux formes ont tout à l'heure passé.
Leurs yeux sont morts et leurs lèvres sont molles,
Et l'on entend à peine leurs paroles.
Dans le vieux parc solitaire et glacé
Deux spectres ont évoqué le passé.
– Te souvient-il de notre extase ancienne?
– Pourquoi voulez-vous donc qu'il m'en souvienne?
– Ton cœur bat-il toujours à mon seul nom?
Toujours vois-tu mon âme en rêve? – Non.
Ah! les beaux jours de bonheur indicible
Où nous joignions nos bouches! – C'est possible.
– Qu'il était bleu, le ciel, et grand, l'espoir!
– L'espoir a fui, vaincu, vers le ciel noir.
Tels ils marchaient dans les avoines folles,
Et la nuit seule entendit leurs paroles.

(Verlaine, *Les Fêtes galantes*)

VI La rime

Lisez la première strophe de *Brise Marine* de Mallarmé et essayez de la traduire, tout en gardant la rime AA, BB, CC, DD, EE

> La chair est triste, hélas! et j'ai lu tous les livres.
> Fuir! là-bas fuir! Je sens que des oiseaux sont ivres
> D'être parmi l'écume inconnue et les cieux!
> Rien, ni les vieux jardins reflétés par les yeux
> Ne retiendra ce cœur qui dans la mer se trempe
> Ô nuits! ni la clarté déserte de ma lampe
> Sur le vide papier que la blancheur défend
> Et ni la jeune femme allaitant son enfant.
> Je partirai! Steamer balançant ta mâture,
> Lève l'ancre pour une exotique nature!

VII Experimentation

Le poète Christian Bök a proposé cinq traductions différentes pour le célèbre poème de Rimbaud, *Voyelles*. Bök les décrit ainsi:[5]

- Une traduction sémantique (qui préserve les rimes de l'original tout en imposant les contours rigoreux et syllabiques de l'alexandrin).
- Une traduction homophonique (qui préserve la séquence des sons mais non pas le sens des mots). Ainsi, les deux poèmes ont les mêmes sons, quand on les lit à haute voix.
- Une traduction homovocalique (qui préserve la séquence des voyelles de l'original mais qui remplace les autres éléments du poème avec les consonnes différents).
- Une traduction qui est un anagramme parfait des *Voyelles* et qui réorganise les lettres de l'original.
- Une traduction qui prend le titre du poème *Voyelles* dans un sens litéral et élimine tout ce qui n'est pas un voyelle (cela inclut les consonnes, la ponctuation et les espaces entres les lettres).

Voici l'original et les cinq versions de Bök:

> A noir, E blanc, I rouge, U vert, O bleu: voyelles,
> Je dirai quelque jour vos naissances latentes:
> A, noir corset velu des mouches éclatantes
> Qui bombinent autour des puanteurs cruelles,
>
> Golfes d'ombre; E, candeurs des vapeurs et des tentes,
> Lances des glaciers fiers, rois blancs, frissons d'ombelles;

I, pourpres, sang craché, rire des lèvres belles
Dans la colère ou les ivresses pénitentes;

U, cycles, vibrements divins des mers virides,
Paix des pâtis semés d'animaux, paix des rides
Que l'alchimie imprime aux grands fronts studieux;

O, suprême Clairon plein des strideurs étranges,
Silences traversés des [Mondes et des Anges]:
– O l'Oméga, rayon violet de [Ses] Yeux! (Rimbaud, *Poésies*)

Vowels

A black, E white, I red, U green, O blue: the vowels.
I will tell thee, one day, of thy newborn portents:
A, the black velvet cuirass of flies whose essence
commingles, abuzz, around the cruellest of smells,

Wells of shadow; E, the whitewash of mists and tents,
glaives of icebergs, albino kings, frostbit fennels;
I, the bruises, the blood spat from lips of damsels
who must laugh in scorn or shame, both intoxicants;

U, the waves, divine vibratos of verdant seas,
pleasant meadows rich with venery, grins of ease
which alchemy grants the visages of the wise;

O, the supreme Trumpeter of our strange sonnet –
quietudes crossed by another [World and Spirit],
O, the Omega! – the violet raygun of [Her] Eyes. . . .

Veils

Anywhere near blank rage
you veer, oblivial.

Jade array, calico azure
evanescent talents.

Unaware, corrosives flow
to my shackled hand.

Key bombing an auto tour
to paint her colour.

Gulfs of amber contours
evaporate the tint.

Linseed glass or oblong
freezing dumbbells.

Upper pressing cashiers
do deliver verbals.

Dance the clear, elusive
rinse of paintings.

Icicle fibre meant divine
daymares varied.

Pity paid to see my dynamo
poised to rid us.

Cool chimes, a primal green
for studios.

Spur my clear plan astride
a stranger.

Cylinders versus diamonds
a decision.

Hollow, my gray ovule does
decide you.

Phonemes

Phantoms, infernal,
without refuge or return – phonemes.

We will hark if such
resurgent souls ordain a dreamt verse:

A (offspring of perfect
murders, so unseen that stranglers

fulfill no crime, and thus
mourners must call the unjust schemes

overdoses); E (charmed
slumber that engulfs the sleepers,

cradled by dreamlike
Sirens who sing mankind, forlorn themes);

I (corrupted archangel,
shriven when mercy redeems

all shadowy spectres
who plunder shipwrecked believers);

U (the Sphinx, beheld
by disciples, then by infidels:

a riddle that grieves
a king; a truth that crippled minstrels

must bewail in epics,
like staunch martyrs whom Furies spurn);

O (untempted Saint,
who lends this typewritten utterance

its fervency
– an endless cycle of perseverance).

O, how the Bards
abolish symbols, when the letters burn. . . .

Vocables

Eternal, you beguile love or ruin – vocables
Jejune vassals quote ten codas in reliquaries:
A (the ceaseless verses at occult monasteries;
requiems of dust, bound to nebulous particles:

Embers of gold); E (graven urns in sanctuaries;
brass bells, unsold, decreed priceless for our canticles);
I (a senseless verse – a spell, garbled in pentacles;
choruses, deemed perverse in desolate nurseries);

U (a universe, expressed as a murmur of tides,
all its perplexing maxims, exquisite suicides;
dim minds, transcended by vivid, hexadic prisms);

O (a vesper, stressing serenades or solitudes;
a clever muse, to generate endless interludes).
O, my elegiac ode, ends in paroxysms. . .

AEIOU

AOIEAIOUEUEOEUOEE
EIAIUEUEOUOAIAEAEE
AOIOEEUEOUEEAAE
UIOIEAUOUEUAEUUEE

OEOEEAEUEAEUEEEE
AEEAIEIEOIAIOOEE
IOUEAAEIEEEEEE
AAOEEOUEIEEEIEE

UEIEEIIEEIIE
AIEAIEEAIAUAIEIE
UEAIIEIIEAUAOUIEU

OUEEAIOEIEIEUEAE
IEEAEEEOEEEAE
OOEAAOIOEEEEU

Qu'est-ce que vous pensez de ces expérimentations de forme? Avez-vous d'autres idées pour d'autres versions?

Notes

1 Copyright permission has kindly been granted by Gallimard.
2 The often-cited dictum is attributed to Robert Frost. David Bellos notes that although this adage is repeatedly used when poetry in translation is discussed, it is actually taken out of context. Frost stated this in an interview to explain his view of *vers libre* in which he says that poetry is that which is lost out of both prose and verse in translation. Bellos concludeds that like "many other received ideas about translation, this one turns out to have little foundation in fact" (2012: 152).
3 Copyright has kindly been granted by Oxford University Press for the translation published in 2008 from *The Flowers of Evil, translated with notes by James McGowan* (Oxford: Oxford University Press).
4 Copyright has kindly been granted by the estate of Sir Kinsley Amis.
5 Copyright permission for these poems have kindly been granted by Christian Bök. These works appear in his 2001 book *Eunoia* (Toronto: Coach House Books).

References

Bassnett, S. (1980). *Translation Studies*. London and New York: Routledge.
Bellos, D. (2012). *Is That a Fish in Your Ear: The Amazing Adventure of Translation*. London: Penguin.
Bök, C. (2001). *Eunoia*. Toronto: Coach House Books.
Ferber, M. (2019). *Poetry and Language: The Linguistics of Verse*. Cambridge: Cambridge Univestiy Press.
Hofstadter, D. (1997). *Le Ton beau de Marot: In Praise of the Music of Language*. New York: Basic Books.
Holmes, J.S. (1998). *Translated! Papers on Literary Translation and Translation Studies*. Amsterdam: Rodolphi.
———(1970). Forms of Verse Translation and the Translation of Verse Form. In: F. de Haan and A. Popovic, eds., *The Nature of Translation: Essays on the Theory and Practice of Literary Translation*. The Hague: Mouton.
Jones, M.H. (2014). *The Beginning Translator's Workbook or the ABCs of French to English Translation*. Lanham, MD and Plymouth: University Press of America, Inc.
Lefevere, A. (1975). *Translating Poetry: Seven Strategies and a Blueprint*. Amsterdam: Van Gorcum.
McGowan, J. (2008). *The Flowers of Evil*. Oxford: Oxford University Press.
Queneau, R. (1947). *Bucoliques*. Paris: Gallimard.
Raffel, B. (1991). The Translation of Poetry. In: M. Larson, ed., *Translation: Theory and Practice, Tension and Interdependence*. ATA Scholarly Monograph Series, vol v. Binghamton, NY: State University.
Shaw, M.L. (2003). *The Cambridge Introduction to French Poetry*. Cambridge: Cambridge University Press.
Sullivan, C. (2019). Poetry. In: R.K. Washbourne and B. Van Wyke, eds., *The Routledge Handbook of Literary Translation*. London: Routledge, pp.268–281.
Valéry, P. (1971). *Tel quel: Rhumbs, Autres Rhumbs, Analecta et Suite*. Paris: Gallimard.

Chapter 7

Audiovisual Translation

Summary

Curiously, audiovisual translated material has long been considered aesthetically inferior to literary works. Audiovisual translation was excluded as a discipline in translation studies and only really started to emerge as late as the 1990s. However, as this chapter will illustrate, the specific challenges and constraints of the medium make screen translation a complex activity which overlaps with many of the strategies and techniques we have highlighted for approaching literary genres (cultural adaptation, omission and compensation, to mention a few,) and demand a sophisticated knowledge of linguistic, pragmatic and cultural dimensions of both the SL and TL. Even if commercial products do not always attend to such detail (fast turnaround time and constraints of the jobs often lead to poor renderings), this chapter will encourage the translator to consider the varied ways of approaching the audiovisual material to produce polished versions that capture the different dimensions of the original. We will not be focusing on technical issues or market requirements of subtitling or dubbing but, rather, will focus on specific linguistic issues arising in interlingual translation. In this respect, we are not interested in mimicking the professional environment of subtitling and dubbing assignments by engaging with the use of particular software in the exercises, nor will we be focusing on amateur practices such as the translations undertaken by fansubbers (such translation also known as subbing which is the domestic subtitling by fans of series, films or cartoons, originally *anime*, before release in the fan's country). Rather, we are encouraging the use of audiovisual translation to practise and reinforce the understanding of important translation issues and analytical procedures. In so doing, we aim to provide greater language awareness and examine issues that stand out in such genres. This kind of activity is also important for language students since it privileges working with the spoken word and can improve listening skills. When looking at subtitling, one of the questions we ask is how the aural dimension of speech might be expressed in writing.

As with the other chapters in this book, we view translation as a cross-cultural, communicative process and therefore argue that the role of the audiovisual translator is as a cross-cultural mediator, even if the various constraints of the medium and certain norms and conventions make this a difficult position to adopt in all instances. This discussion leads us to reflect upon the aesthetic and ideological assumptions upon which Audiovisual Technology (AVT) practices are often built.

1 Introduction

Audiovisual translation is an umbrella term which encompasses "media translation", "multimedia translation" and "screen translation". Subtitling, dubbing, voice-over, surtitling (for opera and other live performances), subtitling for the deaf and the hard-of-hearing, and audio description for the blind and the partially sighted are among the many audiovisual modes that exist. Nowadays, with the wealth of streaming and new television series, TED talks, computer games and interactive software programmes, there is an ever-greater commercial demand for audiovisual translations. In the early days, subtitles were stamped into the film stock by using a wax and and chemical bath method. Towards the end of the 1980s, laser subtitling machines constituted huge progress since prior to this, the only way to correct errors involved striking a new print. With laser, however, the video could be reviewed and corrections made up to the last minute. Electronic subtitles were also used which were transferred onto the screen using a projector that had a time code system to make sure there was proper synchronisation with the written subtitles. Since they were superimposed onto the image, they could be changed more easily than laser captions. Electronic subtitling was more widely used for TV and DVD distribution. Today subtitles are projected digitally and translators have digital copies, usually accompanied with a transcript of the dialogue. The subtitles are created in a file format and can be activated on or off. In cinema, they are transferred from a computer directly onto the cinematic screen. Digitalisation and access to the Internet have certainly changed the way we interact with audiovisual texts. They have created opportunities for subtitling to move out into the public sphere so that consumers have become "prosumers" (Díaz Cintas, 2013: 273). This burgeoning of fansubbers and amateur subtitling by the general public has changed the landscape of audiovisual translating. In certain respects, this has allowed for more freedom and creativity since nonprofessionals can eschew market values, industry standards and constraining practices. In other ways, this has arguably led to an undercutting of professional work (outsourcing to amateurs or using machine translation) and has meant that companies often churn out material of poor quality. Netflix, for example, was recently embroiled in controversy over the subtitling of many of its shows. In February 2019, the vice-president of the *Association des Traducteurs/Adaptateurs de l'Audiovisuel* openly condemned the lamentable subtitling of the acclaimed film *Roma*, stating that what they discovered to be both "shocking and baffling" including a "list of violations of subtitling conventions and industry practice" and an "inventory of translation and adaptation errors".[1] Charting the many subtitling blunders across Netflix, the Twitter account *#traduiscommeNetflix* has emerged. Examples, such as the insult,

"In your fucking face, sucker!" translated as "Tel est pris qui croyait prendre!" and the famous typing scene in *The Shining* where Jack Torrance has been writing nothing but "All work and no play, makes Jack a dull boy" (translated as "Un 'tiens' vaut mieux que deux 'Tu l'auras'") show failures to capture the sense and crucial manner in which the information is expressed.

The focus of the activities will be on screen translation and will revolve around an extract of a now cult film (from Quentin Tarantino's *Pulp Fiction*, 1994). The aim is to examine the speech and dialogue of the characters and identify what difficulties the language poses for the translator. Our choice is motivated partly by the fact that this film has always generated fruitful discussion when used in the classroom. Furthermore, interactive speech often requires a more nuanced understanding of what is happening in the exchange than a static speech from one speaker (for example, with a narrator of a documentary or a speech on a certain topic) and so offers a good level of challenge. These activities can be supplemented with work on other films to extend exposure to a range of speakers in a range of fictional contexts and thereby showcase more styles, register and accents. The particular scene selected is of urbane interlocutors in an American diner setting, but in the vast choice of material available today (be it feature films, cartoons or television series) the styles and lexicon will be as wide ranging as the thematic content is vast. The speech might well resemble or imitate spontaneous speech but is, at the same time, an artistic rendering of reality by screenwriters. Even if writers imitate spontaneous oral conversation, we should remember that this is a hybrid form of conversation, displaying characteristics of both oral and written language. When examining subtitles, our investigation will focus on how this very speech can then be transformed into the written form. It is important also to ask whether features such as voice quality, intonation, accents and other sociocultural markers, including paralinguistic features (such gestures and expressions), are conveyed in the written code. Often dialogue is written to be slick and witty and elicit laughter (particularly for sitcoms), and part of our focus for this chapter will point to rendering different types of humour into the TL. As we are working on interlingual transfer (from one language to another), we will also attend to terms that are culture-bound and look at strategies for dealing with such references and the implications involved in such choices.

2 Methods/modalities

The two most widespread methods adopted for translating products for the screen are dubbing and subtitling. There is also the less common acoustic form of screen translation known as voice-over. In the English-speaking world, films tend to be subtitled rather than dubbed. Dubbing is the standard for imported films and TV programmes in Austria, France, Germany, Hungary, Italy, Slovakia, Spain, Switzerland, the Czech Republic and Turkey but also in the Americas (Brazil, Colombia, Mexico, Venezuela). Dubbing is also predominant in some Asian countries (China, Iran, Japan, Korea) and in some North African countries. In dubbing, the original soundtrack – including both music and special effects – are retained. Voice-over is popular in Russia and Poland, as part of a continuing tradition of this modality but also because lip-synch dubbing is too expensive. Voice-over involves having one narrator interpreting the lines of every character, and the volume of the original audio is turned down while the narrator is speaking.

Works for the screen are polysemiotic in nature, that is to say they are made up of numerous codes (the visual code such as verbal information in written form e.g. letters, placards or graffiti, and acoustic codes such as dialogues but also background noise, sound effects and music). These interact to produce a single effect. For subtitling and dubbing, the translator is concerned mainly with conveying the verbal audio codes of an audiovisual product into another language. These different codes can also be defined as simultaneous "channels" that the translator needs to take into account. These have been categorised as including:

- the verbal auditory channel (dialogue, lyrics, background voices)
- the nonverbal auditory channel (music, sound effects)
- the verbal visual channel (superimposed titles and written signs on the screen)
- the nonverbal visual channel (picture and composition) (Gottlieb, 2001: 245)

Dubbing is a process which uses the acoustic channel for translation purposes, while subtitling is visual and involves a written translation that is superimposed onto the images on the screen (the verbal and visual channel becomes the focus). Dubbing involves the replacement of the original speech by a voice track that encompasses lip synchronisation with the speaker on the screen. This process aims to follow as closely as possible the timing, phrasing and lip movements of the original dialogue. Matching sounds to lip movements is only an issue in close-up shots, but this synchronisation puts limits on the translator's choice for the TL. Interestingly, however, such constraints have been overcome via the latest technology which is able to modify lip sync and voice quality. Software can modify footage in such a way that an actor mouths words not originally spoken so that the lip motions can match up to the new audio. Additionally, there is software that can allow a dubbed voice to be readily assimilated to that of the original actor. This *matching* gives the impression that the original actor is speaking the TL with its particular patterns and intonations. In dubbing, the translation is divided up into segments. These chunks of text are called *takes* or *loops* and known as *boules* in French. Segmenting methods (the way they split the translation into takes, prepare the translation layout, or use dubbing symbols) vary from one country to another and even, sometimes, within the same country, as some dubbing companies have their own conventions. Overall, however, segmenting is done according to audiovisual punctuation marks which marks the start of a new scene or sequence. Dubbing symbols are placed between the dialogue lines so that dubbing actors know when paralinguistic sounds such as crying must be produced. Attention must also be paid to interrupting another character.

Subtitles can be defined as either *open*, which means they cannot be turned off by the viewer (as is the case in cinematic viewing of films), or *closed*, which means that they are optional and can be accessed by the user (i.e. subtitles for hard of hearing or included in DVD menus and on streaming programmes). There are a variety of spatial and temporal factors involved in working with subtitles. This includes specifications on the position of subtitles on the screen (usually horizontal, displayed at the bottom of the screen and centre-aligned), how much space they should occupy and for how long they should be displayed (with specifications for the number of characters per line, usually 37, for European characters). Temporal synchronicity with the utterances they are translating are also important. In addition to all these technical details, the "readability" of the renderings are important (Guillot, 2018: 36–38). The written text needs to be shorter than the audio because the viewer needs the necessary time to read the captions and still watch the action of the film as characters are speaking. Translators need to create subtitles that can be easily understood in the short time they appear on the screen (on technical considerations, see Díaz Cintas and Remael, 2007: 67–99). They need therefore to structure their subtitles in such a way that they are self-contained (semantically and syntactically). Every subtitle should aim to have a clear structure and be a complete sentence. If this is not possible, then the subtitler will have to segment the sentence. Since complex sentences are difficult to keep track of, it makes sense to split them into smaller ones. A sentence may have to be distributed over the two available lines of a subtitle (with a line break) or it may run on into two or more subtitles, though this is less desirable. In any case, subtitles represent a reduced form of the oral ST and can never be a complete and detailed rendering. Text reduction can be partial or total. The former is achieved through condensation and rendering the ST in a more concise fashion. The latter is achieved through deleting or omitting lexical items. In this respect, subtitling means a kind of rewriting. It is important that reformulations are idiomatic and not calques of the SL. Some strategies subtitlers use to simplify sentences include using simple rather than compound tenses, using pronouns to replace nouns and merging two sentences into one (see Cintas and Ramael, 145–172). In terms of omissions, subtitlers will generally remove what is considered redundant or irrelevant. Phatic words tend to disappear (since strictly they do not advance the action), as do hesitations or false starts. Vocatives, greetings and formulas of courtesy (unless crucial to the sense of the scene) are also usually excluded. Since written language is, in general, not the same as spoken language, it can be strange to replicate dialogue that is spoken into a written format. Subtitling can therefore be seen as a peculiar genre in that it reflects speech but does not conform to features of written style (with the latter's greater formality or elaborateness, for example).

3 Challenges: cultural references

Whether working with subtitling, dubbing or voice-over, the screen translator will encounter a range of similar problems. One of the reasons for this is that these products contain both oral and visual elements. Indeed, the acoustic and visual codes are interwoven and need to be understood as working as a whole. Each modality will have their own unique difficulties, but in addition to this, the translator will have to deal with language-specific features (taboo language and terms of address, for example) and references that are highly culture-specific (place names, references to sports and festivities, famous people, monetary systems, institutions, etc.), including overlaps between language and culture. The fact that audiences can match what is on the screen with what they hear or read means that translators cannot veer too far from the original without it being rather discordant. With subtitling, the possibility of comparing the original audio with the subtitles means the discrepancies or omissions are in danger of being noticed and criticised by audiences. Sometimes, however, the visuals or acoustic signs can actually help the translator by clarifying an understanding of the cultural reference. In any case, having a dubbed or subtitled scene that is set in another language and culture does require the audience to accept the inherent incongruity and suspend disbelief to a large extent.

Let us now examine what is known as highly culture-specific references or *items* (CSIs) and look at how these can be handled and which we have already touched upon in earlier chapters. In this context, these can be visual, verbal or both. When audiences are faced with a culture-specific term (e.g. North American *cheerleaders* or *baby showers*, a *6/20* grade given to a student at a French *lycée*, a *chippy* in England) they need to be dealt with so as to be comprehensible to the target audience. Antonini and Chiaro have identified ten areas that are likely to create difficulty (this follows in a trend of scholarly taxonomies, from Newmark onwards). They categorise these as institutions; educational references; place names; units of measurements; monetary systems; national sports and pastimes; food and drink; holidays and festivities; books, films and programmes; and celebrities and personalities (cited in Chiaro, 2009: 156–157). This is not an extensive list since – as Franco Aixelà, who actually coined the term "culture-specific item" (1996: 56–57), makes clear – what makes something a CSI is not its membership to a fixed category of linguistic items but the fact that its translation is problematic due to the nonexistence in the TL culture of an equivalent object, concept, custom or expression.

Many scholars have proposed classifications of CSI translation strategies. Hervey and Higgins (1992), for example, provide a classification, described as degrees of cultural transposition (exoticism, calque, cultural borrowing, communicative translation and cultural translation), which we have already considererd in previous chapters. Franco Aixelà (1996) maps translation procedures on a scale from conservation to substitution. Eirlys Davies (2003: 72–88), building on this, provides a list of seven "individual procedures", but David Katan (1999: 87) only distinguishes three main translation strategies (generalisation, deletion and distortion). This is by no means an exhaustive account, but despite the dizzying array of taxonomies (in many ways, in line with of the work presented by Vinay and Darbelnet which we have already examined in previous chapters), there is no clear agreement among scholars on the number of procedures available to translators or on the labels to attach to them. That said, there is a large degree of overlap between the terms. Whatever categorisation is adopted, translators ultimately can choose from different techniques that exist on a spectrum from the most domesticating to the most foreignising. Let us examine more closely Aixelà's systematisation. As previously mentioned, the procedures are presented on a scale from conservation (more specifically repetition, orthographic adaptation, linguistic [non-cultural] translation and gloss) to substitution (synonymy, limited universalisation, absolute universalisation, naturalisation, deletion and autonomous creation). What do these entail?

- Repetition
  This involves repeating the item without providing a translation. This means retaining the cultural reference in the original language. An example of this would be keeping *Thanksgiving* or *Halloween* in a French subtitling of an American programme that references this.

- Orthographic adaptation
  Here, again, a translation is not provided but a transcription of the sounds presented for languages with different alphabets (e.g. *manga* from the Japanese). Official proper names or neologisms can also be adapted this way.

- Literal translation
  An example of this would be *soirée de filles* for *girl's night out* or *Poufsouffle* for *Hufflepuff* in Harry Potter

- Gloss
  In glossing, of course, the meaning of the Cultural Item (CI) is made explicit. However, glosses or paraphrases are much longer and are therefore can be difficult to use in subtitling where space is at such a premium.

Moving away from these options, the translator can also choose cultural adaptation (or substitution). This is a technique which seeks to neutralise the exoticism of the Cultural Reference (CR) when it is unfamiliar in the target culture. Cultural adaptation can be implemented through using:

- Limited adaptation
  This involves replacing the CI with another CI from the source culture but one that is more well known/accessible to the target culture. An example of this would be replacing *graham cracker* with *oreo* or *petit beurre* with *langue de chat*.
- Absolute universalisation
  This involves using a CI that is not culturally marked and is well known globally. It can be used to replace an item in the source culture that is not familiar in the target culture.
- Cultural substitution or naturalisation
  This involves replacing the CI with a new CI of the target culture (e.g. baseball for football). Practically, however, the visuals on the screen

might prevent this from being a useable strategy, particularly if the CI is a main part of the action.
- Omission
  The translator can erase the CI from the translation. This is a strategy if the CI is unclear or repeated.
- Creation
  The translator can also opt to create a new CI that was not in the original, perhaps as a compensation strategy for something that was erased in another part of the programme or because the overall approach is to "domesticate" the material.

It is worth stressing that the strategies adopted will be dependent on the kind of cultural items that abound within the ST, the specific brief the translator is given and the norms and ways of working within the TL. We will examine the implications of particular approaches in more detail in the conclusion.

4 Challenges (marked language, forms of address, humour, multilingual AVT and songs)

One of the most difficult subjects is the translation of marked speech and language variation. This includes the translation of style, register, dialects, sociolects, idiolects, and emotionally charged language. How does one go about translating spoken language variants into a written form? The general norm tends to be the homogenisation of speech. In other words, a standard variety of the TL is often adopted. This levelling obviously obscures the specific characteristics of the interlocutors and the significance of having them talk in the way they do. In subtitling, the translator can try to mark the speech of certain characters so that the viewer will note that the speech of a particular person is unlike that of others, but overall the practice is to transform variation into a standardised form. However, it must be said that the stylistic features do vary in terms of their relevance. The example cited is often of heritage or literary films. For these, the particular language used is a fundamental feature of the entire work. The literary language of Rostand's *Cyrano de Bergerac* was captured by Anthony Burgess' subtitles. These were based around Burgess' theatrical adaptation of the novel where the alexandrines were replicated by using sprung rhythm (five-beat lines with a varying number of syllables and a regular couplet rhyming scheme). For *Shakespeare in Love*, for example, the dubber or subtitler needs to be particularly attentive to giving a flavour of the Elizabethan styles and particular quotes of Shakespeare. Arguably, however, the characteristic way in which the characters speak is an essential part of any work and when not incidental should be made visible/audible. However, specific accents or dialects can be deemed by distributors to hamper audience's understanding and enjoyment. For this reason, the film *Trainspotting*, for example, in which characters speak with a strong accents in an Edinburgh vernacular, was actually dubbed in parts to make the "pronunciation clearer" when distributed to the American market. Ken Loach's films, similarly, are often dubbed or subtitled for the American market. The gritty authenticity key to such films is no doubt diminished by such tampering. When translating interlingually, however, one does, of course, need to produce another version but if the strategy is to incorporate the features corresponding to those in the ST, one of the main problems lies in the fact that there is never an exact equivalent in the TL. What is the equivalent in French, for instance, of the Queen's English? Or of cockney? How can one convey the Marseille dialect of Pagnol, for instance, or the language in Danny Boon's 2008 film *Bienvenue chez les Ch'tis* which features a dialect closely related to the Picard language of the region in which it is located? In the latter case, the English subtitles of the film did not go unnoticed. Marcelline Block (2018) underlines how Michael Katims, the subtitler, strove "to preserve the linguistic wordplays and misunderstandings that arise from the interactions between standard French and ch'ti speakers", and in a more detailed analysis of the strategies, Ellender (2015) notes that a careful "transposition of pronunciation, juxtaposition of different linguistic registers and national variants" and "rewriting of wordplays" ensured the linguistic specificity and the resulting humour were retained, which certainly is no easy feat. That said, given how crucial language is to the whole thrust of the film, it would have been a major oversight not to engage with such issues and Boon himself was apparently also involved in subtitling the film for foreign release to ensure that such nuances were preserved.

Another example of dealing with the challenge of language variation can be seen in the subtitling of the acclaimed film *La Haine*, previously mentioned in Chapter 5. Here the characters speak a variety of French spoken in the *cités* (commonly described as *banlieue French*). This variety has geographical as well as social connotations, arising as it has, in close-knit communities such as those of the *banlieue's* youth population. The use of slang and of features such as *verlan* are some of the distinguishing features. *Verlan*, which inverts two syllables of a word (and derives from inverting the word *l'envers*), poses considerable challenges as there is no morphological equivalent in English. Pig Latin is a similar playful device (for interlocutors to speak to each other in a coded-like way), although it is not used as prolifically or in equivalent contexts.

The English subtitles written by Alexander Whitelaw and Stephen O'Shea in the Tartan Video version (of 1996) tried to render the speech in the film by using a variety of English, namely African American Vernacular English (a "dialect-for-dialect" approach). Their domesticating strategy also involved transposing cultural references in the script, as we saw in Chapter 5 (*kro* for Kronenbourg, was turned into *Bud*, *les schtroumpfs* becomes *Donald Duck* and *Darty* becomes *Walmart*). As Pierre-Alexis Mével analyses, their approach is not entirely incongruous, since the language and culture of the French youth in the *cités* are certainly influenced by African American street culture and a parallel can be drawn between the world of the *projects* in the U.S. and the *cités* (2007: 52–53). However, the subtitles were criticised, seen as a "sloppy pastiche of black American slang that hinder rather than help understand the film and where the characters speak as if they were 'homeboys in the hood'"(Jäckal, 2001: 227). For instance, *une racaille* becomes a *gansta, un enculé* is a *mothafucka* and *les amis* become *homeys*. As Mével points out, it is not so much the quality of the translation that results in the dissatisfactory nature of the subtitles but rather the limits of the dialect-for-dialect approach and how consistently this is applied. The main problem is that there is a striking visual dissonance between what is seen and what is heard. Indeed, Mével rightly concludes:

> the result of this transposition/translation of the film to fit American culture is that the American viewer is confronted with a language that belongs to his/her national culture, and yet is not given the means to apprehend the specificity of the French situation. The American audience is confronted with a recognisable language that is traditionally associated with African American people, but which is superimposed onto pictures of the French black-blanc-beur trio of characters.

(54)

The specificity of the situation the director is trying to underline is certainly lost in the process of translation. It is unsurprising then that Kassovitz himself requested new subtitles to be written for the DVD that came out in 2006 to mark the film's tenth anniversary. These new subtitles used a much more neutral form of English and the problematic dialect-for-dialect approach was not adopted.

Swearwords are very frequently toned down when translated into another language, particularly in subtitling. Dubbing is more predisposed to soften swearwords than subtitling. Subtitles, rather than adopting this strategy, tend to omit or reduce a considerable amount of them. There are two main reasons for this. Owing to the fact that subtitling has a limited amount of words, it favours omitting what can be deemed extraneous. Furthermore, there is a general belief that these words are more offensive when seen in written form than when uttered in spoken language. Determining the strength and the level of rudeness implied in certain terms is both subjective and culturally determined. You may have noticed that some translations use mollifying childlike insults to replace more violent language or use retrograde language or U.S. slang that is not familiar to British audiences. These can be jarring or even come across as ridiculous if they are clearly mismatched with the original. The context, and what is considered appropriate for the interlocutors, must be taken into account. Before looking at how one might go about handling such language, the translator needs to identify the different pragmatic functions swearing can have. These include expressing emotion (anger, frustration, annoyance, surprise, happiness), asserting power, solidarity or group membership, or to emphasise what is being said. Obviously these functions go far beyond the literal meaning of the actual words (see Andersson and Trudgill, 1990, on this). When the swearwords are used in a connotative way, that is to say, in order to insult, blaspheme, curse or swear, these words ought to be translated to maintain as much as possible the connotation of the word.

Overall, however, what strategies are adopted when such language is encountered?

1   Omission or softening: this involves removing the language altogether or weakening the force of the language or its vulgar connotations. In this way, the slang language is made more neutral. It can seem very incongruous to use mild words as equivalents of the stronger original expression and this mismatch can anger viewers.
2   Compensation: this involves placing a swearword elsewhere in the TT to compensate for omitting words in other parts of the text.
3   Equivalence of the word: this involves replacing the SL word with an established counterpart in the TL. The problem with this is that swearwords in different languages are not always used in the same context. Calques are also commonly used, which can appear odd.
4   Equivalence of function: this involves aiming to reproduce the same pragmatic function the word in the SL fulfilled. This is more nuanced and requires creativity.

The subtitling in Laurent Cantet's 2008 film *Entre les murs* is a good example of the difficulty swearwords can pose. In fact, one of the key moments in the film revolves around the word *pétasse* and how this is interpreted. It is obviously important, therefore, for the translation of it to reflect its different connotations and ambiguities. In the film (which centres on a class of teenagers in an inner-city Parisian school and their teacher Monsieur Marin), the teacher openly insults two of his pupils. Up until this point, M. Marin has had a teasing rapport with his tumultuous class, but he is angered that Esmerelda and Louise (the class representatives) whispered and giggled in the teachers' meeting they got to attend the previous day. In class, angered when he discovers that they have passed on confidential information from the meeting, he criticises the behaviour he witnessed. Esmeralda argues that no one else minded ("Non, non, non. Ça dérangeait que vous") to which Monsieur Marin responds, "Si, si. Moi, je suis désolé, mais rire comme ça en plein conseil de classe, c'est ce que j'appelle une attitude de pétasses". The English subtitles translated this as "to giggle during a meeting like that is behaving like a skank". The choice here works (even if for a British viewer the word stands out as more American than British), in the sense that such a word could credibly trigger the student's shock and lead to the disciplinary proceedings which the teacher subsequently has to face. However, it seems more offensive and rather less ambiguous than the French. It is interesting that when they discuss the insult, the student and the teacher have very different ideas about what they think the word means. Esmeralda says, "Déjà, pour moi, pétasse, ça veut dire prostituée" but Monsieur Marin argues that "Une pétasse, c'est une fille pas maligne qui ricane bêtement". What emerges from this is how different generations and social groups read this insult in different ways. The girls certainly play up this insult and use it to try and destroy the teacher. As Simon Kemp underlines, when discussing the film on the Oxford University blog on Languages and Cultures,[2] *Le Petit Robert* definition is of a "prostituée" but *Le Dictionnaire de la Zone* which specialises in contemporary slang argues that it means "femme d'une allure vulgaire, provocante, aguichante". Given such definitions, even if Monsieur Marin made his interpretation sound more innocent than what he perhaps meant to say, it is very likely that he did not think it as vulgar as Esmeralda believes it was intended to be. Would the translation *bitchy behaviour* have been more appropriate? An extended exchange on the online discussion site *Francofil* when the film came out in the UK showed there was no straightforward consensus for the most apposite term. Some suggested *bimbo*; others thought *slut* would work better. It is clearly very tricky to find an English word that covers the full meaning of the French.

Having looked at handling rudeness and swearwords, let us turn to think more about how pragmatic features which are language-specific, such as politeness and forms of address, can also be problematic. How, for example, do you convey the intended shift from formality to intimacy that is represented by the French "on se tutoie", for example? We will not be delving into the enormity of this subject here, but as Hatim and Mason (1997) who have examined the complexities of forms of address note, if the wrong forms of address are chosen in translation, the power dynamics can be changed. The translator needs to decide on the right form of address in each case by examining the different clues (be they linguistic or visual or in terms of the narration) within the scene.

We have already touched on trying to replicate the tone of a film, paying attention to conveying humour, for instance, which was a key part of linguistic wordplays and misunderstandings of *Bienvenue chez les Ch'tis*, but let us look more broadly about the challenges humour can present in audiovisual translation. Numerous theorists in the field of translation (e.g. Attardo, 2002; Delabastita, 2004; Díaz Cintas and Remael, 2007; Zabalbeascoa, 1996) have dealt with cultural aspects of humour and linguistic differences between the SL and TL and have also engaged with the challenges of creating similar humorous effects in the TT. We will not rehearse all these arguments here, but rather want to signal some key points that need to be addressed. Firstly, it is important to remember that humour does not operate in isolation and emerges through the dialogue/scene, and so both the visual and linguistic features need to be taken into account.

Díaz Cintas and Remael (2007: 217–228) build on Zabalbeascoa's study (1996) to present seven types of humour that are regularly used in audiovisual materials and are useful for pinpointing the different kinds of challenges with which the translator must grapple. These include:

- International or binational jokes where the humour is independent of a language-specific wordplay or knowledge of a specific phenomenon in the source culture, and if not truly international can "travel" between cultures (such as with a famous film star or world-famous politician and can usually be translated literally).

- Jokes referring to a national culture or institution (if the reference is unknown in the target culture, adaptation will be necessary so that the joke is not lost on the audience).
- Jokes reflecting a community's sense of humour (often mocking sub-communities within it and laughing at their expense. More than Zabalbeascoa's definition of "humour typical of a particular country or nationality" (252), this is extended to embrace communities since to understand them, "such jokes rely on a form of intertextuality as one must know the insider national tradition" (the French joking about the British or the Belgians and British making fun of the Irish, for example). The humour (often historical but usually inspired by prejudice) thus targets communities, not just nationalities. Obviously, an entire "community" may not embrace such humour, but they are rehearsed and perpetuated as standard jokes of one group against another).
- Language-dependent jokes (these rely on features of the language and thus include puns, play on words, or idioms. These cannot be translated literally and a counterpart that reproduces the semantic and pragmatic effects that also replicate the wordplay from the SL can be hard to come by. The translator will have to assess how to best replicate this feature or whether to rewrite for a similar effect through a different means).
- Visual jokes (gestures and facial expressions act as "sign systems" and, even if there are cultural differences, these do have a certain universality. Thus in the majority of cases the translator can rely on the image to have the effect on the audience).
- Aural jokes (these rely on sounds, but not ones that are linguistically meaningful and thus do not require translation).
- Complex jokes (this category is used when jokes integrate two or more of the above features. In such cases, combining, for example, visual information, wordplay and cultural-bound references will need untangling and decisions then need to be made about how to replicate each constituent part of the joke).

Overall, strategies to handle these features will be similar to those used to render cultural references (such as addition, substitution and explication). The translator will need to make sense of the material and also be sensitive to clues and comic repertoires, pick up on exaggerations and understatements in the dialogue, and make decisions on how crucial the different elements are and how best they can be rendered. Thus, the overall process involves the translator interpreting the ST humour (often, for sitcoms, detecting the humour is facilitated by the use of "canned laughter", which acts as a prompt for the viewer's laughter); determining how this will be received/understood by the target viewer (subtitlers in one country may have a different view of what their viewer will understand than in another); and then needing to rephrase the humour accordingly. Sometimes, because of space restraints, the exaggeration inherent in much humour of the ST may not be fully replicated in the TT but, equally, to make the joke more comprehensible, the subtitles might need to be more explicit, which will make the joke less subtle than in the ST. Obviously, finding creative solutions, as with all translating, is important but the major thrust and tone of the film/programme should take priority, and an attempt to render all the different humourous elements should not mean sacrificing overall fluency or textual coherence of the TT.

5 Multilingual films

Another challenge the audiovisual translator will have to face involves works where characters speak in a language other than the main language of the programme. *Babel* (Alejandro González Iñárritu, 2006), *It's a Free World* (Ken Loach, 2007), *Inglourious Basterds* (Quentin Tarantino, 2008) and *L'Auberge espagnole* (Cédric Klapisch, 2002) are good examples of multilingual films where characters all speak a range of different languages. This dimension can be difficult to subtitle and even harder to dub. In countries where dubbing is prevalent, the strategy for multilingual films is usually to adopt a mixture of dubbing and subtitling. The predominant language may be dubbed into a TL, and the secondary ones may be either dubbed/subtitled or just remain untranslated, making some scenes convey the sense that there is is a variety of languages involved. However, if one of the languages is the very language into which the translator is rendering the material overall, a solution must be found. In the Spanish version of the British television sitcom *Fawlty Towers*, Manuel, the Spanish employee, is transformed into Paolo, an Italian from Naples. On the other hand, in the film *A Fish Called Wanda* (1988), Wanda demands that her lovers must speak to her in any other language than English. Otto's Italian is transformed into Spanish in the Italian version of the film. In the sitcom *Frasier*, the two doctor Crane brothers pepper their language with French to show their sophistication and erudition. These interjections are kept in the French in the French version of the show, with the rest of their speech transformed from English to French. This means the multilingual dimension of their ostentatious speech is eclipsed.

6 Songs

As a final point for consideration in this chapter, audiovisual translators will have to make decisions about what to do with song lyrics that feature in programmes. Songs in dubbed versions are often translated and sung in the TL (think of Disney feature cartoons, for instance) but they can also be left in the original or subtitled. The choice of how they will be handled must be considered. Firstly, the prominence and importance of the song in the programme needs to be assessed. Songs in musicals contribute explicitly to the story, and so the lyrics are usually translated. Additionally, in other films or even documentaries where the songs capture the essence of the film, it also makes sense to capture the message of the songs by translating the lyrics. However, if the song featured is a well-known international song (by The Rolling Stones for example, or with very simple lyrics), then it may be decided that a translation is not necessary since the target audience will be sufficiently familiar with it. Similarly, if the song is in a language close to the TL (an Italian song for a film to be dubbed into French), it may be decided that the song need not be translated because it is already sufficiently intelligible. In cases where the lyrics of the song are not in the same language as the rest of the film (a Spanish song, for example, included in a French film), these should only be subtitled or dubbed into the TL if they were also subtitled in the original. If not, keeping the flavour of the original song without any gloss makes more sense. Another factor that will impact one's choices will be technical. If the song overlaps with the dialogue, the dialogue needs to be given priority. If the song coincides with opening or closing credits, it could be subtitled but it may eclipse the text on the screen and thus it may be decided not to risk cluttering the screen. Once the decision has been made to actually translate a song, however, the question remains on how to go about doing so. While subtitles that respect the rhythm of the song are easier to read because of the synchrony between the soundtrack and the words, if the rhyme scheme is markedly different from the ST it may attract too much attention. This is problematic because ultimately subtitles should not take centre stage or detract attention too much from the soundtrack or images. In dubbed versions, the translator will have more flexibility, but as with poetry, decisions need to be made about whether to privilege content over rhyme and rhythm or how much of a balance can be struck to replicate the different elements of the text.

Conclusion

Translation, as we have shown throughout the book, is never a neutral act of communication. Particular strategies will carry with them certain assumptions, values and stereotypes, and this is important to think about, whether engaging with audiovisual translation or, indeed, any other media. In domesticating, we are in danger of cultural hegemony or suppression. If we manipulate or adjust what appears foreign to the dominant ideology of the target culture, then surely we are not doing justice to the particularities of the original? On the other hand, of course, in the case of AVT, it is often argued that such strategies allow for a greater audience and makes such audiovisual products more accessible. Normative market pressures and the mighty machinery of Hollywood can dominate. The subtitling/dubbing of a programme can thus be subject to constraining principles with agendas that involve "levelling" or "neutralising". This can include standardising the register used in the target material and "cleansing" foreign accents or sociolects. Furthermore, toning down sensitive material (of language such as expletives, blasphemies or political comments) can be a form of censorship that can be masked as a simple translation solution. Markus Nornes, in *Cinema Babel* (2007: 155–158, 176–187), draws a distinction between two kinds of AVT. The first he calls "corrupt" since he sees this as a violent means of appropriating the ST and forcing it to conform to cultural norms and industrial constraints in a way that conceals the appropriation and underlying ideologies. The other he calls "abusive" (but he means this in a productive rebellious sense) since by experimenting with linguistic features, it reveals the violence that is at the heart of translation. In this latter approach, the translation works to critique ideologies that operate in corrupt practices and steers the viewer back to the ST. This approach goes against the notion that good subtitling should be invisible since it does not attempt to conceal the translation process. Fansubbers are good examples of translators who do not abide by the standard recommendations that subtitles be as inobtrusive as possible.

We have looked at some of the expected approaches and different ways we can handle linguistic and cultural aspects in audiovisual material, but we must not lose sight of the fact that the norms and practices adopted can shape the way many people will experience the material. This means (notwithstanding the pressures and practices imposed on professional translators) that translators, as Díaz Cintas has clearly underlined, "are now considered to be active agents participating in the shaping of the ideological discourse of their culture, whose system of values they may consciously or unconsciously accept, contributing to their dissemination or subversion" (2012: 283).

7 Activités de mise en pratique

Cette activité se base sur une scène du film *Pulp Fiction* réalisé par Quentin Tarantino (1994). Elle met en scène Uma Thurman et John Travolta et précède la fameuse scène de danse entre les deux protagonistes. Dans cette scène de dîner, Mia Wallace, épouse du truand Marsellus, le patron de Vincent, se livre à un jeu de la séduction avec Vincent. Ce dernier est visiblement intéressé mais méfiant, ce qui crée une certaine tension et donne tout son piquant à la scène.

Cette activité est élaborée à partir de la transcription des dialogues de la scène originale, de la version sous-titrée et de la version doublée. Il s'agira ici de 1) tenter de traduire la scène, 2) de comparer ce que vous avez proposé avec ce qui est proposé dans la version sous-titrée, 3) de comparer la version sous-titrée avec la version doublée.

Si vous le pouvez, regardez la scène dans sa version originale. Les sous-titres et les doublages correspondent à ceux qui apparaissent dans la version française du DVD (effectués par la compagnie Murfilms dirigée par Philippe Murcier).

Commentaires liées à la nature du médium: sous-titres vs. doublages

Notons tout d'abord que les sous-titres ne modifient pas la bande-son, les spectateurs d'un film sous-titrés dans une langue étrangère ont le même accès au texte source que les spectateurs du film dans sa version originale; à la différence qu'une petite partie de l'écran est entamée par les sous-titres. Les traductions sous-titrées sont plus succinctes que les traductions doublées; il n'est en effet pas nécessaire, et généralement impossible, de tout traduire. Il faut avant toute chose proposer au spectateur une traduction qui soit lisible dans le temps imparti. Les traductions doublées sont plus complètes, mais pas nécessairement plus fidèles, puisqu'il faut faire plus ou moins correspondre le nombre de syllabes du texte source à celui du texte cible, afin que les mouvements de la bouche des personnages à l'écran correspondent à ce qu'entend le spectateur.

PULP FICTION - Scène au restaurant

> Pas de traduction littérale ici !

                    MIA
        Don't you just love it when you come back
        from the bathroom to find your food waiting
        for you?

> Comparer à ST et DB

                    VINCENT
        We're lucky we got anything at all.
        I don't think Buddy Holly is much
        of a waiter. Maybe we shoulda sat in
        Marilyn Monroe's section.

                    MIA
        Which one, there's two Monroes.

                    VINCENT
        No there's not.

                    VINCENT
        That's Marilyn Monroe...

                    VINCENT
        ...and that's Mamie Van Doren. I
        don't see Jayne Mansfield, so she
        must have the night off or something.

                    MIA
        Pretty smart.

> Modulation SVP !

                    VINCENT
        Yeah I've got my moments.

                    MIA
        So did you think of something to say?

                    VINCENT
        Actually, I did. However you
        seem like a nice person, and I
        don't want to offend you.

> Comment recréer cet effet provocateur ?!

                    MIA
        Oooohhhh, this doesn't sound like the usual
        mindless, boring, getting-to-know-
        you chit-chat. This sounds like
        you actually have something to say.

> Eviter « offenser »

                    VINCENT
        Well, well I do but you have to promise not
        to be offended.

                    MIA
        No, no, no, no. You can't promise something
        like that. I have no idea what you're
        gonna ask me. So you can go ahead and ask me
        what you're gonna ask me, and my natural
        response could be to get offended.

Then, through no fault of my own, I
woulda broken my promise.

> Attention idiome !

            VINCENT
Let's just forget it.

            MIA
That is an impossibility. Trying
to forget anything as intriguing as
this would be an exercise in
futility.

            VINCENT
Is that a fact?

            MIA
Besides, it's more exciting when
you don't have permission.

> Très idiomatique

            VINCENT
 All right, here goes. What do you think about
what happened to Antwan?

            MIA
Who's Antwan?

            VINCENT
Tony Rocky Horror. You know

            MIA
He fell out of a window.

            VINCENT
That's one way to say it. Another
 way to say it would be that he was thrown
 out. Another
way would be he was thrown out by
Marsellus. And yet even another way
is to say he was thrown out of a window
by Marsellus because of you.

            MIA
Is that a fact?

> Eviter une traduction
> littérale

            VINCENT
No, no it's not a fact, it's just what I
heard.

            MIA
Who told you?

> Comment recréer le
> jeu sur le pronom ?

            VINCENT
They.

            MIA
They talk a lot, don't they?

            VINCENT
They certainly do. They certainly do.

            MIA

Well don't be shy Vincent, what
else did they say?

> Que sous-
> entend-
> elle ?

                MIA
Did it involve the F-word?

                VINCENT
No. They just said Antwan
had given you a foot massage.

                MIA
And...?

                VINCENT
And nothing, that's it.

                MIA
You heard Marsellus threw Tony Rocky
Horror out of a four-story window
For giving me a foot massage?

                VINCENT
Yeah.

                MIA
And you believed that?

                VINCENT
At the time I was told, it sounded
reasonable.

                MIA
Marsellus throwing Tony out of a
four-story window for massaging
 my feet seemed reasonable?

                VINCENT
No, it seemed excessive. But that
doesn't mean it didn't happen. I
understand Marsellus is very protective
of you.

> Eviter
> d'utiliser
> un adjectif

                MIA
A husband being protective of his
wife is one thing. A husband
almost killing another man for
touching his wife's feet is
something else.

                VINCENT
But did it happen?

> Proposer
> deux noms

                MIA
The only thing Antwan ever touched
of mine was my hand, when he shook
it, at my wedding then never again. The
truth is, nobody knows why
Marsellus tossed Tony Rocky Horror
out of that window except Marsellus
and Tony. But when

> Comment
> recréer ce
> stéréotype ?

you scamps get together, you're
worse than a sewing circle.

Expression idiomatique dans le TS ?

VERSION SOUS-TITREE

M :C'est pas génial de trouver
sa bouffe servie en revenant ?

V :On a du bol d'être servis,
Buddy Holly m'inspire pas confiance

V : Fallait aller chez Marilyn

M :Y a 2 Marilyn

V : Erreur
Là, c'est Marilyn
L'autre, c'est Mamie Van Doren
Jayne Mansfield a pas l'air
d'être là, ce soir

Quel adjectif dans le TS ?

M : T'es futé, dis donc

V : ça m'arrive

M : T'as trouvé un sujet ?

V : Justement. T'as l'air vraiment sympa,
je veux pas te choquer

TS ?

Raconter des fadaises = to talk twaddle

M : ça ne ressemble pas
à des fadaises de circonstance
T'as vraiment quelque chose à me dire

V : Ben, oui. Mais tu promets
de ne pas le prendre mal ?

= se vexer

= ne pas tenir sa promesse

M : Je peux rien promettre
sans savoir ce que t'as à me dire
Après, tu le diras et si je le prends mal,
je trahirai ma promesse malgré moi

V : N'y pensons plus

M : Pas question
Impossible de plus y penser, ça m'intrigue
trop

V : C'est vrai ?

M : D'ailleurs, c'est moins excitant
si y a pas de risques, non ?

Expression idiomatique

V : Bon, d'accord. Je me jette à l'eau.
Tu penses quoi du coup d'Antoine ?

M : Qui c'est ?

V : Tony Rocky Horror. Tu sais bien

M : Son accident ?

```
V : Accident, si on veut.
Peut-être qu'on l'a poussé
Peut-être même
que c'est Marsellus qui l'a jeté.
Ou mieux encore, que Marsellus l'a jeté
par la fenêtre à cause de toi

M : Tu en es sûr ?

M : Sûr, non, je l'ai entendu dire,
c'est tout.

M : Qui te l'a dit ?

V : Des gens

M : Des gens bavards ?

V : Oh ça, oui !

M : Sois pas gêné, dis-moi tout

V : Je suis pas gêné, mais...

M : C'est très scabreux ?

V : Paraît qu'Antoine t'aurait
massé les pieds, voilà

M : Et puis ?

V : Et puis rien. C'est tout

M : On t'a dit que Marsellus
avait balancé Tony du 4ème
pour m'avoir massé les pieds ?
Et t'y as cru ?

V : Sur le moment, ça m'a paru crédible

M : Que Marsellus ait jeté
Tony par la fenêtre
pour m'avoir massé les pieds ?

V : Ca m'a paru radical,
mais pas impossible
J'ai cru comprendre que Marsellus
te couvait beaucoup

M : Qu'un mari couve sa femme,
d'accord mais de là à tuer un homme
pour un massage, y a une marge

V : Il l'a fait ou pas ?

M : Antoine m'a jamais touchée,
sauf pour me serrer la main.
Ie jour de mes noces. En fait, personne sait
pourquoi Marsellus l'a fait sauf Marsellus et
Tony.
```

Qui parlent beaucoup !

Difficile à dire ou à traiter décemment

La poule couve ses œufs ou ses petits. Couver quelqu'un = *to overprotect sbdy*

= mariage

= un truand

Les <u>malfrats</u>, y a pas plus <u>pipelettes</u>

Un personne très bavarde

VERSION DOUBLÉE

Expression idiomatique

M : *Génial, je <u>crevais de faim</u> et puis j'aime bien quand on est servi quand je reviens des toilettes.*

V : *Mouais, on a eu de la chance d'avoir quelque chose. Je pense que Buddy Holly <u>pédale dans le yaourt</u>.*

Expression familière; =pédaler dans la semoule

V : *Fallait aller chez Marilyn*
Pour moi, on aurait été mieux chez Marilyn.

Laquelle ? Y a deux Monroe.

Ah, non pas du tout.

Là, c'est Marilyn Monroe

Et celle-là, c'est Mamie Van Doren

Mais je vois pas Jayne Mansfield, c'est sûrement son soir de congé.

ST: futé

M : *T'es <u>malin</u>*

V : *Ouais, j'ai mes moments*

M : *T'as décidé de quoi t'allais parler ?*

blesser, choquer

V : *Je crois oui… sauf que t'es tellement gentille que… j'ai peur, je voudrais pas te <u>vexer</u>*

M : *Oh, dis donc ça nous change du tout au tout des <u>banalités que tout le monde dit quand on lie connaissance</u>. T'as tout l'air d'avoir un message à faire passer.*

Pas aussi fort que le TS

V : *Ben ouais, ouais, je crois, je le crois, seulement tu dois me promettre de ne pas te <u>vexer</u> ?*

TS: *to be offended*

M : *Non, non, non, non, ce genre de promesse c'est pas tenable. J'ai aucune idée de ce que t'as à me dire alors si toi tu te décides pas à me dire ce que t'as à me dire, comment savoir d'avance si je me vexerai pas, ce qui fait que je risque de me vexer quand même en oubliant ma belle promesse.*

V : *Non, laisse tomber.*

M : *Ah non, impossible. Ce que tu viens de dire là est si intrigant*

V : *Ah, ouais, c'est vrai ?*

M : *Et puis d'ailleurs est-ce que c'est pas
plus excitant de faire les choses sans
permission ?*

TS: *here goes*

V : *D'accord si tu veux, allons y. Qu'est-ce
que tu penses de ce qui est arrivé à
Antoine ?*

M : *Qui est Antoine ?*

V : *Tony Rocky Horror. Tu le connais.*

M : *Il est passé par la fenêtre.*

V : *C'est une façon de le dire. Une autre
façon serait peut-être de dire qu'on l'a
jeté, ou alors on pourrait peut-être dire
qu'il s'est fait jeter par Marsellus, et une
dernière version serait qu'il s'est fait
jeter d'une fenêtre par Marsellus à cause de
toi.*

M : *Tu crois que c'est vrai ?*

M : *Non, non, non, non j'en sais rien mais je
l'ai entendu. Je l'ai entendu.*

M : *Où tu l'as entendu.*

TS: *they talk a lot don't
they?*

V : *Chez des gens.*

M : *Les gens disent tant de choses.*

V : *Oh ça c'est sûr, c'est sûr !*

M : *Sois pas gêné Vincent, dis-moi la suite*

TS: traduit bien le sous-
entendu

V : *Je suis pas gêné*

M : *Ils racontent qu'on était amoureux ?*

M : *T'as décidé de quoi t'allais parler ?*
V : *Non, non non non. Ils ont dit qu'Antoine
t'avait fait un massage.*

M : *Et ?*

TS: *foot massage*

V : *Et non, rien. C'est tout*

M : *On t'a dit que Marsellus avait fait jeter
Tony Rocky Horror d'une fenêtre du troisième
pour m'avoir fait un massage et t'as pu
avaler ça ?*

TS: *four story*

V : *Je sais pas. Quand on m'a raconté ça, ça
m'a paru possible.*

M : *Marsellus aurait jeté Tony d'une fenêtre
du troisième étage pour un massage qu'il m'a
fait et ça te parait normal ?*

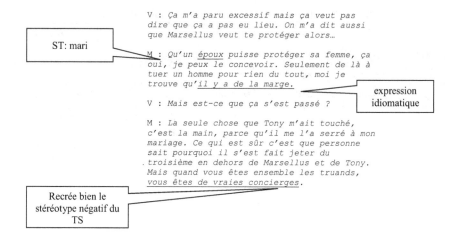

ST: mari

> V : *Ça m'a paru excessif mais ça veut pas dire que ça a pas eu lieu. On m'a dit aussi que Marsellus veut te protéger alors…*
>
> M : *Qu'un <u>époux</u> puisse protéger sa femme, ça oui, je peux le concevoir. Seulement de là à tuer un homme pour rien du tout, moi je trouve qu'<u>il y a de la marge.</u>*
>
> V : *Mais est-ce que ça s'est passé ?*
>
> M : *La seule chose que Tony m'ait touché, c'est la main, parce qu'il me l'a serré à mon mariage. Ce qui est sûr c'est que personne sait pourquoi il s'est fait jeter du troisième en dehors de Marsellus et de Tony. Mais quand vous êtes ensemble les truands, <u>vous êtes de vraies concierges.</u>*

expression idiomatique

Recrée bien le stéréotype négatif du TS

Commentaires sur deux éléments du TS particulièrement difficiles à traduire: "f-word" et "sewing circle":

Nous avons signalé certaines difficultés, d'ordre lexical pour la plupart dans les transcriptions. Deux énoncés sont particulièrement difficiles à traduire. Le premier: *did dit involve the f-word*, en grande partie parce qu'on peut être tenté de chercher une équivalence formelle à "f-word". Il est en fait utile de bien replacer l'énoncé en contexte, Vincent vient d'expliquer à Mia qu'il a entendu dire quelque chose qu'il ne peut ouvertement lui dire, sans la choquer ou prendre de risques. C'est alors que Mia pose la question à Vincent visiblement gêné. Cette question contient un fort sous-entendu; il est important de voir qu'ici c'est sur le mode implicite que Mia pose la question, elle ne veut en effet pas parler à sa place, l'utilisation de l'euphémisme lui permet de cultiver le mystère et le non-dit propre au jeu de la séduction. Afin de bien traduire cet énoncé, on peut se poser la question du type d'information qu'elle essaie d'obtenir et la reformuler en termes explicites: *ils ont dit que nous avions eu une relation sexuelle?* que nous pouvons décliner sur le mode implicite, comme c'est fait dans la version doublée: *ils racontent qu'on était amoureux,* ou dans la version sous-titrée: *c'est très scabreux,* (proposition peut-être un peu trop allusive).

De la même façon, lorsque Mia, faussement excédée, dit à Vincent: *But when you scamps get together, you're worse than <u>a sewing circle</u>;* après qu'il lui a révélé ce qu'il a entendu dire, plutôt que de chercher une traduction littérale, il est important se demander ce que Mia essaie de faire. La valeur pragmatique de son énoncé est en fait celle d'une critique, elle l'attaque sur le fait que lui et ses acolytes parlent trop, faisant appel à un stéréotype négatif et les comparant à un *sewing circle,* traditionnellement constitué de femmes.

Afin de proposer un stéréotype négatif permettant à Mia d'attaquer Vincent, on peut donc aller chercher du côté des termes à connotation péjorative qu'on utilise dans la culture francophone pour désigner quelqu'un qui parle trop: la pipelette ou la concierge.

Notes

1 Available at: https://beta.ataa.fr/blog/article/roma-french-subtitles (accessed 11 February 2020).
2 Available at: https://bookshelf.mml.ox.ac.uk/tag/entre-les-murs/ (accessed 11 February 2020).

References

Aixelà, J.F. (1996). Culture-specific items in translation. In: R. Alvarez and C.-A. Vidal, eds., *Translation, Power, Subversion*. Clevedon: Multilingual Matters, pp. 52–78.

Andersson, L. and Trudgill, P. (1990). *Bad Language*. London: Penguin.

Attardo, S. (2002). Translation and humour: An Approach based on the general theory of verbal humour. *The Translator*, 8(2), 173–194.

Block, M. (2018). One of the most elaborate, protracted and relentlessly side-splitting linguistic adventures ever attempted onscreen: Language contact and conflict in the blockbuster French film *Bienvenue chez les Ch'tis* (2008). In: W. Finke and H. Kitasbayashi, eds., *Language Contact, Conflict, and Development: Volume 1, second edition*. Raleigh, North Carolina: American Society of Geolinguistics Publications, pp.41–65.

Chiaro, D. (2009). Issues in Audiovisual Translation. In: J. Munday, ed., *The Routledge Companion to Translation Studies*. London: Routledge.

Crichton, C., dir. (1988). *A Fish Called Wanda* [Film]. Metro-Goldwyn-Mayer.

Davies, E. (2003). A Goblin or a dirty nose?, *The Translator*, 9(1), 65–100.

Delabastita, D. (2004). Wordplay as a translation problem: A linguistic perspective. In: H. Kittel, A.P. Frank, N. Greiner, T. Hermans, W. Koller, J. Lambert and F. Paul, eds., *Übersetzung, translation, traduction*. Berlin: Mouton de Gruyter, pp. 600–606.

Díaz Cintas, J. (2012). Clearing the smoke to see the screen: Ideological manipulation in audiovisual translation. *Meta*, 57(2), 279–293.

———(2013). The technology turn in subtitling. *Translation and Meaning*, 9, 119–132.

Díaz Cintas, J. and Remael, A. (2007). *Audiovisual translation: Subtitling*. London: Routledge.

Ellender, C. (2015). Dealing with dialect: The subtitling of *Bienvenue chez les Ch'tis* into English. In: J. Cintas and J. Neves, eds., *Taking Stock: Audiovisual Translation*. Newcastle: Cambridge Scholars Publishing, pp.46–68.

Gottlieb, H. (2001). Subtitling. In: M. Baker, ed., *Routledge Encyclopedia of Translation Studies*. London and New York: Routledge, pp.244–248.

Guillot, M.-N. (2018). Subtitling on the cusp of its futures. In: L. Pérez-Gonzalez, ed., *The Routledge Handbook of audiovisual translation*. London: Routledge, pp.31–46.

Hatim, B. and Mason, I. (1997). Politeness in screen translating. In: L. Venuti, ed., *The Translation R.* London: Routledge, pp.46–68.

Hervey, S.G.J. and Higgins, I. (1992). *Thinking French Translation: A Course in Translation Method: French to English*. London and New York: Routledge.

Iñárritu, A.G., dir. (2006). *Babel* [Film]. Anonymous Content.

Jäckal, A. (2001). The subtitling of *La Haine*: A case study. In: Y. Gambier and H. Gottlieb, eds., *(Multi) media Translation: Concepts, Practices and Research*. Philadelphia, PA: Benjamins, pp.223–235.

Katan, D. (1999). *Translating Cultures, An Introduction for Translators, Interpreters and Mediators*. Manchester: St. Jerome Publishing.

Klapisch, C., dir. (2002). *L'Auberge espagnole* [Film]. France: Mate Production.

Loach, K., dir. (2007). *It's a Free world* [Film]. Tournasol Films.

Mével, P.A. (2007). The Translation of identity: Subtitling the vernacular of the French cité. *Modern Humanities Research Association*, 2, 49–56.

Nornes, M. (2007). *Cinema Babel*. Minneapolis: University of Minnesota Press.

Tarantino, Q., dir. (1994). *Pulp Fiction* [Film]. A Band Apart Jersey Films.

Tarantino, Q., dir. (2008). *Inglourious Basterds* [Film]. A Band Apart, Studio Babelsberg, Visiona Romantica.

Zabalbeascoa, P. (1996). Translating jokes for dubbed television situation comedies. *The Translator*, 2(2), 235–267.

Conclusion

The impetus behind writing this book was the desire to provide an engaging text-book for students, inspired by work we had undertaken with students. As this goes to press, we are well aware that the COVID-19 crisis has brought about some major changes and challenges across the world, including, most certainly, for university students to whom we dedicate this book. In-person teaching and the year abroad for language degrees have been compromised by the pandemic. We firmly hope that social distancing and the inability to learn together on campuses and in the TL countries will be short-lived. In the immediate future, however, we believe this book can contribute to a learner's individual progress when used in the context of independent study but, equally, that it can be used as a basis for group work that can be conducted through online synchronous learning and vir-tual forums. We are by no means implying that our textbook can stand in place of interaction within the classroom with fellow students and teachers. Rather, we sincerely hope the different analyses across the chapters can be fruitfully used for discussions and activities that take place collectively. We hope it motivates students and teachers to undertake close readings of the texts and systematically tackle the range of important issues that we have sought to highlight in the act of translation. The fully immersive experience of the year abroad cannot be repli-cated in one's own country but, in our humble way, we hope that the activities in the TL will provide more contact with the language and encourage sustained work and thought in French. Furthermore, our approach of selecting texts from a range of sources (magazines, novels, poems, adverts, etc.) models what we believe to be a very useful activity that any language learner should adopt (and most certainly does so when abroad when, for example, confronted with adverts in the subway or newspaper articles lying around or through the more active exploration of art and culture with films and literary texts). Exposure to a variety of authors, periods, genres, registers and subject matter increases one's competency in the language and enriches one's ability to navigate through the complexities any text might present. If the idea of selecting texts and putting them under the microscope seems like a daunting task, Chapters 1 through 4 of this book can help break down the task by providing a framework for examining recurring structural patterns in both languages. These sections help identify linguistic procedures that can be used when translating. However, to avoid the risk of adopting too myopic a vision and of exclusively focusing on linguistic forms, it is important to remember that stylistic, cultural and ideological issues also need to be examined. Indeed, when working to understand a text and transform it into another language, linguistic features cannot productively be divorced from these other considerations. Chapters 5 through 7 of this book point to these broader issues, and these sections can be used to sharpen the learner's ability to understand the role, responsibilities and "task" of the translator in a more comprehensive fashion.

Surveying the work across this book, it is clear that we have devoted considerable attention to the translation of literary texts. This choice has been driven by:

- the pedagogical necessity of preparing our students to handle such texts for the requirements of their degree
- our knowledge of a range of literary texts across both languages as avid readers and researchers
- our explicit desire to expose students to the benefits of working with literary texts to alert them to features which can be applied across a multitude of text types.

As we have stated from the start, this book is a practical guide but it is not designed to be a handbook for the professional translator or student seeking to pursue a career in this field. That said, we realise that many readers, like our students, will have a strong interest in pursuing this subject and might very well uncover their talents in this area when working on translation assignments in class and more extended translation projects at university. In these concluding comments, it therefore seems apt to draw attention to the changing world of the profession and appreciate its ever-growing importance in the globalised world in which we live. The economic impact of the pandemic has and will continue to affect many professional translators, the majority of whom work as freelancers. Income and key clients have been lost, and it will certainly be hard to recover from this. In-house positions for translators and interpreters will be even more scarce, and independent publishers that specialise in literary texts in translation will struggle.

However, viewed from another angle, there has never been a greater need for translators. *Translators without Borders*, a nonprofit organisation set up to provide translation services for humanitarian bodies, has underlined that the pandemic has been fuelled by what the WHO calls an "infodemic". Unreliable and inaccurate information has spread like wildfire. The organisation works to translate critical public-facing content in 89 languages. Additionally, to help stop the spread of rumors and inaccurate information, they also monitor COVID-19-related social media conversations in multiple languages. The world needs trained linguists to better survive.

On a more prosaic note, in a post-Brexit world, if the UK removes itself from common EU rules, practices and reciprocal arrangements, it is foreseeable that there will be a significant need to produce a higher volume of bespoke trade, contractual and legal documentations, and thus there will be a greater and urgent need for professional translators to deliver this. The English language will still play a crucial role in the EU, but it is also likely that the expectation for everything to be conducted in English will lessen. Owing to this, there will be an ever-greater need for trained linguists to help communicate with European countries.

More poetically, but no less urgently, the world also needs stories. Stories from around the globe that present a picture of the myriad perspectives and experiences lived in different cultures, contexts and socioeconomic landscapes. We will continue to rely on translators to help access these narratives and make them come alive for a new target audience.

The medieval writer Bocaccio's collection of novelle in the *Decamerone* reminds us that recounting stories can be therapeutic and a bonding experience in a time of plague. More generally, the curative power of storytelling should not be forgotten, both for a narrator and for a reader/listener. The translator can inhabit both these spaces, positioning themselves alongside the voice of the narrator, while also occupying the space of reader, when decoding the text. If this "healing" or bridging position is rewarding for the translator and also the reader of the translated product, it does not come about without considerable effort or skill. As if the act of reading were not challenging enough, the translator must, of course, also grapple with the difficulties of communicating the *fond* and the *forme* into another language. Yet, we argue, such toil is productive and can allow for an intimate encounter with texts and a deeper understanding of the way language shapes the telling.

On a final note, we believe it is important to signal that the "invisible translator" (as evoked by Venuti) is increasingly being challenged, and rightly so. As Daniel Hahn argues, "a new breed of translator has emerged: confident, vocal and media-savvy"[1] (2019). The campaign for the previous anonymous translator to be named on book covers and in reviews (with the hashtag #NameTheTranslator) continues to grow. We can see that literary translators are increasingly in the spotlight discussing their versions, providing book prefaces, and voicing their thoughts in speaker panels and across digital spaces (e.g. on Twitter and through blogs). The translator is visible. In this vein, we also hope our book contributes to make the translation process itself ever more visible.

Note

1 Available at www.economist.com/prospero/2019/05/21/daniel-hahn-on-the-art-of-translation (accessed 2 June 2020).

Key answers – Réponses aux questions

Chapter 1

I Hyperonymes et hyponymes

1 Le prince charmant avait reçu une éducation privilégiée.
  L'éducation d'Aladdin avait été basique.
2 La maison de grand-mère, qui se trouve dans les bois, comporte deux pièces en haut et deux en bas.
  Bien que la princesse n'ait aucune envie de dormir, elle devait rester dans sa chambre et se reposer.
3 Hansel a les cheveux châtains et porte des chaussures marron.
  Gretel aime le sucre roux et a les cheveux roux.
  Ils vivent dans une maison en pain d'épices.
4 Cendrillon s'est fait mal à la jambe en quittant le palais à minuit.
  Sais-tu combien de pattes ont les licornes?
5 La Belle au bois dormant n'a pas entendu la cloche de l'église ce matin.
  Le Chat du Cheshire[1] n'avait pas de grelot autour du cou.
6 Pauvre Petite Poule rousse, chaque fois qu'elle demande de l'aide aux autres animaux, ils refusent de l'aider!
  Le Grand méchant loup s'est approché du Petit Chaperon rouge et lui a demandé où elle allait.
7 Sais-tu quelle pointure fait le géant?
  Le dragon vit dans une maison de la taille d'une montagne.
8 Une fille qui fait des tâches ménagères en attendant le prince charmant, c'est sexiste!
  La Bête avait une grave blessure qui nécessitait des points de suture.
9 Le Chat botté, c'est l'histoire d'un chat qui utilise de vils stratagèmes pour arriver au pouvoir.
  "Oublie les bottes de sept lieues, nous ne vivons pas dans un conte de fées. Je vais mettre mes chaussures d'escalade et grimper en haut de la tour", dit le prince à Raiponce.

10   L'exposition canine nationale venait de commencer quand les 101 dalmatiens arrivèrent.
Jack est allé acheter des haricots au Salon international de l'agriculture de Paris.[2]

Chapter 2

I Identification des procédés de traduction

1   Dire des choses belles et fausses est le véritable but de l'art.
2   S'aimer soi-même, c'est se lancer dans une histoire d'amour qui durera toute la vie.
3   Une critique est dur à prendre, particulièrement venant d'un parent, un ami, une connaissance ou un inconnu.
4   Il n'y a qu'un remède à l'amour: aimer davantage.
5   Je ne veux pas atteindre l'immortalité grâce à mon œuvre. Je veux atteindre l'immortalité en ne mourant pas.
6   La vie, c'est comme rouler à bicyclette, il faut avancer pour ne pas perdre l'équilibre.
7   L'argent est plus utile que la pauvreté, ne serait-ce que pour des raisons financières.
8   Si vous voulez être aimé, aimez et soyez digne d'être aimé.
9   Un baiser est un tour délicieux conçu par la nature pour couper la parole quand les mots deviennent superflus.
10   Inspiré par l'amour, tout le monde devient poète.
11   On ne mesure pas un homme par ses actions dans le confort et la commodité, mais dans le défi et la controverse.
12   Le cours de l'amour véritable n'a jamais été sans écueils.

II Transposition

1   Lors de <u>mon séjour</u> en Allemagne, j'ai vu beaucoup . . .
2   Après <u>son départ</u>, elle fait le pain et continue le nettoyage de la maison.
3   Un an après son <u>départ à la retraite</u>, elle divorce Pierre.
4   <u>À sa mort</u> en 1896, Alfred Nobel ne lègue pratiquement rien de sa fortune à ses héritiers directs.
5   Elle a souvent <u>le mal de mer</u>.
6   Quand j'étais à la faculté de droit <u>à la fin des</u> années 1960 et <u>au début des</u> années 1970 . . .
7   La femme voulait qu'on la garde en vie de toutes les façons possibles et son époux ne voulait pas <u>qu'on la réanime</u>.
8   Je ne désirais pas <u>que l'on se rendît compte</u> de l'état de la pauvre Lucy.
9   Les défenseurs se sont battus <u>avec bravoure</u> avant d'être forcés de capituler.

10 Je suis complètement étonnée par <u>la rapidité et la compétence</u> avec laquelle ils agissent.

11 Il a <u>fait preuve de courage</u> mais a terminé dernier.

12 La violence des médias pousse les enfants à se conduire <u>de manière plus aggressive</u>.

13 Donald éleva ses enfants <u>avec amour et fermeté</u>.

14 Elle a hoché la tête <u>d'un air entendu</u>.

15 Quand on lui demande comment elle occupe son temps libre, Dina répond <u>d'un air penaud</u>: " Je ne vous mentirai pas; je ne fais pas grand chose".

16 J'adore rire, dit-il <u>d'un air joyeux</u>.

17 Il riait <u>avec plaisir</u> des blagues qu'on pouvait raconter.

18 En vous inscrivant, vous avez fait un geste <u>d'une générosité exceptionnelle</u>.

III *Transposition et phrasal verbs*

1 Il est entré dans la maison en courant.

2 Elle est sortie de la maison avec fracas.
  Elle est sortie en trombe.

3 Il traversa la pièce à tâtons.

4 Comme elle était dans l'incapacité de marcher, elle a dû descendre l'escalier en rampant.

5 La dame gravit les marches et entra dans la maison.

6 Un cycliste a percuté un piéton et a tenté de lui dérober son sac.
  Un cycliste <u>à vélo</u> a percuté un piéton et a tenté de lui dérober son sac.*
  Un cycliste a percuté un piéton avec son vélo et a tenté de lui dérober son sac.*

7 Elle monta dans la voiture et sortit du garage.
  Elle monta dans la voiture et sortit du garage <u>en voiture</u>.*

8 J'ai ouvert la porte d'un coup de pied.

9 Pour le ranimer, le policier a mis des claques à un homme qui avait perdu connaissance.

10 Il avait été tué à coups de pieds.

11 La voiture a explosé après avoir percuté la palissade.

12 Est-ce que tu peux sortir la poubelle?

13 Quand je repense à mon enfance, je me dis que j'aurais dû étudié davantage.

14 Il s'est enfui quand il avait 15 ans.

IV *Transposition et étoffement – traduction des prépositions*

Préposition simple en anglais → locution prépositionnelle en français

1 Pour lutter contre la piraterie <u>au large de</u> la Somalie, le gouvernement a décidé de . . .

2 La réservation des places est obligatoire pour tous les trains <u>en partance pour</u> l'Italie.

3   Une hôtesse de l'air dans un vol <u>en provenance de Chicago</u>, a trouvé un colis suspect laissé dans les toilettes.
4   En partance pour le Pérou le mois prochain, pour arpenter de nouvelles ruines.
5   Nous espérons recevoir de l'argent <u>en provenance de</u> partenaires internationaux.
6   Toute plainte doit être présentée <u>dans un délai de</u> deux ans à partir de la date à laquelle vous avez eu connaissance des faits.
7   Par conséquent, bon nombre de ces entreprisses se sont écroulées <u>en l'espace de</u> quelques mois.
8   Il y a eu des accusations <u>portées</u>/<u>lancées</u> contre lui.
9   La femme vêtue d'une robe jaune.
10 Elles n'ont pas le droit de quitter leur maison sans être <u>accompagnée d'</u>un homme de la famille.
11 Envoyez votre formulaire de demande <u>accompagnée d'</u>une lettre à votre centre fiscal.
12 Leur regard sensible sur le monde <u>qui les entoure</u> mérite d'être partagé.
13 C'était le seul homme marié <u>qui avait</u> des enfants.
14 Je sais que j'ai raison dit-elle <u>en souriant.</u>

V Modulation

VI Modulation par le contraire

1   Savait-elle que j'étais triste et que je pleurais <u>sans cesse</u>?
2   Eh bien, elle a <u>sans cesse</u> des maux de tête et ne peut pas aller l'école.
3   Les deux garçons <u>n'arrêtaient pas</u> de rigoler.
4   <u>N'oubliez pas</u> de saluer et de remercier le public et vos supporters.
5   Ce produit ne comporte pas <u>moins de risques</u> que la cigarette.
6   Ceci n'eût/aurait <u>pas manqué de</u> le surprendre.
7   Ce que fait ce cascadeur <u>est dangereux.</u>
8   <u>Que ne ferions-nous pas</u> pour nos lecteurs!

VII Modulation métonymique

1   Il s'est très vite habitué à son école, il y est comme <u>un poisson</u> dans l'eau.
2   Pourquoi les êtres humains ont-ils <u>la chair de poule</u>?
3   Je n'ai pas pris de petit-déjeuner ce matin et maintenant <u>j'ai une faim de loup.</u>
4   On ne réveille pas le <u>chat</u> qui dort.
5   Il est inconcevable que le president se comporte <u>comme un éléphant</u> dans un magasin de porcelain/<u>comme un chien</u> dans un jeu de quilles.
6   Elle est très gentille mais <u>myope comme une taupe.</u>
7   On n'apprend pas à un <u>vieux singe à faire la grimace.</u>
8   Se jeter <u>dans la gueule du loup.</u>
9   Quand <u>les poules auront des dents.</u>

10 Etre <u>gai comme un pinson</u>.
11 Le <u>chat parti, les souris dansent</u>.
12 Monter sur <u>ses grands chevaux</u>.
13 <u>Une hirondelle</u> ne fait pas le printemps.

Chapter 3

I Coordination et subordination

1 Les enfants devaient obéir et regarder pour apprendre.
2 Lire le texte puis souligner les pronoms personnels et les verbes.
3 J'ai obtempéré, mais ils m'ont dit qu'ils ne pouvaient pas venir ni m'aider.
4 Viens me chercher!
5 Notre entreprise emploie aujourd'hui 91 salariés et a transformé en 2003 100 millions de litres de lait pour réaliser un chiffre d'affaires de 70 millions d'euros.

IV Voix passive

1 Ici on parle français.
2 On ne nous a pas facilité l'accès à l'Ambassade.
3 Le jambon se vend à la charcuterie.
4 Les baskets s'achètent dans les magasins de sport.
5 Cela ne se fait plus.
6 La vengeance est un plat qui se mange froid.
7 Il est interdit de fumer.
8 Il est défendu de stationner/Stationnement interdit.
9 Il est interdit de porter des chaussures de ville sur le court.
10 Elle s'est vu refuser la possibilité de se représenter elle-même durant son procès.
11 L'Union européenne s'est vu accorder une plus grande souplesse adminis-trative.
12 Elle s'est vu accorder une bourse de recherche de cinq ans.
13 Peu de temps après son licenciement, son ex-employeur l'a contacté.
14 Plusieurs modifications apportées au navire après sa construction n'avaient pas été signalées.
15 L'autorisation entrainera un afflux de demandes d'assouplissement des règles.
16 On nous a donné une récompense.
17 J'ai beaucoup de musique sur mon téléphone qui n'a jamais été écoutée.
18 Elle était embêtée qu'on lui ait parlé ainsi.
19 Elle n'a pas été contactée.

V Le participe présent

1 J'entendais des chiens qui aboyaient toute la nuit.
2 Je le vois qui tâche d'ouvrir la porte.
3 Selon/en fonction de votre décision, je partirai ou resterai.
4 Au sujet de l'euro, je signalerai deux choses.
5 Si l'on tient compte (compte tenu) de l'inflation aux Etats-Unis, on ne peut s'attendre à aucune baisse substantielle des taux d'intérêts.
6 Ils se sont joints à nous pour offrir leurs condoléances et leur soutien.
7 Sa carrière et son palmarès font de lui l'un des plus grands noms de l'histoire de la natation tricolore.
8 Il sauta sur son cheval et s'en alla au galop.

Chapter 4

III Traduction des temps dans un article de journal

1 vivais, emmenait, allais, pouvais.
2 étiez, étais, était, était, restais, expérimentais, trouvais, testais.

Chapter 5

I Traduisez les slogans politiques ci-dessous

1 Pas d'imposition sans représentation.
2 Une poule dans chaque pot.
3 Le retour des beaux jours.
4 Avec les Travaillistes, pas de travail.
5 Ça ne peut que s'améliorer.
6 C'est possible! /Oui, on peut.
7 Un changement, un vrai.
8 C'est l'économie, imbécile.
9 Ne partez pas perdant, faites le choix gagnant.
10 Trop, c'est trop!/Ça suffit!
11 L'avenir nous appartient.
12 L'heure est au changement.
13 Priorité au peuple.
14 Agissez local, pensez global.

III Traduction d'éléments lexicaux culturellement marqués

1 Originaire de la petite bourgeoisie de banlieue, ou pauvreté et prétention vont de pair, je comprends maintenant le sort enviable de la bonne bourgeoisie.

2   Le bureau – que mes parents m'ont acheté quand j'ai passé mon baccalauréat –, je l'ai trimballé de squat en squat, de hlm en location partagée, jusqu'à ce qu'il atterrisse ici, ce premier bien que j'ai jamais possédé.

3   Mais mes premières semaines à l'université m'ont sonné comme un électro-choc. Je devais rentrer à la maison pour lire des manuels pédagogiques et telle ou telle matière "expliquée aux enfants".

4   Je devrais peut-être me rappeler que je file à l'anglaise et que mon nom ne figure pas sur le catalogue de disques *Desert Island*.

5   Je me suis mis à faire la tournée des hôpitaux. Je sais maintenant où ils sont tous, ou presque.

IV Analyse d'un texte non-standard et de sa traduction

Marqueurs linguistiques "non-standard" dans le texte Kiffe Kiffe demain:

- Sur le plan lexical: certains termes appartiennent à un registre familier *se casser* (1), *conne* (6), voire vulgaire *destin de merde* (55), *se faire couiller* (57). On notera également l'utilisation du verlan: *meuf* (8), du terme tronqué *mytho* (45), ainsi que de formules stéréotypées associées au parler des banlieues: *comme une crapule* (11), *il y avait pas moyen* (12).

- Sur le plan morphologique: utilisation de *ça* plutôt que de *cela*: *ça lui faisait exotique* (34), *si ça se trouve* (48), absence du *ne* de négation *je sais plus son nom* (3), *il y avait pas moyen* (12), utilisation de *bizarre* comme adverbe: *Il regardait bizarre les bibelots* (35).

- Sur le plan syntaxique: le texte comprend de nombreux détachements à gauche:

    - La nouvelle, je sais plus son nom. (2–3)
    - Moi, comme une crapule, je lui ai répondu. (11–12)
    - Il ressemblait à Laurent Cabrol, celui qui présentait "La Nuit des héros". (19–20)
    - Il regardait bizarre les bibelots qui sont posés sur le meuble, ceux que ma mère a rapportés du Maroc après son mariage. (34–37)
    - Sauf que lui, il avait des pieds bioniques. (40–41)
    - Le destin, c'est la misère parce que t'y peux rien. (55–56)
    - Si mon père nous a abandonnées, c'est parce que c'était écrit. (58–59 = détachement + pseudo clivée)

Notes

1 Connu également sous le nom de Chafouin ou de Chat de Chester.
2 Couramment désigné, le "Salon de l'agriculture".

Index

CPSIA information can be obtained
at www.ICGtesting.com
Printed in the USA
LVHW081719300822
727207LV00004B/144